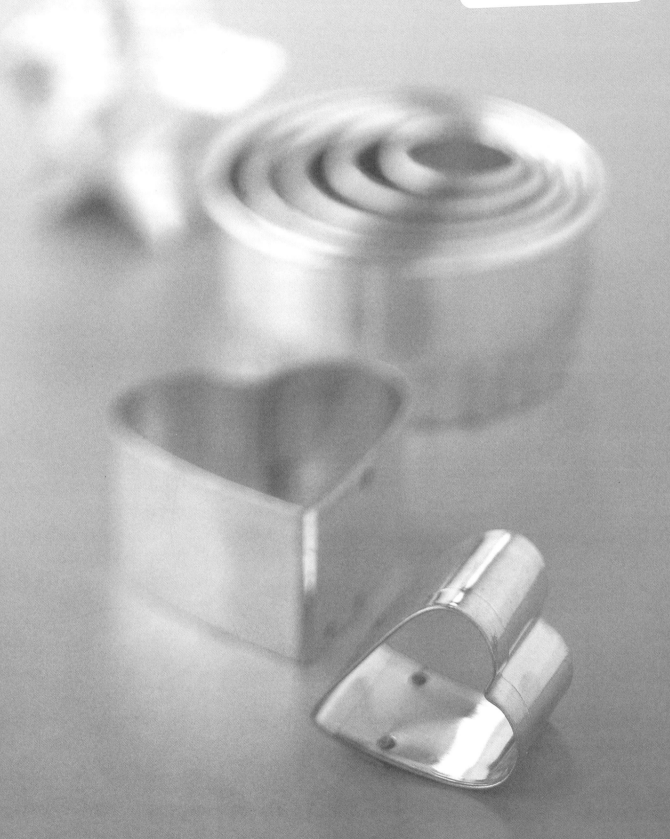

best-ever
PASTRY

over 135 fantastic recipes for pies, pastries, tarts and flans

cookbook

CATHERINE ATKINSON

JG PRESS

Published by World Publications Group, Inc.
140 Laurel Street
East Bridgewater, MA 02333
www.wrldpub.net

Produced by Anness Publishing Ltd
Hermes House, 88–89 Blackfriars Road
London SE1 8HA
tel. 020 7401 2077; fax 020 7633 9499

www.annesspublishing.com

If you like the images in this book and would like to investigate using them for publishing, promotions or advertising, please visit our website www.practicalpictures.com for more information.

Publisher: Joanna Lorenz
Managing Editor: Linda Fraser
Senior Editor: Margaret Malone
Special Photography: Janine Hosegood
Food Styling: Emma Patmore (recipes) and Annabel Ford (reference)
Stylist: Helen Trent
Designer: Isobel Gillan
Additional Recipes: Alex Barker, Angela Boggiano, Carla Capalbo, Jacqueline Clarke, Carole Clements, Trish Davies, Roz Denny, Matthew Drennan, Joanna Farrow, Christine France, Sarah Gates, Brian Glover, Nicola Graimes, Christine Ingram, Lucy Knox, Norma MacMillan, Sue Maggs, Sally Mansfield, Maggie Mayhew, Norma Miller, Sally Morris, Keith Richmond, Liz Trigg, Hilaire Walden, Laura Washburn, Steven Wheeler and Elizabeth Wolf-Cohen
Additional Photography: Karl Adamson, Steve Baxter, James Duncan, Gus Filgate, Ian Garlick, Michelle Garrett, Amanda Heywood, Dave Jordan, Dave King, William Lingwood, Thomas Odulate, Craig Robertson and Sam Stowell
Copy Editors: Rosie Hankin and Jenni Fleetwood
Editorial Reader: Joy Wotton
Production Controller: Wendy Lawson
Indexer: Caroline Noakes

ETHICAL TRADING POLICY

Because of our ongoing ecological investment programme, you, as our customer, can have the pleasure and reassurance of knowing that a tree is being cultivated on your behalf to naturally replace the materials used to make the book you are holding. For further information about this scheme, go to www.annesspublishing.com/trees

A CIP catalogue record for this book is available from the British Library.

Front cover shows Summer Berry Tart, for recipe see page 188

Previously published as *Pastry*.

ISBN-10: 1-57215-518-3
ISBN-13: 978-1-57215-518-3

Printed and bound in China

NOTES

Bracketed terms are for American readers.
For all recipes, quantities are given in both metric and imperial measures and, where appropriate, measures are also given in standard cups and spoons. Follow one set, but not a mixture because they are not interchangeable.
Standard spoon and cup measures are level. 1 tsp = 5ml, 1 tbsp = 15ml, 1 cup = 250ml/8fl oz
Australian standard tablespoons are 20ml. Australian readers should use 3 tsp in place of 1 tbsp for measuring small quantities of gelatine, cornflour, salt etc.
Medium (US large) eggs are used unless otherwise stated.

CONTENTS

INTRODUCTION 6

PASTRY ESSENTIALS 8

THE ART OF PASTRY MAKING 10

BASIC EQUIPMENT 12

MAKING PASTRY 16

MAKING FLANS AND PIES 28

SHAPING AND BAKING CHOUX PASTRY 38

SHAPING AND BAKING HOT
WATER CRUST 39

MAKING PARCELS AND
SHAPED PASTRIES 40

SAVOURY FILLINGS 48

SWEET FILLINGS 52

SAUCES FOR SAVOURY PASTRIES 60

SAUCES FOR SWEET PASTRIES 64

THE PASTRY KITCHEN 68

SMALL SAVOURY PASTRIES 70

QUICHES AND SAVOURY TARTS 88

SINGLE- AND DOUBLE-CRUST PIES 104

PARCELS AND SHAPED PASTRY CASES 122

SWEET SHORTCRUST AND
CHOUX PASTRIES 142

SWEET PUFF AND FILO PASTRIES 160

ELEGANT FRUIT TARTS 178

RICH AND INDULGENT
PASTRY DESSERTS 196

CLASSIC DECORATED PIES 212

PUFF, CHOUX AND
FILO PASTRY DESSERTS 232

INDEX 252

INTRODUCTION

FEW CAN RESIST the display in the window of a good quality pâtisserie, and many of us have fond memories of the savoury pies and rich, fruit-laden tarts served up by our mothers at dinnertime. Be it a humble apple pie or a hearty chicken and mushroom pie, there is something irresistible about well-made pastry that makes it popular with people of all ages.

Just as eating good pastry is a hugely enjoyable experience, making your own can be equally satisfying. For anyone who likes to cook, learning how to make melt-in-the-mouth pastry is to discover a culinary art that is full of traditions and classic recipes, but is also full of creative possibilities. It's not necessary to be an experienced pastry cook to make good pastry, and this book has all the necessary information to get started, as well as containing many fabulous classic and contemporary recipes for you to delight your friends and family.

A BRIEF HISTORY OF PASTRY

Pastries were made as long ago as the 5th century BC and, in ancient Greece, pastry cooks were considered to be a separate trade to bakers. As the ancient Romans and Greeks used oil, not butter, in their cooking, it would not have been possible to shape the pastry as we do today. Consequently, pastry was used primarily as a container for the filling.

For some time, pastry was used chiefly as a means of enclosing food, to protect it from the heat of the fire and to ensure that the precious juices would not be lost during cooking. These pastry cases or "coffers" were often simply a mixture of flour and water, which cooked to a leaden covering that was broken off and discarded. However, as ovens improved and the temperature became more controllable and less fierce, it was possible to release pastry from its original role as fire-retardant and explore ways of making it a more edible and appealing part of the dish. In Northern Europe, hard fats such as butter and especially lard were used in cooking, and it was this important addition to the basic pastry recipe that made stiffer, more pliable pastries, such as raised pies, possible.

As the art of pastry- and pie-making developed, there was little distinction made between sweet and savoury, and the two flavours were often combined. It was not uncommon, for example, for a meat or fish pie to be topped with a sweet pastry with a sugary glaze. For instance, right up until Victorian times in England, mince pies, often served at Christmas time, always contained pieces of minced (ground) meat and shredded suet combined with chopped dried fruits, mixed nuts, spices and sugar, all encased in a rich, sweet

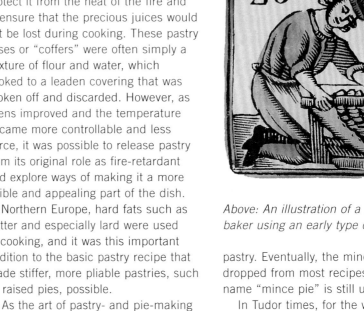

Above: An illustration of a 17th-century baker using an early type of rolling pin.

pastry. Eventually, the minced meat was dropped from most recipes, but the name "mince pie" is still used today.

In Tudor times, for the wealthy at least, pastry once more reverted to the inedible. Pies were often used as spectacular centrepieces at banquets, with the result that the emphasis was on the appearance of the pies rather than the taste. When these beautifully moulded crusts were opened, the "filling" was always a dramatic surprise, which often included live animals or performers, and so it is little wonder that no one wanted to eat the pastry.

Meanwhile, the poorer classes continued to rely on pastry as both a source of nourishment and a useful way of packaging food: pastry parcels often contained a savoury filling at one end and a sweet one at the other. This enterprising method was used by those travelling to work in the fields and, a few centuries later, in factories and mines. Cornish miners who emigrated to the USA from England took this custom with them.

Over the years, pastry became richer and much more flavoursome; by the 17th century, butter, eggs and myriad spices were being added to the basic flour and water paste. Trial and – more often – error led to many happy

Left: This painting shows the interior of a Dutch cake shop in 1866, with a variety of cakes, breads and pastries.

outcomes: puff pastry is believed to have been created around this time by a young French pastry apprentice who forgot to add the butter to the dough and hastily attempted to disguise his error by wrapping it inside the pastry. The result was a gloriously golden, flaky pastry, the recipe for which quickly spread throughout France and then the rest of Europe.

The 19th century saw the creation of many classic recipes. One of the greatest pastry chefs of all time, Antonin Carême from France, is credited with creating the vol-au-vent, mille-feuilles and croquembouche – all of which are still eaten with pleasure today.

As chefs experimented with different ingredients and techniques, pastry-making became simpler and less time-consuming, and a number of short-cut recipes such as rough puff pastry came into being. For the average cook, this was a welcome development as the exquisitely decorated pies typical of Victorian times were really possible only with a large household staff. As staff numbers fell and working conditions and hours improved, the fashion for making ornate pies declined.

PASTRY-MAKING TODAY

Time-saving machines such as food processors and refrigeration have further simplified pastry-making. Trends have come and gone, but at heart all sweet and savoury pastries still rely on a well-made pastry. Indeed, the rules of pastry-making have not changed much since the 19th century and still apply to classic and contemporary recipes.

Easy travel and communication has increased our knowledge of pastries from around the world. Ready-made pastry such as filo is as easily available as shortcrust, and modern cooks are as likely to serve a rich Turkish baklava for dessert as a tarte tatin. It is interesting to see how certain combinations or uses for pastry constantly reappear. Dishes such as apple pie and blueberry pie are found the world over, as are turnovers, and layered pastries. The potential combinations of pastry and filling are limited only by the cook's imagination.

This book contains a wonderfully detailed reference section showing how to make all the major types of pastries, and their variations, as well as tips and suggestions for flavouring the basic pastry. All the essential techniques are explained, from rolling out and lining to decorating and shaping pastry, so that you can feel confident about every aspect of making good pastry. Once you have mastered the art of pastry-making, turn to the recipe chapters for a very comprehensive selection of all-time

Above: A typical Viennese pâtisserie in the mid 20th century, with a range of cakes and pastries.

classics and new and contemporary treats. Many are delightfully simple to make, such as a rustic Mediterranean One-crust Pie or Almond Cream Puffs, while others are sumptuous indeed – for example the classic pastry gâteau, Saint-Honoré. Whatever the filling, each recipe is a delicious example of the pleasure to be had from pastry-making.

PASTRY ESSENTIALS

There is no reason why even beginners should not be able to create delicious pastry; pastry-making is based on a few golden rules, which, if adhered to, will ensure success every time.

First, always measure ingredients accurately – even professionals with years of experience rely on weighing scales. Secondly, keep everything cool: the work surface, ingredients, utensils, your hands and even your temper, as pastry needs careful, light handling (this does not apply to choux or hot-water crust pastry, however). Lastly, most pastries need to be rested and chilled after every stage of making and assembling. Don't be tempted to cut down on the times suggested for this, or your pastry may suffer.

PASTRY INGREDIENTS

Good quality ingredients are at the heart of successful pastry-making, as only a few are needed.

For traditional crisp pastries, plain (all-purpose) flour is best. Self-raising (self-rising) flour produces a softer pastry, such as suet crust. Wholemeal (whole-wheat) flour makes a heavier dough, which is difficult to roll out, so a mix of half wholemeal, half white flour is recommended. White bread flour is used for puff pastry and its variations, as it contains a higher proportion of gluten (the proteins in the flour). As the pastry is rolled and folded, the gluten develops and becomes elastic, making it possible for the dough to be rolled out without tearing.

Pastry can be made with one fat, or a mixture of fats. These include butter, lard, white vegetable fat and margarine. Butter on its own gives pastry a rich flavour and a wonderful colour and is absolutely essential in puff pastry, rich shortcrust and pâte sucrée. Shortcrust pastry has an excellent flavour when made with all butter, but you may prefer to be more traditional and use a mixture of butter and white vegetable fat or lard, which will give the pastry a shorter (crumblier) texture. White vegetable fats are whipped from blended vegetable oils and are flavourless. They give light, "short" results, hence they may be referred to as shortening. If margarine is preferred, it should be the hard block variety rather than soft-tub margarine.

Both the whole egg and the yolks on their own are used in pastry. Eggs make pastry more pliable; give it a golden colour; and set it during cooking so that it holds its shape.

Sugar is added to pastry to produce crisper baked results, but it is essential to watch the pastry during cooking as it colours more quickly. Salt is sometimes added to pastry to enhance its flavour; this is most often done in savoury pies. Care must be taken when adding liquid to the dry ingredients. It is impossible to give the exact quantity needed, as the absorbency of flour varies – too much and the result will be tough; too little and the pastry will be crumbly.

Left, clockwise from top left: Essential pastry ingredients include water, flour, butter, salt, eggs, sugar and lard.

Above, from top: Rich shortcrust, plain shortcrust, French flan pastry and pâte sucrée.

TYPES OF PASTRY

There are many types of pastry, but all are based on a mixture of flour and fat, with eggs or water for binding.

Shortcrust pastry This crisp and light pastry is made with half the weight of fat to flour, with eggs or water to bind. It is easy and quick to make; indeed speed is very important, as overworking toughens the dough. There are many variations on the basic shortcrust recipe, varying the flour and fat used, and their ratios to each other.

Rich shortcrust or pâte brisée By adding a little more butter and moistening the mixture with eggs instead of water, a plain shortcrust is transformed into rich shortcrust or pâte brisée, a flavoursome and firm pastry that will stay crisper for longer, making it ideal for pastries that aren't going to be eaten straight away. *Brisée* means "broken", as the fat is broken into the flour, or rubbed in.

French flan pastry or pâte à foncer This is another variation of shortcrust made with egg yolk and a dash of lemon juice to develop the gluten and make a firm pastry. As the name suggests, it is used for flans as it is robust enough to hold sweet and savoury fillings for a long time without becoming soft and soggy.

Pâte sucrée This rich and crisp-textured sweet pastry is sometimes known as biscuit pastry because of its crumbly texture when baked. It is a soft pastry and needs chilling before use due to its higher proportion of butter and sugar. It is used mainly for tarts and tartlets, especially those that are partially baked (baked blind) and then filled with fruit.

Suet pastry is a light, spongy pastry used for steamed puddings. It is made with suet, a heavy grated fat, which is balanced by the use of self-raising flour.

Puff pastry This is a very light, crisp pastry made with equal quantities of fat and flour. Air is incorporated into the dough by trapping it between the layers during the rolling and folding stage. The layers are separated by butter, always added in one piece. When baked, puff rises higher than any other pastry, as the trapped air and steam from the water force the layers apart. Puff is used in many sweet and savoury recipes.

Short-cut puff pastry is a quick version of puff and has a crisper texture. It uses a mixture of half butter and half white

vegetable fat or lard. It is excellent for single-crust pies when time is short.

Rough puff pastry Quicker and easier to make than puff, rough puff pastry has a lower proportion of fat to flour, and has a rich buttery, flaky texture. It does not rise as well as puff, so is used for pie and flan crusts.

Flaky pastry This pastry is made in a similar way to puff, but here the butter is dabbed on to the dough during the rolling process, rather than added in one piece. It has fewer layers so can be used instead of puff when the rise is less important, such as meat cooked "en croute" and pasties and turnovers.

Short-cut flaky pastry This has the same crispness as flaky, but the butter is chilled then grated into the flour. It does not rise as well, but is quick to make.

Choux pastry This is unlike any other pastry. It is cooked in a pan, looks like a soft dough and is never rolled out. It is one of the easiest pastries to master and can be piped into small shapes, with hollow centres ready to be filled. It is used for pastries such as profiteroles and in savoury dishes such as gougère.

Strudel pastry and filo This paper-thin pastry is used for making strudels and small pastries. The home-made strudel pastry is best used for making strudels only and has to be used immediately after making. Filo pastry is store-bought and, though similar, it can be stored for a week in the refrigerator and freezes well. It can be cut, folded or scrunched into shape to make baskets, wrapped pastries and small pies.

Hot water crust pastry This hard, slightly bland, pastry is traditionally used for raised pies and is flavoured by the meat juices and fat that seep out from the filling during cooking. It is made using lard or white vegetable fat and, unlike other pastries, must be kept warm during shaping so that it stays pliable. It is

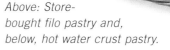

Above: Store-bought filo pastry and, below, hot water crust pastry.

moulded into a pie crust or used to line a hinged mould to hold substantial fillings of meat or game.

Pâte à pâté is the French version of hot water crust pastry.

KEEPING AND FREEZING PASTRY

Most types of pastry – except choux, home-made strudel and hot-water crust – can be kept chilled for several days, providing they are well wrapped in clear film (plastic wrap) to prevent them from drying out. Pastry can also be frozen for several weeks. To thaw, leave the dough in the refrigerator overnight, then rest it for 10–15 minutes at room temperature before rolling out. You can also freeze rolled-out pastry, by sliding it on to baking parchment set on a baking sheet and freezing uncovered until firm. Wrap in freezer paper and store flat. To defrost, unwrap and leave on a baking sheet overnight in the refrigerator.

Above, from top: Puff, rough puff, and flaky pastry.

What's in a name?

The difference between a pie and a flan can be confusing. A pie is usually defined as having both a pastry base and a top with a filling inside, or it can be made with just a single crust, which covers a filling in a pie dish.

A flan – or tart – is an open pastry case with a filling. It may have a decorative lattice on top with the filling peeping through. These descriptions vary from country to country, however, and there are exceptions, such as pecan pie and key lime pie – both of which, technically, are flans.

Right: Choux pastry

THE ART OF PASTRY MAKING

There's a lot of truth in the old adage — as easy as pie. Making pastry isn't difficult if you follow a few simple rules and master the basic techniques. Any good pastry cook knows that practice really does make perfect. You don't need fancy equipment: a bowl, a set of scales or measuring cups and a rolling pin are all you need to begin with, plus one or two pie plates or dishes in sizes to suit your style of cooking. As you become more proficient and discover how satisfying and creative making pastry can be, you may want to expand your range of utensils, but remember, when it comes to good pastry making, cool, competent hands are the cook's most valuable assets.

BASIC EQUIPMENT

Using the right baking equipment simplifies and enhances the art of pastry making. Few specialist items are essential but, as with all things, having the correct tool for the job makes it considerably easier and helps to ensure success.

Most of the basic items you will probably already possess, such as accurate weighing scales or calibrated measuring cups and jug (pitcher), a good-size mixing bowl, measuring spoons, a fine sieve or sifter, heavy pans for making choux or hot water crust pastry, and a few sharp knives in different sizes.

Among the specialist equipment available, there is much that you may find very handy, particularly as you develop your skills and start to make more elaborate dishes. The following is a brief discussion of the more useful items, all of which are easily available from large department stores.

Timers

This is a useful piece of equipment for any cooking; with pastries it can mean the difference between an overcooked crust and a perfectly light and crisp

Below: Timer with rotating dial

one. You may already have a timer on your stove; otherwise a timer with a rotating dial which registers any time between one and sixty minutes is ideal.

Baking sheets

Heavy baking sheets and trays are used as a base for small individual tartlets and choux pastries, as well as for large "free-form" pies not cooked in tins, such as jalousies and vol-au-vents. They are also handy as trays for quiches and flans to help lift them in and out of the oven. When choosing a baking sheet, make sure the metal is thick enough so that it won't develop hot spots or buckle and twist at high temperatures; if it does liquid fillings in open pies may tip out. To avoid

Above: Baking sheets and tray, at front. Sheets are either entirely flat or have a lip along the length of one of the long sides only; trays have a lip all round.

baking individual pastries in several batches, buy baking sheets that are large but will fit easily in your oven.

Pastry boards

These should be as large as you can accommodate and completely flat and smooth. They come in many materials including wood and toughened glass, but marble is considered the most suitable because it is cool to the touch, whatever the weather. If your kitchen is really warm, you can cool a marble board by placing a tray of ice cubes on top until you are ready to use it.

Nowadays, however, formica work surfaces installed in many kitchens have a very smooth finish. These are a good alternative to using a pastry board.

Rolling pins

A thick, heavy, wooden rolling pin is best for rolling out pastry. You may choose one without handles made from a single piece of wood or one with a fixed handle at either end. You can also get "cool" rolling pins. Some of these are made from marble while others are hollow and designed to be filled with chilled water. These have no advantage over the traditional wooden pin as long as you chill your pastry thoroughly before starting to roll it out on a lightly floured surface.

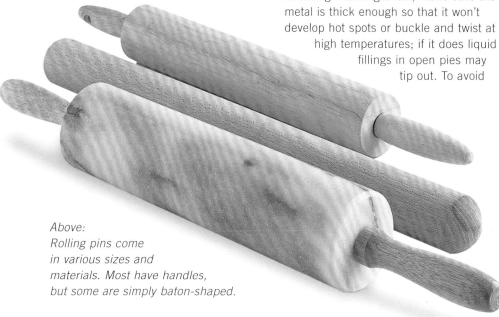

*Above:
Rolling pins come
in various sizes and
materials. Most have handles,
but some are simply baton-shaped.*

Left: Balloon whisk

Whisks

An electric whisk or hand-held balloon whisk are useful for whisking sauces, cream fillings and meringue toppings.

Pie dishes, tins and moulds

Pie dish The traditional pie dish is oval with a small rim and sloping sides and is often made from glazed earthernware. The rim is wide and flat, so that the pastry crust can be attached easily. Pie dishes can, however, also be round, square or rectangular and may also be made of glass or metal.

Springform tins Also known as spring-clip tins, these are round and straight-sided, with a removable base and a clip on the side to release the pie. They are useful for very deep pies.

Raised pie moulds

These moulds are hinged on one side, which simplifies the removal of raised meat and game pies. They range in size from about 20cm/8in to 25cm/10in and may be a pointed oval or a rectangular shape. Very often raised pie moulds have patterned sides, which gives the pie an attractive embossed appearance when turned out.

Wooden pie moulds These thick cylinders are used as a mould for shaping raised pies. Though traditional, a greased and floured jam jar makes a perfectly good substitute.

Right: Tins come in a range of sizes and shapes. They may have loose bases or clipped sides for easy removal of the pie or tart.

Pie plates These have a wide rim and are usually made of metal to conduct the heat to the pastry. They are not as deep as pie dishes, so are used to bake shallow, lidded pies or open tarts with decorated edges.

Above: Glass, metal and earthenware pie dishes, and a metal pie plate.

Flan tins and rings

Flan tins Also known as quiche pans, these metal tins come in all shapes and sizes including square, heart and petal-shaped, but the easiest to obtain is the fluted round. The best flan tins have loose bases, which make the turning out of fragile tarts simple. Fluted sides are easier to line than straight sides and the shape also adds strength to the pastry cases. The most popular sizes are 20cm/8in, 23cm/9in and 25cm/10in. It is important to choose the right size of tin when following a recipe; check not only the diameter, but also that the depth of the tin (if given) is correct. If possible, use flan tins with a dull finish, rather than shiny aluminium ones, as they will produce a crisper crust.

Flan rings These come without bases and are designed to be set directly on a baking sheet. Make sure you use a thick, heavy baking sheet that will not warp during cooking.

Tranche tins From the French, meaning slice, these are long rectangular tins often with fluted edges. They make for easy serving as the finished flan can be simply cut across in slices.

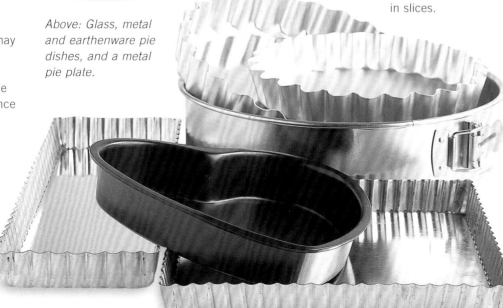

Pastry cutters

There is a wide range of cutters of various sizes available from plain or fluted round pastry cutters, to leaves, flowers and animals. These cutters are ideal for making small pastries and for decorating the tops of larger ones.

Cornet moulds

These metal cones, just over 10cm/4in long, are used to shape pastry horns. The pastry is wrapped around them and then baked. The pastry cones can be filled with cream or a savoury filling.

Cannoli forms

These 10cm/4in metal cylinders are used to shape and bake pastry. They are similar to cornet moulds, but are open at both ends. The little tubes of baked pastry are often filled with piped sweetened cream or a mixture of soft cheese, chopped candied fruits and mixed nuts.

Pie funnels

When making a pie with a lid, a ceramic pie funnel can be used. The hollow funnel pokes up through the pastry lid to act like a chimney letting out steam from the pie's filling, which might otherwise make the pastry soggy and prevent it from rising properly. The shoulders of the pie funnel give further support to the pastry.

Made of porcelain, pie funnels usually have semi-circular holes cut out of the base, so that the juices in the filling can mingle freely in the dish. A singing blackbird, with its beak open as a steam hole (and representing one of the 24 baked in a pie in the traditional nursery rhyme), is a popular design.

Above: Pie funnel with small holes cut out of its base to allow sauces to mix.

Left: Though attractive, porcelain flan dishes are best kept as serving dishes as they absorb heat too slowly to produce good pastry.

Porcelain flan dishes These have unglazed bases so that the heat can penetrate. Even so, they absorb heat much more slowly than metal ones, so are not ideal for baking pastry but are best used as a serving dish. Bake the flan in a metal flan tin (quiche pan), then remove the flan, leaving it on its metal base and slide into the porcelain flan dish for serving.

Tartlet tins These come in a multitude of shapes and sizes. Single portion, 10cm/4in round ones are popular, but boat-shape moulds, known as bateau and barquette moulds, are also available. Tiny fluted tins are usually reserved for making petits fours. They come in diamond, triangular and oval shapes, and can be as small as 4cm/ 1½in, the perfect size for a tartlet to be topped with nothing more than a single fresh strawberry.

Above: Round and fluted, or boat-shaped and smooth, tartlet tins offer lots of opportunity for creative pastry-making.

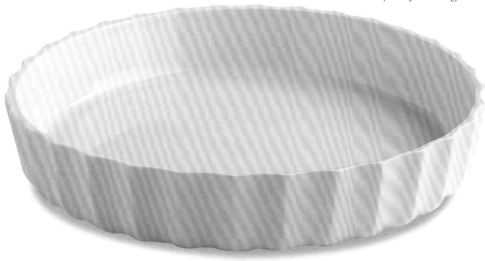

Pastry blender

This is a tool that can be used to cut fat into flour in the same way as you would rub it in with your fingertips. It is useful if you have very hot hands or if you are dealing with softer fats such as lard, white vegetable fat or shortening.

Baking beans

To ensure pastry cases cook through and become crisp, they are usually lined with foil or baking parchment and weighed down with baking beans, and baked blind. You can buy ceramic or aluminium beans that last for ever, are good heat conductors and are washable. Dried beans or pulses are a very good alternative.

Above: Ceramic baking beans

Pastry brush

An essential item for brushing egg or milk glazes on pastry or jam glazes over fruit tartlets. The best brushes are made from natural bristles set in a wooden handle (although nylon bristles are considered more hygienic). Rinse brushes that have been used for egg glazing in cold water before washing in warm soapy water, rinse well, then flick dry and leave to air.

Pastry prickers

Also known as dockers, these consist of a large number of spikes set in a roller, or six or more prongs at the end of a wooden handle. Used to make tiny holes in the bases of tarts and flans before baking, they're handy if you've got a lot of pastry to prick; otherwise an ordinary fork does the job equally well.

Pastry wheel

This makes cutting pastry quick and easy. It has a zig-zag edge that patterns the pastry, making it useful for cutting lattice strips.

Lattice cutter

This easy-to-use pastry tool has a series of wheels that cut a pattern of broken lines on rolled-out pastry. After marking the pattern, you rest the dough on your hands and gently ease the pastry open, starting from the middle and working your way outwards. In this way, a net-like lattice is formed.

Below: Wire rack, palette knife and piping nozzles

Above, from left: Lattice cutter, pastry brush and pastry blender.

Wire rack

The best way to cool all baked pastries and pies is to rest them on a wire rack. The rack allows air to circulate, thus preventing trapped warmth turning to moisture, which would make the pastry base soggy.

Palette knife

This wide, round-bladed metal spatula is used for mixing pastry dough and for smoothing fillings in flans and tartlets. It is also useful for removing small or delicate items, such as jam tarts, from their tins after baking.

Piping nozzles and bags

Nozzles can be plain or fluted and are used in a piping (pastry) bag for piping cream and adding meringue toppings to pies. Large plain ones, about 1cm/½in in diameter are ideal for using with piping bags for piping choux pastries and for filling them after baking.

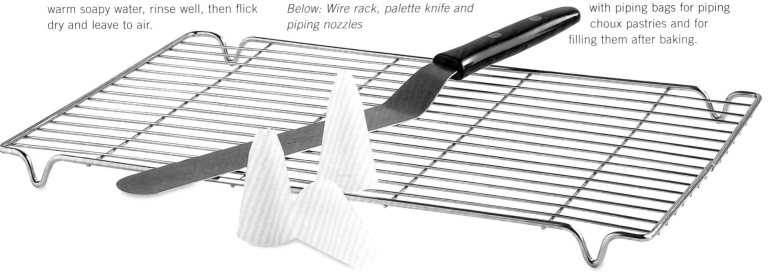

MAKING PASTRY

There is no need to feel apprehensive when first working with pastry – the dos and don'ts are well-known and there is no better – or more enjoyable – way to learn than by making your own.

This section contains recipes for classic shortcrust and its enriched variations; flaky, rough puff and puff pastries; choux; and strudel. There are also traditional pastries, such as hot-water crust and suet, and others with a more modern twist including chocolate and olive oil pastry.

SHORTCRUST PASTRY

This short, crumbly pastry is probably the best known and most frequently used type. Although the simplest of all pastries, perfect shortcrust needs a cool light hand, as over-handling the dough will develop the gluten in the flour, making it heavy and hard. The following makes enough for a 25cm/10in flan tin (quiche pan) or ten 7.5cm/3in tartlet tins (mini quiche pans).

MAKES ABOUT 375G/13OZ

INGREDIENTS
   225g/8oz/2 cups plain
     (all-purpose) flour
   pinch of salt
   115g/4oz/½ cup chilled butter,
     diced, or half butter and half lard
     or white vegetable fat
   45–60ml/3–4 tbsp chilled water

1 Sift the flour and salt together into a mixing bowl. Cut the fat into the flour using a pastry blender or use your fingertips to rub it in. Shake the bowl occasionally to bring any large pieces of fat to the top. Blend until the mixture resembles fine breadcrumbs.

2 Sprinkle 45ml/3 tbsp of the water evenly over the mixture and mix lightly with a round-bladed knife or fork until the dough comes together. Add a little more water if the mixture is still too dry; it should just begin to hold together.

3 Using one hand, gather the dough together to form a ball. Incorporate any loose pieces of the rubbed-in mixture. Knead on a lightly floured surface for just a few seconds until smooth.

4 Wrap the dough in clear film (plastic wrap), and chill for about 30 minutes, or until firm but not too stiff to roll. The shortcrust pastry is now ready to use.

Variations
Once you've mastered making shortcrust, try adding flavourings to vary the rubbed-in mixture.
Cheese pastry Add 50g/2oz/½ cup grated mature Cheddar or 45ml/ 3 tbsp freshly grated Parmesan and a pinch of mustard powder.
Fresh herb pastry Add 45ml/3 tbsp chopped fresh herbs such as parsley, sage or chives or 15ml/ 1 tbsp stronger flavoured herbs such as rosemary or thyme.

RICH SHORTCRUST PASTRY

Also known as pâte brisée, this is a richer version of shortcrust pastry with a higher proportion of fat. It is usually made with an egg yolk and chilled water, but a whole egg may be used. This quantity is enough for a 25cm/10in flan tin (quiche pan) or ten 7.5cm/3in tartlet tins (mini quiche pans).

MAKES ABOUT 400G/14OZ

INGREDIENTS
   225g/8oz/2 cups plain
     (all-purpose) flour
   pinch of salt
   150g/5oz/10 tbsp chilled butter,
     diced
   1 egg yolk
   30ml/2 tbsp chilled water

1 Sift the flour and salt into a large bowl. Rub or cut in the butter until the mixture resembles fine breadcrumbs.

2 Mix the egg yolk and water together. Sprinkle over the dry ingredients and mix in lightly to form a soft dough.

3 Gather the dough together into a ball. Knead on a floured surface until smooth. Wrap in clear film (plastic wrap) and chill for 30 minutes before using.

MAKING SHORTCRUST PASTRY IN A FOOD PROCESSOR

This method of making pastry is good for rich shortcrust, especially where the higher proportion of fat and sugar may make it harder to handle. If you have hot hands, or the weather is warm, the food processor ensures that the dough stays cool.

1 Put the sifted flour, salt and sugar, if using, into the food processor. Process for 4–5 seconds. Scatter the cubes of fat over the dry ingredients. Process for 10–12 seconds only, or until the mixture resembles fine breadcrumbs.

2 Sprinkle the water or other liquid (such as egg and water) over the flour mixture and, using the pulse button, process until it starts to hold together. Pinch a little of the mixture between your finger and thumb; if the dough is too dry and crumbly, add a little more water and process for just 1–2 seconds more. Do not allow the pastry to form a ball in the food processor.

3 Remove the mixture and form into a ball. Lightly knead on a floured surface for just a few seconds until smooth, then wrap in clear film (plastic wrap) and chill for 30 minutes.

Steps to shortcrust success
• It is best to make shortcrust pastry as and when you need it.
• If you need a large amount, make in batches as large quantities are difficult to handle and may become overworked and tough.

• Sift flour before using; this will remove any lumps and incorporate air, thus making your pastry lighter.
• Store flour in a cool, dry place, preferably in an airtight container. Keep an eye on the use-by date.
• When making pastry, use fat that is cool but not hard.
• The fat may be all butter – which makes the best-flavoured pastry – or a combination of butter and white vegetable fat or lard, which results in a pastry with a much shorter (crumblier) texture.
• Use chilled water when mixing the rubbed-in fat and flour together, so that it will not soften or melt the fat.
• Always sprinkle the water evenly over the rubbed-in mixture, then toss with a fork to moisten, before gathering the mixture into a ball.
• Take care when adding the water. If the pastry is too wet, it will be sticky to handle and tough when cooked; if too dry, it will crumble and be difficult to roll out. As different types and brands of flour vary, it is impossible to give an exact amount of water – always add the minimum amount suggested, then add a little more as necessary.
• When kneading pastry, use either the tips of your fingers or the heel of your hand.

• If using the heel of your hand, knead lightly and for a few seconds only before wrapping and chilling.
• When using the pastry, roll it out in short gentle strokes. Avoid stretching it as much as possible.
• Always chill shortcrust pastry before rolling, even if only for a short time, and again after rolling and before baking. This is an important step as it allows the gluten to "relax" and helps prevent the pastry from shrinking when it is cooked.
• After chilling the pastry, if your kitchen is fairly cool and airy, leave the pastry at room temperature for 10 minutes before rolling out. On a warm day, leave for just 2 minutes.

Using ready-made shortcrust
Although there is nothing quite as satisfying as making your own pastry at home, good-quality, ready-made shortcrust pastry is available.

• It can be bought either frozen in blocks, "fresh" in the chilled cabinet of the supermarket or as a ready-rolled sheet. Simply unroll and use.
• Usually, brands of ready-made shortcrust pastry are available in two sizes: the 375g/13oz packet is roughly equivalent to home-made shortcrust or rich shortcrust pastry made with 225g/8oz/2 cups flour, a 450g/1lb packet is the equivalent of shortcrust pastry made with 275g/10oz/2½ cups flour.
• Bought shortcrust should always be left at room temperature for about 20 minutes before rolling or it will crack and be difficult to work with.

FRENCH FLAN PASTRY

Also known as pâte à foncer, this pastry is traditionally used for lining flan tins (quiche pans) and tartlet cases. It is always made with all butter to ensure a good flavour. Because it has a high proportion of fat, it needs to be well chilled before use, and care must be taken when rolling out. After making, the pastry is kneaded by a process known as fresage. The following makes enough for a 25cm/10in flan tin or ten 7.5cm/3in tartlet tins (mini quiche pans).

MAKES ABOUT 300G/11OZ

INGREDIENTS
    200g/7oz/1¾ cups plain
      (all-purpose) flour
    1.5ml/¼ tsp salt
    115g/4oz/½ cup chilled butter, diced
    1 egg yolk
    1.5ml/¼ tsp lemon juice
    30–45ml/2–3 tbsp chilled water

1 Sift the flour and salt into a mixing bowl. Rub or cut in the butter until the mixture resembles fine breadcrumbs.

2 Whisk the egg yolk, lemon juice and 30ml/2 tbsp of the water together in a bowl. Sprinkle over the dry ingredients. Stir in with a fork to mix.

3 Shape the moistened dry ingredients into a rough ball with your hand, adding the remaining water if the mixture is too dry. Place on a lightly floured surface.

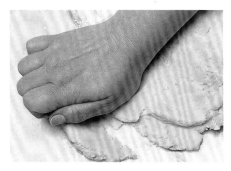

4 With the heel of your hand, lightly knead the dough for 1 minute, pushing small portions of dough away from you and smearing them on the surface until the dough is smooth and pliable.

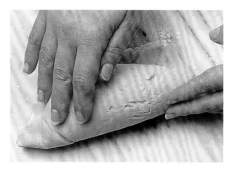

5 Shape the dough into a ball, then flatten into a round. Wrap in clear film (plastic wrap) and chill for an hour.

COOK'S TIP
To make in a food processor, blend the dry ingredients for 10 seconds, then add the butter and process for about 12 seconds. Mix the liquid ingredients and add gradually, pulsing until the dough is beginning to hold together.

French flan pastry variations
These simple recipes add texture and flavour and can be used for savoury or sweet dishes.

Light nut crust Nuts such as walnuts go particularly well with savoury cheese quiches and flans. Use chopped toasted almonds or hazelnuts in fruit flans. Stir in 40g/1½oz/⅓ cup finely chopped nuts to the basic French flan flour mixture before adding any liquid.
Rich flan pastry This pastry has an extra egg yolk and more butter. It is ideal for lining larger flan and tranche tins. Use 200g/7oz/ 1¾ cups plain (all-purpose) flour, 2.5ml/½ tsp salt, 150g/5oz/10 tbsp chilled butter, diced, 2 egg yolks and 15–30/1–2 tbsp water.

Sweet flan pastry This sweetened pastry is perfect for fruit, nut or frangipane-filled tartlets. To make, sift 200g/7oz/1¾ cups plain (all-purpose) flour with a pinch of salt and add 15g/½oz/1 tbsp caster (superfine) sugar. Rub or cut in 150g/5oz/10 tbsp butter and add 2 egg yolks mixed with 15–30ml/ 1–2 tbsp water and 2.5ml/½ tsp vanilla essence (extract).

PATE SUCREE

This rich and crisp-textured sweet pastry, also known as biscuit pastry, is used mainly for making flan and tartlet cases, as it holds its shape well during cooking. Because pâte sucrée has a high proportion of sugar, it is a much softer pastry than shortcrust and needs to be chilled for 1 hour before using. It is made with icing (confectioners') sugar, but caster sugar may be used. As with French flan pastry, it is lightly kneaded by a process known as fresage using the heel of the hand. Mix the pastry either in a bowl or – the classic way – on a marble slab or other cold surface. This quantity is enough for a 23cm/9in flan tin (quiche pan) or eight 7.5cm/3in tartlet tins (mini quiche pans).

MAKES ABOUT 275G/10OZ

INGREDIENTS
  150g/5oz/1¼ cups plain
    (all-purpose) flour
  pinch of salt
  75g/3oz/6 tbsp chilled butter, diced
  25g/1oz/¼ cup icing (confectioners')
    sugar, sifted
  2 egg yolks

1 Sift the flour and salt together to make a mound on a marble slab, pastry board or cold work surface. Make a well in the centre and put in the butter and sugar, then place the egg yolks on top.

2 Using your fingertips only, and using a pecking action, work the butter, yolks and sugar together until the mixture resembles scrambled eggs. As you do this, pull in a little of the surrounding flour to prevent the mixture from becoming too sticky.

3 When the mixture begins to form a smooth paste, pull in more of the flour to make a rough dough, gradually working in all the flour. Work quickly, using just your fingertips, so that the butter does not become oily. If the pastry is slightly crumbly at this stage, you can remedy this by working a small amount of egg white into the dough.

4 Lightly knead the dough with just the heel of your hand for about 1 minute, pushing small portions of dough away from you and smearing them on the surface until smooth and pliable.

5 Shape the dough into a ball, then flatten slightly into a flat round – this makes it easier when you start rolling it out. Wrap in clear film (plastic wrap) to prevent the pastry from drying out and chill for about 1 hour before using.

Top tips for making and baking pâte sucrée
• Always allow plenty of time for the pastry to chill and relax in the refrigerator – at least 1 hour.
• If the pastry has been chilled for more than 1 hour, allow it to soften at room temperature for about 10 minutes before using, or it may crack when you roll it out.

• If you find pâte sucrée difficult to handle at first, roll it between sheets of clear film (plastic wrap) or simply press it into the tin with your fingers instead.

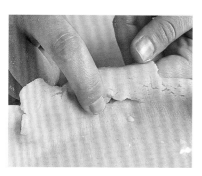

• Although pâte sucrée is slightly trickier to handle than shortcrust, it is much easier to patch; just press any small tears together with your fingers – they won't show when baked.
• Pies made using sweet pastry should be taken out of the oven as soon as the pastry is golden brown and crisp. Once it reaches this stage the pastry will burn very quickly because of the high sugar content, and if overcooked it will have a slightly bitter flavour.

WHOLEMEAL PASTRY

Pastry made with all wholemeal flour can be heavy in both taste and texture. A mixture of flours together with a little fat gives lighter results. This is enough for a 25cm/10in flan tin (quiche pan).

MAKES ABOUT 400G/14OZ

INGREDIENTS
   115g/4oz/1 cup wholemeal
     (whole-wheat) flour
   115g/4oz/1 cup plain
     (all-purpose) flour
   pinch of salt
   pinch of mustard powder
   115g/4oz/½ cup chilled butter, diced
   25g/1oz/2 tbsp white vegetable
     fat or lard
   1 egg yolk
   30ml/2 tbsp chilled water

1 Sift the flours, salt and mustard powder into a mixing bowl. Rub or cut in the butter and fat until the mixture resembles breadcrumbs. Mix the egg yolk with the water and sprinkle over the dry ingredients. Mix to a dough.

2 Knead on a lightly floured surface for a few seconds until smooth. Wrap the dough in clear film (plastic wrap) and chill for about 20 minutes before using.

OLIVE OIL PASTRY

Choose a well-flavoured olive oil for this crisp pastry. It is best used for savoury tarts and complements vegetable fillings especially well. This quantity is enough for a 23cm/9in flan tin (quiche pan).

MAKES ABOUT 275G/10OZ

INGREDIENTS
   225g/8oz/2 cups plain
     (all-purpose) flour
   pinch of salt
   1 egg
   60ml/4 tbsp olive oil
   30ml/2 tbsp lukewarm water

1 Sift the flour and salt into a bowl. In a separate bowl, use a fork to whisk the egg, olive oil and water together.

2 Make a well in the centre of the flour and salt, add the egg mixture and stir with a fork, gradually incorporating the surrounding flour until all the liquid has been worked in and a dough is formed.

3 Knead on a lightly floured surface for a few seconds until smooth, then cover with a damp dishtowel and leave to rest for 30 minutes before using. Knead only until smooth and do not overwork, or the pastry will be tough.

SUET PASTRY

This pastry can be used for both sweet and savoury steamed puddings and has a light, spongy texture. It is wonderfully easy to make as there is no rubbing-in. Because suet is a heavy fat, self-raising flour is always used for this recipe. Lower-fat or vegetarian suet may also be used. This quantity is sufficient to line a 1.75 litre/3 pint/7½ cup ovenproof bowl.

MAKES ABOUT 500G/1¼LB

INGREDIENTS
   275g/10oz/2½ cups self-raising
     (self-rising) flour
   2.5ml/½ tsp salt
   150g/5oz/1 cup shredded suet
   175ml/6fl oz/¾ cup chilled water

1 Sift the flour and salt into a large mixing bowl.

2 Stir in the shredded suet, followed by most of the chilled water (you may need a little less or more) and mix with a fork or spoon to form a soft dough.

3 Knead on a lightly floured surface for a few seconds until smooth. Roll out the suet pastry and use straight away. Don't be tempted to roll the pastry too thinly. It needs to be about 1cm/½in thick.

POTATO PASTRY

This substantial pastry has a crumbly texture when baked. It's rolled out more thickly than shortcrust pastry and is ideal as a topping for meat or other savoury pies. This makes enough for a 25cm/10in pie crust.

MAKES ABOUT 450G/1LB

INGREDIENTS
  115g/4oz floury potatoes, diced
  225g/8oz/2 cups plain
   (all-purpose) flour
  115g/4oz/½ cup chilled butter, diced
  ½ beaten egg
  10ml/2 tsp chilled water

1 Cook the diced potatoes in a pan of salted boiling water until tender. Drain well and mash until smooth.

2 Sift the flour into a mixing bowl. Rub or cut in the butter until the mixture resembles breadcrumbs.

3 Mix together the beaten egg and water, and stir into the mashed potato. Add to the flour mixture and stir with a round-bladed knife to mix to a smooth, pliable dough. Wrap the dough in clear film (plastic wrap) and chill for about 30 minutes before using.

CORNMEAL PASTRY

This pastry can be used in savoury or sweet dishes. It is particularly good in fruit pies, especially apple or pear. The yellow cornmeal gives the pastry an attractive colour. Use the following in a 25cm/10in flan tin (quiche pan).

MAKES ABOUT 350G/12OZ

INGREDIENTS
  115g/4oz/1 cup plain
   (all-purpose) flour
  75g/3oz/¾ cup fine yellow cornmeal
  5ml/1 tsp salt
  5ml/1 tsp soft dark brown sugar
  90g/3½oz/7 tbsp chilled butter, diced
  1 egg yolk
  30ml/2 tbsp chilled water

1 Sift the flour with the cornmeal and salt into a mixing bowl. Stir in the sugar. Rub or cut in the butter until the mixture resembles breadcrumbs.

2 Mix the egg yolk with the chilled water, add to the dry ingredients and mix to a dough, adding a little more water if needed. Gather the dough into a ball, then flatten slightly into a flat round, to make it easier to roll out. Wrap in clear film (plastic wrap) and chill for 30–40 minutes before using.

CREAM CHEESE PASTRY

This moist, flaky pastry is very easy to make and use, provided it is well chilled before being rolled out. It is perfect for tiny tartlets with rich fillings and also makes a wonderful shoofly pie. This quantity is enough for a 25cm/10in flan tin (quiche pan) or ten 5–7.5cm/2–3in tartlet tins (mini quiche pans).

MAKES ABOUT 375G/13OZ

INGREDIENTS
  150g/5oz/1¼ cups plain
   (all-purpose) flour
  pinch of salt
  5ml/1 tsp caster (superfine) sugar
  115g/4oz/½ cup full-fat cream
   cheese, at room temperature
  115g/4oz/½ cup butter, at room
   temperature, diced

1 Sift the flour, salt and caster sugar into a mixing bowl. Add the cream cheese and diced butter to the bowl.

2 Using the back of a fork, mix the butter and cream cheese into the flour to make a soft, smooth dough. Form into a ball and flatten slightly to make rolling out easier. Wrap the dough in clear film (plastic wrap) and chill for about 1 hour before using.

CHOCOLATE PASTRY

This rich, dark pastry is ideal for tarts or flans with creamy fillings or fruit such as pears or mixed soft summer berries. This quantity is enough for a 23cm/9in flan tin (quiche pan).

MAKES ABOUT 300G/10OZ

INGREDIENTS
    115g/4oz/1 cup plain
      (all-purpose) flour
    25g/1oz/¼ cup icing
      (confectioners') sugar
    25g/1oz/¼ cup cocoa powder
      (unsweetened)
    75g/3oz/6 tbsp chilled butter, diced
    2 eggs
    2.5ml/½ tsp vanilla essence (extract)

1 Sift the flour, icing sugar and cocoa powder into a mixing bowl. Rub or cut in the butter until the mixture resembles fine breadcrumbs.

2 Mix the eggs with the vanilla essence. Add to the dry ingredients and mix to a dough with a round-bladed knife.

3 Knead the dough on a lightly floured surface until smooth. Form into a ball, then wrap in clear film (plastic wrap) and chill for 20 minutes before using.

ALMOND PASTRY

This dough resembles pâte sucrée and is especially good with fruits such as apples and cherries. The addition of ground almonds makes it fairly soft to handle, so it must be well chilled before using. This quantity is sufficient for a 23cm/9in flan tin (quiche pan).

MAKES ABOUT 350G/12OZ

INGREDIENTS
    150g/5oz/1¼ cups plain
      (all-purpose) flour
    pinch of salt
    25g/1oz/2 tbsp caster
      (superfine) sugar
    50g/2oz/½ cup ground almonds
    90g/3½oz/7 tbsp chilled butter, diced
    1 egg
    1–2 drops almond essence (extract)

1 Sift the plain flour and salt into a mixing bowl. Stir in the caster sugar and ground almonds. Rub or cut in the butter until the mixture resembles fine breadcrumbs.

2 Beat the egg and almond essence together in a bowl. Stir into the dry ingredients to make a soft dough. Wrap in clear film (plastic wrap) and chill for 40 minutes until firm, before using.

SPICED ORANGE PASTRY

This spicy pastry works well with winter fruit fillings. The following is enough for a 23cm/9in flan tin (quiche pan).

MAKES ABOUT 275G/10OZ

INGREDIENTS
    175g/6oz/1½ cups plain
      (all-purpose) flour
    pinch of salt
    75g/3oz/6 tbsp chilled butter, diced
    4 green cardamom pods
    pinch of ground cloves
    finely grated rind of 1 orange
    25g/1oz/2 tbsp caster
      (superfine) sugar
    2 egg yolks
    10ml/2 tsp fresh orange juice

1 Sift the flour and salt into a mixing bowl. Rub or cut in the butter until the mixture resembles fine breadcrumbs.

2 Using a pestle and mortar, crush the black seeds from the cardamom pods to a powder. Stir them into the flour with the cloves, orange rind and sugar.

3 Mix the egg yolks with the orange juice. Add to the bowl and mix to a dough. Knead until smooth, then wrap and chill for 40 minutes before using.

PUFF PASTRY

Light and crisp, with a distinctly buttery flavour, puff pastry (pâte feuilletée) is the richest, yet lightest, of all pastries. It contains an equal amount of butter to flour. Air is trapped between the layers of dough and this, together with the steam created as the water heats, makes the pastry rise up when baked.

Although you need to allow plenty of time, puff pastry does not require continuous work; just a few minutes of re-rolling about every half hour.

It is essential that everything be kept cold when you are making puff pastry. The water should be chilled and the butter cold, but not so cold that it will break up and tear the dough; before commencing let the butter stand at room temperature for 10 minutes. Never make puff pastry on a hot day. This makes enough for two single-crusts in 1.5 litre/2½ pint/6¼ cup pie dishes or fifteen 8.5cm/3½in vol-au-vents.

MAKES ABOUT 500G/1¼LB

INGREDIENTS
  225g/8oz/2 cups strong white
    bread flour
  pinch of salt
  225g/8oz/1 cup chilled butter
  15ml/1 tbsp lemon juice
  150ml/¼ pint/⅔ cup chilled water

1 Sift the flour and salt into a mixing bowl. Rub or cut in 25g/1oz/2 tbsp of the butter into the flour until the mixture resembles fine breadcrumbs.

2 Place the remaining butter between two sheets of clear film (plastic wrap) and gently beat it out into a 15cm/6in flat square with a rolling pin.

3 Make a well in the centre of the dry ingredients. Stir the lemon juice into the water and add most of it to the bowl. Mix together with a round-bladed knife, adding a little more water if necessary to make a soft, but not sticky, dough.

4 Using a floured rolling pin, roll out the dough on a lightly floured surface to a 25cm/10in square. The dough may look a little lumpy at this stage, but don't knead it. Place the butter diagonally in the centre of the dough, so that it looks like a diamond. Bring each corner of the dough to the centre of the butter to enclose it completely.

5 Roll out the dough to a 40 × 15cm/ 16 × 6in rectangle, then fold the lower third of the pastry over the centre third, and the top third of the pastry down over that. Seal the edges by pressing down with the rolling pin. Brush off any excess flour with a dry pastry brush, then wrap the pastry in clear film and chill for 30 minutes.

6 Roll out the pastry to the same size again, with the sealed edges at the top and bottom. Fold up and chill as before. Repeat the rolling, folding and chilling process five more times. After this, the pastry is ready to be used.

Puff pastry perfection

• Strong white bread flour is usually used when making puff pastry as this flour contains extra gluten to strengthen the dough, enabling it to withstand the rolling out and folding. However, plain (all-purpose) flour will still give good results, or you can use a mixture of the two.

• Lemon juice softens the gluten in the flour and makes the dough more supple. Measure it carefully; too much will make the pastry difficult to handle.

• When chilling the pastry between rollings, do not leave it for longer than 30 minutes or the butter will harden and may break up when rolling out. If you do chill it for longer, leave the puff pastry at room temperature for about 10 minutes to soften slightly before re-rolling.

• It is easy to forget how many times you have rolled puff pastry out. To avoid confusion, mark the pastry each time by pressing it with the appropriate number of fingertips before chilling.

• Allow the pastry to stand for 15 minutes at room temperature before rolling it out for use.

• Always roll out puff pastry at least 5mm/¼in thick. If it is too thin, it won't rise sufficiently.

• If you are not going to use the pastry straight away, wrap it tightly in some clear film (plastic wrap), then in foil. It will keep in the refrigerator for up to three days.

SHORT-CUT PUFF PASTRY

This quick version of puff pastry forms light flaky layers. It uses a mixture of half butter, for flavour, and half white vegetable fat or lard, to give it a crisper texture as compensation for the reduced rolling-out and resting time. It is crucial that all the ingredients are kept cold, so mix the initial dough together quickly. This is enough for two single-crusts in 1.5 litre/2½ pint/6¼ cup pie dishes.

MAKES ABOUT 500G/1¼LB

INGREDIENTS
   115g/4oz/½ cup butter
   115g/4oz/½ cup white vegetable fat
    or lard
   225g/8oz/2 cups plain
    (all-purpose) flour
   pinch of salt
   10ml/2 tsp lemon juice
   150ml/¼ pint/⅔ cup chilled water

1 Dice both the fats. Spread out on a plate and freeze for 10 minutes.

2 Sift the flour and salt into a mixing bowl. Add the diced fat and stir to coat in flour. Make a well in the centre. Stir the lemon juice into the water and add to the dry ingredients. Mix together with a round-bladed knife to make a dough.

3 Put the dough on to a pastry board or work surface, along with any loose flour left in the bowl. Gently shape to a block, then roll out the pastry to a 35 × 20cm/14 × 8in rectangle.

4 Fold the lower third of the pastry over the centre third, then fold the top third over that. Press the edges firmly with the rolling pin to seal. Wrap in clear film (plastic wrap) and chill for 10 minutes.

5 Roll out the pastry to the same size again, with the sealed edges at the top and bottom. Fold up and chill as before. Repeat the rolling, folding and chilling process three more times. Wrap in clear film. Chill for at least 3 hours, but preferably overnight, before using.

ROUGH PUFF PASTRY

This is much simpler to make and far less time-consuming than puff pastry, and has a lower proportion of fat to flour. You will get lovely buttery, flaky results using rough puff pastry, but not a good rise, so use it for sweet and savoury pie and flan crusts. This makes enough for two single-crust pies in 1.5 litre/2½ pint/6¼ cup pie dishes.

MAKES ABOUT 500G/1¼LB

INGREDIENTS
   250g/9oz/2¼ cups plain
    (all-purpose) flour
   pinch of salt
   175g/6oz/¾ cup chilled butter, diced
   5ml/1 tsp lemon juice
   120ml/4fl oz/½ cup chilled water

1 Sift the flour and salt into a mixing bowl. Add the butter and mix with your fingertips to coat the butter with flour.

2 Stir the lemon juice into the water, then add to the dry ingredients and mix in with a round-bladed knife to make a soft dough. Don't worry if the dough is slightly lumpy; the rolling and folding will gradually incorporate the fat.

3 Put the dough on to a lightly floured surface and knead for a few seconds to bring it together.

4 Roll out the pastry to a 30 × 10cm/ 12 × 4in rectangle. Fold the lower third over the centre and the top third over that. Seal the edges. Wrap in clear film (plastic wrap) and chill for 15 minutes.

5 Place the pastry on a lightly floured surface with the sealed edges at the top and bottom. Roll, fold and chill, as before, four more times. After this, the pastry is ready for use.

FLAKY PASTRY

When baked, this pastry looks a little like puff pastry, but has fewer layers. Instead of adding the fat at the start, it is incorporated by dotting it over the rolled-out dough. This creates pockets of air and helps to separate the layers. Half white vegetable fat or lard and half butter can be used instead of all butter for an even flakier texture. This makes enough for two single-crusts in 1.2 litre/ 2 pint/5 cup pie dishes.

MAKES ABOUT 450G/1LB

INGREDIENTS
 225g/8oz/2 cups strong white
  bread flour
 pinch of salt
 175g/6oz/¾ cup chilled butter
 150ml/¼ pint/⅔ cup chilled water

1 Sift the flour and salt into a mixing bowl. Rub or cut in 40g/1½oz/3 tbsp of the butter until the mixture resembles fine breadcrumbs. Pour over 120ml/ 4fl oz/½ cup of the water and, using a round-bladed knife, mix to a soft dough, adding more water if needed.

Using bought puff pastry
If you do not have the time to make your own pastry, ready-made chilled and frozen puff pastry can be bought instead, usually in two sizes: 375g/13oz and 450g/1lb. Ready-rolled puff pastry is also available; check the packet first to make sure it will be large enough for your needs. All-butter varieties are worth searching out.

2 Put on a lightly floured surface and knead until smooth. Wrap in clear film (plastic wrap) and chill for 15 minutes.

3 Roll the dough out to a 30 × 10cm/ 12 × 4in rectangle. Cut another 40g/ 1½oz/3 tbsp of the remaining butter into small pieces and dot them evenly all over the top two-thirds of the pastry, leaving a 1cm/½in margin at the edge.

4 Fold the lower third of the pastry up and over the centre third, and the buttered third down over that. Press the edges together to seal. Wrap in clear film and chill for 10 minutes.

5 Repeat the rolling out and folding process (without adding any more of the butter) once more. Roll out two more times, with the folded edges at the sides, using 40g/1½oz/3 tbsp of the butter each time. Roll out and fold once again (without adding any fat). Chill for at least 1 hour before using.

COOK'S TIPS
• If the pastry still looks streaky after the final rolling and folding, roll and fold it once more.
• Should the pastry become warm and sticky at any time, wrap and chill for about 15 minutes before continuing.

SHORT-CUT FLAKY PASTRY

In this version, instead of dotting the dough with the fat, the butter is chilled and grated or shredded into the flour. This pastry has the same buttery flavour and crispness of flaky, but it isn't as light. This makes enough for two single-crusts in 1.2 litre/2 pint/5 cup pie dishes.

MAKES ABOUT 450G/1LB

INGREDIENTS
 175g/6oz/¾ cup chilled butter
 225g/8oz/2 cups plain
  (all-purpose) flour
 pinch of salt
 90ml/6 tbsp chilled water

1 Put the butter into the freezer for about 40 minutes, or until very hard. Sift the flour and salt into a mixing bowl and chill while the butter is hardening.

2 Holding the butter in a piece of foil, coarsely grate it into the flour, working quickly. Stir in the butter with a round-bladed knife. Sprinkle the water over the mixture and stir to make a dough, adding a little more water if needed.

3 Bring the dough together with your hand. Wrap in clear film (plastic wrap) and chill for 40 minutes before using.

CHOUX PASTRY

Elegantly light and crisp, choux pastry puffs up during baking to at least double its original size, creating a hollow centre, perfect for both sweet and savoury fillings.

Choux is one of the easiest pastries to make; follow the instructions and you can't go wrong. Unlike other pastries, where the fat is rubbed into the flour, choux is made on the hob (stovetop). The butter is melted with water then brought to the boil before adding the flour. Beating the mixture over a low heat partially cooks the flour. Finally, eggs are gradually incorporated to make a thick glossy paste, ready for spooning or piping into puffs and éclairs, or for making an impressive gâteaux such as Paris-Brest and Gâteau Saint-Honoré. This quantity is sufficient for 20 small puffs, 14 large puffs or 12 éclairs.

MAKES ABOUT 150G/5OZ

INGREDIENTS
    65g/2½oz/9 tbsp plain
      (all-purpose) flour
    pinch of salt
    50g/2oz/¼ cup butter, diced
    150ml/¼ pint/⅔ cup water
    2 eggs, lightly beaten

1 Preheat the oven to 200°C/400°F/ Gas 6. Sift the flour and salt on to a small sheet of baking parchment. Put the butter and water in a pan and heat very gently until the butter has melted.

2 Increase the heat and bring to a rolling boil. Remove the pan from the heat and immediately tip in all the flour and beat vigorously until the flour is mixed into the liquid.

3 Return the pan to a low heat and beat the mixture until it begins to form a ball and leave the sides of the pan. This will take about 1 minute. Remove the pan from the heat again and allow to cool for 2–3 minutes.

4 Add the beaten eggs a little at a time, beating well between each addition, until you have a very smooth shiny paste, thick enough to hold its shape. (You may not have to add all the egg.)

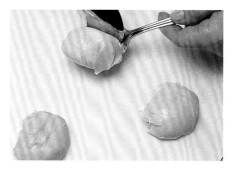

5 Spoon or pipe the pastry on to a baking sheet dampened or lined with baking parchment. Space well apart.

VARIATIONS

For a savoury choux pastry, sift up to 2.5ml/½ tsp mustard powder with the flour. Alternatively, add 75g/3oz/¾ cup grated mature Cheddar or Parmesan.

Top choux pastry tips

• As the choux pastry cooks, the water in the dough turns to steam and puffs up the pastry so, when making, don't let the water boil before the butter fully melts or some of this essential water will evaporate and be lost.

• When adding the flour, beat only until the mixture begins to leave the sides of the pan; over-beating will make the paste oily.
• Eggs lighten the pastry and should be added a little at a time. The mixture will be slightly lumpy at first, but beat vigorously after each addition until the egg and paste are thoroughly mixed. This will ensure you have a smooth and glossy texture.

• Spoon or pipe choux pastry into the required shapes while it is still warm. For the best results, it should be baked straight away.
• When making choux pastry, it may not be necessary to add all of the beaten egg; use just enough to ensure the paste holds its shape.
• If short of time, choux pastry can also be made with a hand held electric mixer.

STRUDEL PASTRY

Although ready-made filo pastry is easily available, the home-made variety is well worth making. Strudel is one pastry that doesn't need gentle handling; the more you bash and beat the pastry dough, the more flexible it will be. It isn't too difficult to make, but requires careful rolling-out on a very large work surface until almost transparent. Have the filling ingredients prepared before you start rolling, as strudel pastry must be used straight away for best results. This makes enough for one large strudel.

MAKES ABOUT 275G/10OZ

INGREDIENTS
    225g/8oz/2 cups strong white
      bread flour
    2.5ml/½ tsp salt
    1 egg, lightly beaten
    10ml/2 tsp sunflower oil
    about 150ml/¼ pint/⅔ cup slightly
      warm water

1 Sift the flour and salt into a mixing bowl. Make a well in the centre. Stir the egg and oil into the water, add to the flour and mix to form a sticky dough.

2 "Beat" the dough by lifting it and slapping it down on to a lightly floured surface. Continue until the dough no longer sticks to your fingers, then knead for 5 minutes until smooth and elastic. Shape into a ball, place on a dishtowel and cover with an upturned bowl. Leave to rest in a warm place for 30 minutes.

3 Lightly flour a very large clean cloth, such as a tablecloth, and roll out the dough as thinly as possible, lifting frequently to prevent it from sticking.

4 Gently stretch the dough with your hands spread out flat underneath it. Work around the dough, stretching until it is paper thin and forms a square of about 65cm/26in. Trim off the thick edges with scissors.

HOT WATER CRUST PASTRY

This traditional British pastry is used for cold meat and game pies – known as standing or raised pies because they hold their shape and stand unsupported by a tin or dish. The following makes enough for a 20cm/8in raised pie mould or loose-based cake tin or a 25 x 7.5cm/10 x 3in oblong raised pie mould.

MAKES ABOUT 450G/1LB

INGREDIENTS
    275g/10oz/2½ cups plain
      (all-purpose) flour
    1.5ml/¼ tsp salt
    65g/2½oz/5 tbsp lard or white
      vegetable fat
    150ml/¼ pint/⅔ cup water

1 Sift the flour and salt into a bowl and make a well in the centre. Gently heat the fat and water in a pan until the fat has melted. Increase the heat and bring to the boil. Pour the hot liquid into the dry ingredients and mix to a soft dough.

2 Knead in the bowl for a few seconds until smooth. Wrap the dough in clear film (plastic wrap) and leave to rest in a warm place for 10 minutes, or until the dough feels firmer. Use while still warm.

PATE A PATE

This is the French equivalent of the British hot water crust pastry. It's a rich, buttery pastry that is robust enough to be used for lining game pie tins as it can hold a heavy filling. The following makes enough for a 20cm/8in raised pie mould or loose-based cake tin or a 25 x 7.5cm/10 x 3in raised pie mould.

MAKES ABOUT 450G/1LB

INGREDIENTS
    225g/8oz/2 cups plain
      (all-purpose) flour
    2.5ml/½ tsp salt
    165g/5½oz/11 tbsp butter, softened
    2 egg yolks
    30–45ml/2–3 tbsp chilled water

1 Sift the flour and salt together to make a mound on a marble slab, pastry board or cool work surface. Make a well in the centre and add the butter. Place the egg yolks on top of the butter.

2 Using just your fingertips, and using a light pecking action, work the butter and yolks together, pulling in a little of the surrounding flour to prevent the mixture from getting too sticky.

3 Add a little of the water and gradually work in all the flour, adding more water if necessary, then knead for 30 seconds until a smooth, soft dough is formed. Wrap in clear film (plastic wrap) and chill for 30 minutes before using.

MAKING FLANS AND PIES

Once the shortcrust, puff or filo pastry is prepared, you are ready to roll and line or cut and layer it into flans, pies or tartlets. Then, there's any number of decorative ideas from simple edgings to lattice tops, pastry cut-outs and glazes.

ROLLING OUT PASTRY

Whether a type of shortcrust or one of the puff pastries, it is not difficult to roll out pastry properly. Try and ensure a cool and airy kitchen, keep the work surface and rolling pin lightly floured, and the dough well chilled. Dust the work surface and the rolling pin with flour as needed; never flour the pastry.

1 Roll out the pastry lightly and evenly in one direction only, rolling from the centre to the far edge, but not actually over the edge. Always roll away from you and rotate the pastry frequently. When rolling out a round, turn the pastry 45 degrees each time to keep an even shape and thickness. (If rolling out pastry to a square or a rectangle, rotate the pastry by 90 degrees each time.)

2 Once or twice during rolling out, push in the edges of the dough with your cupped palms, to keep the shape. Avoid pulling the pastry as you roll it, or it will shrink during cooking.

LINING A FLAN TIN

A traditional flan tin (quiche pan) has straight sides – either fluted or plain – and no rim. Most come with removable bases, making it easy to remove the flan without disturbing the base of it.

Less commonly used is a flan ring, which is a straight-sided metal ring that is set directly on a heavy baking sheet. They are often used by professional pastry cooks, and are a little more tricky to line with pastry.

When lining a very deep-sided flan tin, roll the pastry large enough to cover the base and sides of the tin, then fold it in half, then in half again. Lift the dough into the tin with the point in the centre, then unfold.

1 Remove the chilled pastry from the refrigerator. If it has been chilled for longer than 1 hour, let it stand at room temperature for 15 minutes to soften.

2 On a lightly floured surface, roll out the pastry to a thickness of 3mm/⅛in, and to a round about 5–7.5cm/2–3in larger than the flan tin, depending on the depth of the tin.

3 To transfer the pastry to the flan tin, fold the edge over the rolling pin, then roll the pastry loosely around the pin.

4 Hold the edge of the pastry round and rolling pin over the far edge of the flan tin and carefully unroll the pastry towards yourself, letting it settle easily into the tin without being stretched.

5 Lift the outside edge of the pastry and gently ease it into the base and sides of the tin. Press the pastry against the side of the tin so there are no gaps between the pastry and the tin.

6 Roll the rolling pin over the top of the tin to cut off the excess dough. Prick the base all over with a fork, to stop it rising up during baking.

7 Cover the pastry case with clear film (plastic wrap) and chill for at least 30 minutes to rest the pastry. This will prevent the pastry case from shrinking during cooking.

LINING PIE DISHES

There are three main ways to make a pie. The first is to line the tin with pastry and then fill it; the second is to have a single piece of pastry covering the pie filling (single-crust); and the third is to enclose the filling between two layers of pastry (double-crust).

You can use any of the shortcrust-type pastries when simply lining the tin, though French flan pastry is especially ideal. For single- and double-crust pies, plain or a rich shortcrust pastry is best.

Puff pastry also makes a good pie covering. Use the same techniques as those for shortcrust pastry, but roll the dough slightly thicker, so it rises well.

Making a pastry base for a pie

Roll out the pastry until it is 5cm/2in larger all round than the pie dish. If using shortcrust or one of its variations, the pastry should be 3mm/⅛in thick.

1 Wrap the pastry loosely around the rolling pin. Holding the rolling pin over the pie dish, gently unroll the pastry away from you so that it drapes into the dish, centring it as much as possible.

2 With floured fingertips, press the pastry over the base and up the sides. Trim off the excess with a sharp knife.

Making a single-crust pie

Roll out the pastry on a lightly floured surface until it is 3mm/⅛in thick and 5cm/2in larger all round than the dish.

1 Place the pie funnel in the dish, if using. Cut a 2cm/¾in strip from the rolled out pastry. Brush the rim of the pie dish with water and place the pastry strip around the rim, pressing it down. Brush with water, then add the filling.

2 Using a rolling pin, place the pastry over the filling, using the pie funnel to support it. If you are not using a funnel, fill the dish so that the filling is dome-shaped, then cover with the pastry.

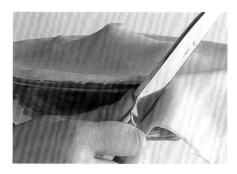

3 Seal the pastry edges together. Trim the excess pastry with a knife, angling it slightly. Finish the edge as wished. Glaze, make steam holes and bake.

Making a double-crust pie

Cut the pastry in half and roll out one half on a lightly floured surface to 3mm/⅛in thick, and 5cm/2in larger all round than the pie dish. Keep the other half wrapped in clear film (plastic wrap).

1 Lift the rolled out pastry into the pie dish using a rolling pin, easing the pastry in without stretching it. Do not worry about the pastry hanging over the edge as this will be trimmed later.

2 Spoon the filling into the pastry case in a domed shape. Brush the edge of the pastry with water to moisten it. Roll out the remaining pastry to a round larger than the top of the pie. Roll it up around the rolling pin and unroll over the pie. Press the edges together.

3 Hold the pie dish in one hand and cut off the excess pastry with a knife, holding the blade at a slight angle. Reserve the trimmings for use as pastry decorations. Finish the edge as wished. Glaze, then make steam holes and bake.

Quantity guide for flans and tarts

The following pastry weights are a guide only, and refer to shortcrust pastry and its variations only. Figures given are the combined weight of ingredients.

Tin size	Pastry weight
18cm/7in	200g/7oz
20cm/8in	275g/10oz
23cm/9in	350g/12oz
25cm/10in	400g/14oz
four x 10cm/4in	250g/9oz
six x 7.5cm/3in	250g/9oz

LINING TARTLET TINS

Use pâte sucrée, chocolate or almond pastry for sweet tarts and rich shortcrust or French flan pastry for savoury ones.

1 When lining tartlet tins (mini quiche pans) that are less than 5cm/2in in diameter, place the tins closely together, then roll out the pastry until it is about 3mm/⅛in thick and able to cover all the tins. Wrap the pastry around the rolling pin, then drape it over the tins.

2 Using a floured thumb, gently press the pastry into the tins. Roll over the top with a rolling pin to trim the edges.

Lining a tin with fragile pastry

If your pastry is too fragile to roll out and lift into a loose-based flan tin (quiche pan) with a rolling pin, remove the loose base and dredge it lightly with flour. Put the pastry on top then roll it out, so that it overhangs the base by 5cm/2in all round. Fold in the overhanging pastry then place the base back in the tin. Unfold the pastry over the edge of the tin, gently pressing into the sides of the tin to fit. Roll a rolling pin over to trim the edges.

LINING A HEATPROOF BOWL OR PUDDING BASIN WITH SUET PASTRY

This spongy pastry is normally used for steamed puddings but it can also be used as a single-crust topping for a baked pie. Its slightly stretchy texture is easy to shape in a pudding basin, but because it is made with self-raising (self-rising) flour it must be rolled out and used immediately.

1 Roll out a scant three-quarters of the suet dough on a floured surface to a 1cm/½in thick round, large enough to line the bowl or basin. Lift it into the bowl, overlapping the edge by 1cm/½in. Press out the folds with your fingers.

2 Spoon the filling into the bowl; it should come nearly to the top. Lightly brush the pastry edge with cold water.

3 Roll out the remaining pastry to make a lid. Carefully place it on top of the filled pastry, pressing down gently with your fingertips to seal the edges. Trim off the excess pastry with a sharp knife.

4 Cover the bowl or basin with a pleated, double layer of baking parchment, securing it under the rim with string. Top with pleated foil – the pleats will expand to allow the pastry to rise.

LINING A TIN WITH FILO PASTRY

Before lining the tin, remove the filo pastry from the refrigerator and leave, still in its wrapper, for 15 minutes at room temperature. Unwrap and unroll and place the filo stack on a board, covering it with a damp dishtowel.

1 Lightly brush a sheet of filo pastry with cooled melted butter or oil, then use to line the base and sides of the tin. There's no need to grease the tin first if it is shallow, but when lining a deeper tin it is easier to position the first sheet of pastry if the tin is lightly greased.

2 Brush a second sheet of pastry with butter or oil as before, then place on top of the first sheet. Layer the pastry to the desired thickness; this will depend on the tin's depth and on the filling, but four or five sheets are usually enough.

3 Neaten the edges by trimming with a pair of scissors. If the filo pastry only slightly overhangs the edge of the tin, it will look attractive if left a little jagged.

4 If the sheets of filo pastry aren't large enough to completely cover a tin, such as a tranche tin, layer up the pastry by covering each end, and overlapping slightly in the middle.

MAKING FILO PASTRY PIES

Filo can be used to make all manner of pies from light and crisp pastry toppings to free-form and double-crust pies. Use the melted butter sparingly, so that the finished pastry is crisp and golden.

Making simple filo toppings

For an incredibly quick and easy way to make a pie, top with either smooth or crumpled sheets of buttered or oiled filo. The filling should require little cooking as the pastry will be crisp and brown in around 30 minutes.

One-crust toppings A savoury or sweet filling can be spooned into a pie dish and covered with a smooth filo pastry topping. You will need six filo pastry sheets, slightly larger than your chosen pie dish – you can use the upturned dish as a guide. Spoon the filling into the dish. Place the sheets of filo on top, lightly buttering between the layers and neatly tucking them down the sides of the dish to fit smoothly.

Scrunch topping Loosely crumple sheets of buttered or oiled filo. Use five to six sheets of filo, placed buttered-side up, to cover the filling. The filling must not be too wet, or steam will spoil the crisp texture of the filo.

Making a free-form pie

Filo pastry can be used to make a free-form pie without using a dish or tin. Pies can be any size you choose, depending on how many people you wish to serve.

1 Melt and cool 50g/2oz/¼ cup butter. Take eight large sheets of filo pastry. Lay the first sheet on a damp dishtowel or baking sheet. Brush with butter.

2 Cover with a second sheet of pastry at a slightly different angle and brush with a little butter. Add three more sheets in the same way.

3 Put the filling into the centre. Cover with the remaining sheets, brushing each layer with butter. Draw up the pastry edges around the filling, twisting and scrunching them to seal. Brush with the remaining butter before baking.

Making double-crust filo pies

Rather than using separate sheets of filo for the bottom and top covering, a single sheet can be draped over the base and sides of a flan tin (quiche pan) or tartlet tins (mini quiche pans) and folded over to enclose the filling.

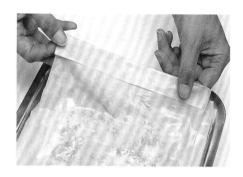

Brush the flan or tartlet tins with melted butter. Fit a square sheet of filo pastry into each tin, draping it so that it hangs over the sides. Brush with butter, then add another sheet at right angles to the first. Spoon in the filling, then draw the overhanging pastry edges together and scrunch to cover the filling. Brush with melted butter before baking. For tins larger than 13cm/5in you will need to use at least four square sheets of filo.

Working with filo

Extremely easy to use, filo comes stacked into sheets, factory-rolled to a thinness that only a pastry chef could achieve.

• Don't be deterred by the flimsy appearance of filo; providing you keep the stack covered with a slightly damp dishtowel and peel off only the sheets that you're working with, it can be cut, folded or layered into shape for quick and easy results.

• To add flavour and to make the pastry light and crisp, lightly brush sheets of bought filo with melted butter or oil, as you layer them.

• Bought pastry is available in various sizes; smaller sheets are about 30 x 18cm/12 x 7in and larger ones are normally about 50 x 24cm/20 x 9½in.

CREATING DECORATIVE EDGES

The edges of flans and pies in pie dishes can be finished in a number of attractive ways, ranging from a simple embossed pattern made with the prongs of a fork to more intricate twists and braids. For some patterns, the pastry will be naturally thick enough around the edge – this is usually the case with puff pastry – but shortcrust and rich shortcrust need a double thickness. If the pie or tart has only a single layer of pastry on the rim, you can leave a slight overhang of pastry when trimming that can be tucked under the edge to create a double thickness.

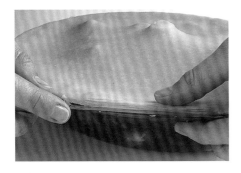

Knocking up After trimming the pastry, finish the pastry edge by holding the blunt edge of a knife horizontally against the pastry edge and tapping to make shallow indentations. Do this all the way around: it seals the join and makes the edge look thicker and neater.

Crimped edges Trim the pastry to leave an overhang of 1cm/½in all round. Fold under. Push your thumb or forefinger into the rim of the pastry and, using the thumb and forefinger of the other hand, pinch the pastry so that forms a "V" shape. Work the pattern all around the edge of the pastry case.

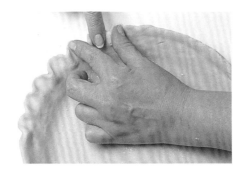

Ruffled edges Trim the pastry to leave an overhang of about 1cm/½in all round and fold under. Place the thumb and forefinger inside the pastry's edge and use the forefinger of the other hand to pull the dough between them, to the edge of the rim. Continue all round.

Scalloped edges Instead of using thumb and forefinger, a knife can be used to finish the edge. Trim the pastry to leave an overhang of 1cm/½in all round and fold it under. Press your forefinger and middle finger on the edge of the pastry. Pressing the blunt edge of a small knife between them, mark a pattern around the edge at 2.5cm/1in intervals.

Forked edges Trim the pastry to leave a slight overhang all round and fold it under. Lightly press the back of a fork evenly all around the edge.

Gabled edges Trim the pastry even with the rim of the dish. Use a knife to make an even number of cuts about 1cm/½in apart all the way around. Fold alternate pieces of pastry inwards. Use on dishes with a rim of more than 1cm/½in.

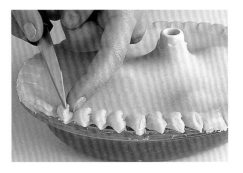

Zig-zag edges Make small cuts in the pastry edge in the same way as for gabled edges. Brush with water, then fold each section over on to itself to form a small triangle. Use on dishes with a rim wider than 1cm/½in.

Ribbon edges Trim the pastry even with the rim. Cut long strips of pastry about 2cm/¾in wide. Moisten the edge of the rim with water. Gently twist a pastry strip and attach it to the rim, twisting and attaching as you go. Use another pastry strip, if necessary, to cover the pie. Press the ends together to seal.

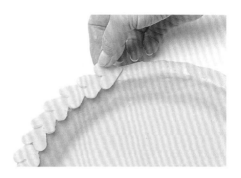

Cut-out edges Trim the pastry even with the rim. With a small floured pastry cutter, stamp out pastry shapes from the re-rolled pastry trimmings. Lightly moisten the edge of the pastry case with water and press the cut-outs in place. Overlap them slightly, if you like.

Braided edges Cut three pastry strips about 1cm/½in wide. Lay the strips on the work surface and pinch the ends together. Take the strip on the right and lay it over the strip in the centre. Take the left piece and lay that over the new centre piece. Continue until the braid is complete, then attach it to the pastry.

Twisted edges Roll a little pastry with your hands to make two thin sausage shapes. Twist the pieces together and seal at both ends. Press into position on the moistened edge of the pastry case.

DECORATING A PIE WITH A LATTICE TOP

A pastry lattice makes a stunning finish and allows the filling to be seen. Roll out half the pastry dough, using either shortcrust or a variation, and use to line the pie dish. Trim to leave a 1cm/½in overhang all round. Add the filling.

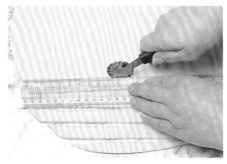

1 To make the lattice top, roll out the remaining pastry to a round that is 5cm/2in larger all round than the dish. Cut strips of pastry 1cm/½in wide using a knife or a fluted pastry wheel and a ruler.

2 To make a square woven lattice, lay half the strips across the pie, keeping them evenly spaced and parallel.

3 Fold back to the centre every other strip. Lay another strip across the centre, on the flat strips, at right angles to them. Lay the folded strips flat again.

4 Next, fold back those strips that were not folded the first time. Lay another strip across those now flat, spacing this new strip evenly from the centre strip.

5 Continue folding the strips in this way until half of the lattice is completed. Repeat on the other half of the pie.

6 Trim the ends of the strips even with the rim of the pie dish. Moisten the edge of the pastry case with water and press the strips gently on to it to seal. Decorate the edge as wished.

7 To make a diamond lattice, weave as above, laying the intersecting strips diagonally instead of at right angles. Seal as above. Or, for the simplest and quickest lattice, arrange half the strips over the filling in one direction and the remaining strips on top at right angles.

MAKING PASTRY DECORATIONS

After the pie or flan has been filled and given a decorative edge or lattice topping, turn the pastry trimmings into attractive motifs to add a final flourish. Where possible, choose a motif to match the filling; fish and shells for a seafood pie, for example. This not only looks attractive, but also lets the diner know what is underneath the crust.

Ordinary shortcrust pastry spreads slightly during cooking and puff pastry rises, so keep designs for these types of pastry fairly simple. To make intricate designs, choose pâte sucrée for sweet pastries, and rich shortcrust for savoury.

Making tassels

These are often used as a decoration on meat and game pies to cover the hole in the centre through which the jelly has been poured.

1 Cut a long rectangle of pastry, about 15 × 2.5cm/6 × 1in. Make 2cm/¾in long neat cuts, at intervals of 5mm/¼in.

2 Brush a little beaten egg or water on the uncut portion of one end, then roll up tightly, and lightly press the end to seal. Open out the tassels. Either bake separately, or position over the pie hole, but don't press into place.

Making leaves

These are extremely simple to make and work well with all types of pastry. Leaf-shaped cutters are available from kitchenware shops in a range of designs including maple and oak leaves. Making your own card (cardboard) template is an easy and creative alternative. Place the template on the pastry and cut round it with a sharp knife. For the easiest leaves of all, however, just follow the instructions below.

Cut rolled-out pastry into strips no more than 2.5cm/1in wide, then cut these diagonally into diamonds. Use the back of a knife to mark veins and pinch each leaf at one end to form a stalk. Curve the leaves slightly when attaching.

Making shells

These spiral shells look wonderful on any pie with a fish or shellfish filling and are very easy to make.

Cut long strips of pastry measuring 10 × 1cm/4 × ½in. Wrap each strip around the pointed end of a cornet mould, overlapping the edge of the pastry strip slightly, as you go. Trim the end to a curve and press to seal. Bake the shells on the cornet moulds and cool before removing.

Making roses

A little patience and practice is needed to achieve perfect pastry roses. They are traditionally used to garnish pâtés enclosed and cooked in pastry (en croûte). They also look good on sweet pastries, with pastry leaves and stems.

1 Mould a marble-size piece of pastry into a cone. Take a second piece of pastry, about twice the size, and shape it into a thin petal.

2 Brush the base of the petal with water and wrap it around the cone to fully enclose it. Make a second petal and place the centre edge opposite the join line of the first petal and slightly above it. Fix one side to the cone and leave the other side free.

3 Place the centre of the third petal over the closed side of the second petal. Fix it on both sides. Place the centre of the fourth petal over the edge of the third and under the second petal's open side. Close the edge of the second petal then curl back all the petal tips. Lastly, add three or four slightly larger petals.

4 Squeeze the base of the rose slightly, flattening it if the rose is to be laid on its side or cutting it to stand upright.

GLAZING PASTRY BEFORE BAKING

The appearance of almost every pie can be improved with a glaze. Even a simple brushing of milk or egg white will give the pastry case a lovely finish. This is true of all shortcrust pastries, whether savoury or sweet, as well as for puff pastry and its variations. The exception is filo, which is given its golden shine by the butter that is brushed over the pastry before it is baked.

Brush the decorated pastry before baking. This removes any stray pieces of flour, seals the surface and gives it a sheen. Glaze the surface of pies before positioning cut-out pastry decorations, then brush the decorations with more glaze. Always glaze thinly and evenly, avoiding any drips. This is important when glazing puff pastry, as any glaze on the sides of the pastry will make the layers stick together and prevent rising.

Each of these glazes gives a slightly different result. Egg wash adds a deep golden colour as well as gloss, lightly beaten egg white gives a clear finish, and milk gives a dull shine. For a richer colour, saffron can be infused with milk and used on its own or with beaten egg. After glazing, sweet pies can be sprinkled with sugar.

Egg wash Whole beaten egg can be used or, for a very rich, glossy finish, lightly beat 1 egg yolk with 5ml/1 tsp cold water in a bowl, then beat in a pinch of salt or caster (superfine) sugar. A double coating of glaze will give an even deeper colour; after applying the first coat of glaze, chill the pastry, then apply a second coat. Brush the egg glaze thinly, taking care that it doesn't pool around any decorative edges, or they will be much darker after baking.

Egg white Lightly beaten egg white gives a clear, shiny finish. On sweet pastries, sprinkle the egg white with caster sugar.

Milk This can be used when a very light glaze with little shine is needed. Use on sweet pies made with rich shortcrust pastry or pâte sucrée as these will already have a good colour from the egg yolks in the pastry. Sprinkle the pastry with caster sugar, or with granulated or demerara sugar to give a crunchy finish.

Saffron egg glaze This gives pastry a vibrant golden colour and is ideal for fish pies. Add a pinch of saffron threads to a small bowl containing 15ml/1 tbsp hot milk or water. Leave for 20 minutes, then strain into a little beaten egg or egg yolk. Add a pinch of salt for savoury pies or caster sugar for sweet ones, before using to glaze.

Tips for baking pastry decorations

• Trimmings can be cooked in place on the pie, or separately on a baking sheet lined with baking parchment. Always chill them for at least 30 minutes before baking.

• Support fragile roses and tassels with crumpled kitchen foil. Just before baking, use a tiny brush to thinly and carefully glaze the decoration with egg wash.
• Cover pastry decorations that are attached to a pie with small pieces of oiled foil. This will prevent them from colouring too much before the pie is cooked.
• Bake shortcrust, pâte brisée and pâte sucrée decorations on the middle shelf of a preheated oven at 190°C/375°F/Gas 5.
• Puff pastry decorations require a slightly higher temperature of 200°C/400°F/Gas 6. Allow 5–6 minutes for leaves, 12–15 minutes for tassels, spiral shells and roses. Check the decorations frequently

• When re-rolling puff pastry trimmings, pile them up on top of each other, so that the layers are arranged laterally, giving the pastry an even rise.

HOW TO BAKE FLANS AND PIES

Whatever type of pastry you are baking, always allow time to preheat the oven; it will take about 15 minutes to reach the required temperature (fan ovens may heat more quickly). As a general rule, bake pastry on the middle shelf or just above the middle of the oven, unless the recipe tells you otherwise. If you are blind-baking or cooking a double-crust pie, it's a good idea to put a heavy baking sheet in the oven to heat up. The hot baking sheet will give the base of the pie an initial blast of heat to help ensure the bottom of the pastry is crisp. It will also make it easier to slide the pie in and out of the oven.

When following a recipe, baking times may vary slightly depending on your oven and how chilled the pie was when cooking commenced. Always check the pie at least 5 minutes before the end of the suggested cooking time. Don't keep opening the oven door though, or the temperature will drop, the pastry will be less crisp and it will inevitably take longer to cook.

BAKING SHORTCRUST PASTRY

Shortcrust pastry and its variations should be well chilled before baking to mimimize shrinkage. Between 30–60 minutes is adequate for a flan or pie that is filled prior to baking; left much longer, the filling may start to soak into the pastry. If a flan case is to be blind-baked or filled just before baking, chill the pastry for an hour uncovered, or cover with clear film (plastic wrap) and chill overnight.

Shortcrust-type pastries are usually baked at 200°C/400°F/Gas 6, but often the temperature is reduced part-way through baking to allow the filling to cook sufficiently. Take care with pastries that contain added sugar; these need to be removed from the oven as soon as the pastry is golden brown because once this stage is reached, they can burn very quickly.

Don't cook any foods that will release a lot of steam in the oven at the same time as the shortcrust is cooking since this could prevent the pastry from becoming crisp.

Baking blind

This process is used for a number of reasons. It is used to partly cook an empty pastry case so that it does not become soggy when the filling is added and the final baking is done. It is also used to completely bake a pastry case when the filling cooks in a relatively short time and you need to ensure that the pastry is fully cooked through, and when the pastry case is to contain a precooked mixture or one that does not require any cooking.

Lining the pastry case with baking parchment or foil and filling it with baking beans stops the pastry from rising up during cooking.

1 Cut out a round of baking parchment or foil about 7.5cm/3in larger than the flan tin (quiche pan). Prick the base of the pastry case all over with a fork.

2 Lay the baking parchment or foil in the pastry case and press it smoothly over the base and up the side.

3 Put either the commercially made ceramic baking beans, or dried beans or peas in the case, spreading them out evenly to cover the base. Whichever kind you choose, they can be used over and over again.

4 To partially bake the pastry, bake in a preheated oven at 200°C/400°F/Gas 6 for 15 minutes, or until the pastry is set and the rim is dry and golden. Lift out the paper and beans. Return the case to the oven for a further 5 minutes. The pastry case can now be filled and the baking completed.

5 For fully baked pastry, bake the case at 200°C/400°F/Gas 6 for 15 minutes, then remove the paper and beans and return to the oven. Bake for a further 5–10 minutes, or until golden brown. Cool completely before filling.

6 To bake tartlets, bake blind in the same way as flans, but allow only 6–8 minutes for partial baking, and 12–15 minutes for fully baked pastry.

> **Planning ahead**
> Fully baked pastry cases, both large and small, may be baked up to two days ahead if carefully stored in airtight containers. Interleave them with greaseproof (waxed) paper, or use baking parchment, if you are keeping several, and always make sure that they are cooled before storing.

Shortcrust baking tips for success

• If you find any small holes in a cooked pastry case, repair them by brushing with a little beaten egg, then return the case to the oven for 2–3 minutes to seal. Any larger holes or tears that appear during baking should be repaired by pressing a little raw pastry in the gap, brushing with beaten egg, and then returning to the oven.

• If the pastry starts to bubble up during baking, remove the pastry case from the oven, prick again with a fork to allow the trapped air to escape and return to the oven. If it has bubbled up when you take it out after cooking, don't try to press it flat, or you will crack the pastry. Make a very small slit in the case with a knife and leave it to shrink back on its own.

• If the pastry has fully browned before the filling is completely cooked, protect it by covering with foil. Cover single- or double-crust pies completely, making a hole in the top of the foil to allow steam to escape. On open flans, cover the pastry edge only with strips of foil.

BAKING PUFF PASTRY

The baking method for puff, rough puff and flaky pastry has much in common with that used for shortcrust. Chilling the pastry before baking is essential, and shaped puff pastries should be chilled for at least an hour to prevent the pastry becoming mis-shapen during baking. Take great care when brushing the pastry with egg glaze; any that runs down the sides of the pastry will make the layers stick together and prevent the pastry from rising well and evenly.

Layered pastries must be cooked in a preheated hot oven, so that the air trapped within the layers expands and, together with the steam produced by the water, lifts up the pastry. If the oven is too cool the butter will melt before the dough has a chance to cook, preventing the pastry from rising well. The oven temperature is usually 230°C/450°F/ Gas 8, but small pastries are sometimes cooked at 220°C/425°F/Gas 7. Reduce the temperature after about 15 minutes, to give the filling time to cook through.

When baking single- and double-crust pies, up to three (depending how moist the filling is) slits or holes should be made in the pastry top to allow the steam from the filling to escape. Don't make too many steam holes though, or too much air will be lost and the pastry won't rise well. After baking, cover steam holes with cooked pastry decorations.

Unlike shortcrust pastries, a steamy atmosphere helps the pastry to rise. Put a dish of hot water on the lowest shelf when preheating the oven. Remove it for the last few minutes of cooking. If the pastry starts to sink after cooking, it hasn't cooked sufficiently and should be returned to the oven for a little longer.

BAKING FILO PASTRY

Unlike shortcrust and puff pastries, filo pastry does not require chilling before baking. The most important point to remember is that filo must never dry out, or it will become brittle and hard to fold and shape. Keep the sheets you are not working with covered with a damp dishtowel. It may also crumble if it is too cold so, before using, remove the unopened packet from the refrigerator and allow to stand for 1 hour.

Filo must always be lightly brushed with melted butter before baking to give it a shiny glaze – unsalted (sweet) butter is perfect because it has a lower water content, or oil can also be used. Choose a flavoursome oil, such as groundnut (peanut) or sunflower oil, or try olive oil when making well-flavoured savoury pastries. Don't overdo the fat though; it should be brushed as thinly and evenly as possible to create light crisp layers. Never brush filo with egg or milk as this would make it soggy.

The usual temperature for baking filo pastry is 200°C/400°F/Gas 6, although it can be cooked at a slightly lower temperature without its crisp texture being affected. It colours quickly, so check frequently towards the end of the cooking time. If the pastry has browned sufficiently before the filling is cooked, cover it loosely with foil, then remove again for the last few minutes to make sure the top of the pie is dry and crisp.

Wrap any unused filo in clear film (plastic wrap) and return it to the refrigerator. It will keep for seven to ten days. It is possible to re-freeze filo, but don't do this more than once. To thaw, allow 4 hours at room temperature, or leave overnight in the refrigerator.

SHAPING AND BAKING CHOUX PASTRY

This thick, smooth and glossy paste can be piped or spooned into a variety of shapes including round puffs, finger-lengths and rings. It can also be fried to make churros and French aigrettes, which are crunchy on the outside and soft in the centre. Choux is made on the hob (stovetop) and should be shaped while warm for the best results.

PIPING CHOUX PASTRY

Before piping, you may find it helpful to draw faint guidelines on the baking parchment first, then place the paper pencil-side down on the baking sheet.
Rounds Use a piping bag fitted with a 1cm/½in plain or fluted nozzle to make small puffs and, for large puffs, use a 2.5cm/1in plain nozzle. Use a wet knife to cut off the pastry at the nozzle.

Eclairs Spoon the pastry into a piping bag fitted with a 2.5cm/1in plain nozzle. Pipe 10cm/4in lengths on to baking parchment, using a wet knife to cut off the pastry at the nozzle.

Ring Draw a 18cm/7in circle on baking parchment. Place pencil-side down on a baking sheet. Spoon the choux pastry into a piping bag fitted with a 1cm/½in nozzle and pipe a ring using the pencil marking as a guide.

SHAPING CHOUX PUFFS

Whether spooned or piped, these balls of choux pastry will rise to about three times their original size, creating a hollow centre that is ready for filling. Make small ones into profiteroles with a cream filling and a chocolate sauce or pile into a pyramid held together with caramel for the classic French dessert croquembouche. Larger ones can be turned into cream buns.

Small and large puffs To make small puffs, use two small spoons dipped in water. Drop the paste in 2.5cm/1in wide balls on to a greased baking sheet, or one lined with baking parchment, leaving a 4cm/1½in space between each. For large puffs, use two large spoons to make balls 5cm/2in wide. Neaten the puffs with a spoon, dipped in water.

FRYING PIPED CHOUX

Choux pastry can be deep-fried in hot oil rather than baked, giving a crisp, golden outside and a soft, light centre.

Spoon the choux into a piping bag fitted with a large star nozzle. Pipe four or five 7.5cm/3in lengths of pastry at a time into hot oil, using a pair of scissors to snip off each length. Fry for 3 minutes until crisp, then drain on kitchen paper.

BAKING CHOUX

No matter what shape or size, choux pastry should be dark golden and crisp on the outside and cooked sufficiently so that it holds its shape when removed from the oven. For this reason, choux is usually baked at a higher temperature first, to cook the outside, then at a lower one to firm and dry the pastry.

Bake small puffs in a preheated oven at 200°C/400°F/Gas 6 for 15–20 minutes; large puffs, eclairs and rings will take 25–30 minutes. Turn down the oven to 180°C/350°F/Gas 4, remove the tray from the oven, make small slits in the sides of the pastries, then return and bake small puffs for a further 5 minutes; large puffs, eclairs and rings for a further 8–12 minutes.

It is important not to open the oven during the first 15 minutes of baking time or the choux may collapse. When you remove the pastries to make slits in them, check that they are fully cooked and set first.

The more steam in the oven at the start of baking, the more successfully the pastry will rise. Try dampening the baking sheet by sprinkling with cold water before spooning or piping the pastry, or place an ovenproof dish of water on the lowest shelf of the oven. Remove the dish for the last 5 minutes of cooking time to allow the pastries to become properly crisp.

Choux pastries are best freshly made, but will keep for a day or two in an airtight container. Put them on a baking sheet in a medium oven for 3–4 minutes to regain their crispness. Once filled, serve them as soon as possible, or they will become soggy.

SHAPING AND BAKING HOT WATER CRUST

This pastry is used for traditional cold meat and game pies as it holds its shape and can withstand long cooking.

MOULDING HOT WATER CRUST PASTRY

Keep this pastry warm while moulding; if the lard starts to set, the pastry will become unmanageable and may crack.

1 Make a basic quantity of dough, and cut off one-third. Wrap it in clear film (plastic wrap) and leave in a warm place. Shape the remaining two-thirds of the pastry into a ball. Lightly grease and flour the outside of an empty 900g/2lb jam jar, turn it upside-down, mould the dough over the base and two-thirds down the sides.

2 Cover with clear film and chill for 20 minutes, then invert the pastry case and jar on to a baking sheet and ease out the jam jar. Spoon the filling into the pastry mould, packing it firmly. Roll out the reserved pastry to a round and trim to fit the top of the pie.

3 Wrap the trimmings and set aside. Dampen the edges and place the lid on top. Crimp the edges together neatly. Make a hole in the top of the pie with a 1cm/½in plain pastry cutter. Attach pastry trimmings, if you wish.

4 Secure a double layer of baking parchment, cut to size, around the pie with paper clips to keep the pastry in shape during cooking.

LINING A TIN WITH HOT WATER CRUST PASTRY

To line a 15cm/6in round cake tin, you need to use 350g/12oz/3 cups plain (all-purpose) flour, 1.5ml/¼ tsp of salt, 75g/3oz/6 tbsp fat and 190ml/6½fl oz/ generous ¾ cup warm water.

To line a 23cm/9in long pointed oval pie tin, or a 20cm/8in round springform tin, use the following: 450g/1lb/4 cups plain flour, 2.5ml/½ tsp salt, 115g/4oz/ ½ cup fat and 250ml/8fl oz/1 cup water.

1 Make the pastry as before. Cut off slightly less than a third, wrap in clear film (plastic wrap) and set aside in a warm place. Roll out the remaining pastry to a round large enough to line the tin. Carefully lift the pastry in, allowing the edges to hang over the sides. Gently press with your fingers to mould the pastry into place, then spoon in the filling, packing it down firmly.

2 Trim off the overhanging pastry edges, angling the knife outwards. Wrap the pastry trimmings and set them aside for later use as decorations.

3 Roll out the reserved pastry to make a lid slightly larger than the top of the tin. Brush the edges with water and place the lid over the pie. Gently press the edges together to seal, then lightly crimp the pastry to give it a fluted edge.

BAKING HOT WATER CRUST PASTRY

As hot water crust pastry cooks the outside becomes crunchy and golden and the juices and fat from the pie filling seep into the pastry and flavour it.

Hot water crust pies are usually cooked at 200°C/400°F/Gas 6 for the first 20–30 minutes, then at a reduced temperature of 180°C/350°F/Gas 4 or lower for the remaining cooking time.

1 Use a small cutter to make a steam hole, or cut a cross in the lid and fold back the corners. Make decorations with the reserved pastry trimmings and bake them separately, or place them on the crust to cook.

2 After baking put a funnel through the hole in the pastry lid and carefully pour in jelly or aspic until it reaches the level of the pastry lid. Replace or add the cooked pastry decorations and then chill until set. If the jelly starts to leak through a crack in the pastry, seal it by filling with butter.

MAKING PARCELS AND SHAPED PASTRIES

Without the restrictions of flan tins (quiche pans) and pie dishes, there are an infinite number of ways to shape pastry packages. Shortcrust and puff pastries and their variations, as well as filo can all be simply and easily used to create delicious parcels in a range of sizes, from mini mouthfuls through to individual portions and larger pastries.

SHAPING SHORTCRUST PASTRY

Rounds, strips, crescents and squares of shortcrust pastry provide the perfect package for sweet and savoury fillings. Mini baked circles of pastry also serve as delightful bases to toppings of fresh fruit and cream.

Making round parcels

This little round pastry parcel is ideal for sweet fillings of thinly sliced raw fruit such as apples and pears tossed in a little sugar, or cooked, then drained, juicier fruits such as gooseberries. The hole in the top allows the filling to be seen as well as providing a steam hole.

1 Roll out 450g/1lb shortcrust pastry to a thickness of 3mm/1⅛in and cut out four 10cm/4in rounds and four slightly larger rounds, about 13cm/5in in diameter. Using a small, round pastry cutter, stamp a small hole out of the middle of the larger rounds. Spoon a little filling in a rounded heap on the smaller rounds.

2 Brush the edges of the filled pastry rounds with a little water, cover with the larger rounds of pastry and crimp the edges together. Bake at 200°C/400°F/Gas 6 for 20 minutes if using a cooked filling, or at a lower temperature for a longer time if the filling is uncooked.

Making pasties

In these traditional single-serving pies, shortcrust pastry completely encloses the filling, which is usually a mixture of either raw or cooked minced (ground) meat and vegetables. The name comes from the Latin "pasta" meaning dough. Originally the crust was a container only and would have been discarded.

1 Roll out 450g/1lb shortcrust pastry to a thickness of 5mm/¼in and cut into four 20cm/8in rounds. Spoon the filling into the centre of each round and brush the edges with water. Bring the edges together to seal, then flute.

2 Transfer to a baking sheet, brush with beaten egg and make a hole in the top of each one for the steam to escape. If using uncooked filling, bake the pasties at 220°C/425°F/Gas 7 for 15 minutes, then reduce the temperature to 160°C/325°F/Gas 3 and bake for 1 hour more. If the filling is already cooked, bake at 200°C/400°F/Gas 6 for 20–25 minutes.

3 You can also cook pasties on their side, in which case spoon the filling on to one half of each circle, lightly brush the edges with water, then fold over the other pastry half and press to seal. Finish and bake as before.

Making turnovers

These triangular-shaped pastries are usually made with a pre-cooked filling such as apple. Savoury vegetable and meat mixtures are also popular.

1 Roll out 300g/11oz rich shortcrust pastry to a 25cm/10in square 3mm/⅛in thick. Cut into four squares. Place the filling on one side of a diagonal centre line, brush with water, then fold over.

2 Press the edges to seal, then mark a pattern on them with a fork. Brush with beaten egg and make a slit in the top to allow the steam to escape. Bake at 200°C/400°F/Gas 6 for 25 minutes.

Making crescents

Rich shortcrust pastry is used to make these crescent-shaped pastries as it is a flexible pastry. They are ideal for richer fillings such as cream or curd cheese with dried fruits.

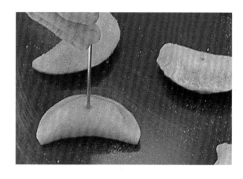

Roll out 450g/1lb pastry to a thickness of 3mm/⅛in and stamp out nine rounds, using a plain or fluted 7.5cm/3in cutter. Place the filling on one side of each. Brush with a little milk, then fold over and press the edges together to seal. Make a steam hole in each and bake at 200°C/400°F/Gas 6 for 18–20 minutes.

Making fruit dumplings

Whole peeled and cored fresh fruit is delicious wrapped in pastry and then baked. Choose firm ripe fruit, such as eating apples or pears, which won't disintegrate during cooking.

1 Roll out 400g/14oz rich shortcrust pastry to a 35cm/14in square. Cut into four squares. Place a small apple or a squat pear on each pastry square – the hollowed-out centre of the fruit can be stuffed if you like.

2 Brush the pastry edges with beaten egg and pull up the four corners to meet at the top, gently pressing the edges together to seal well, then flute. Chill for 40 minutes before brushing with beaten egg and baking at 220°C/425°F/Gas 7 for 30 minutes. Reduce the oven temperature to 180°C/350°F/Gas 4 and bake for 20 minutes more until the pastry is golden and the fruit is tender when pierced with a fine skewer.

3 Alternatively, encase whole fruit in strips of pastry. Cut the rolled-out pastry into 1cm/½in strips and wind around the prepared fruit, slightly overlapping and dampening with a little water to hold together. Wind from the base to the stalk end. Chill and bake as before.

Wrapping larger fillings

Known as en croûte, wrapping meat in pastry keeps it moist and succulent. Beef Wellington is probably the best-known example, but a leg of lamb, whole salmon or even lamb cutlets can also be cooked in this way. These dishes can be prepared up to a day before cooking, providing the meat or fish is very fresh, as the pastry stops the meat from drying out. Cover with clear film (plastic wrap) and chill until needed, but allow to stand at room temperature for 25 minutes before baking.

Brown the outside of larger cuts such as beef and lamb, then cool; this isn't necessary for smaller pieces of meat or fish. Use about 450g/1lb rich shortcrust pastry or puff pastry for a 1.3kg/3lb fillet (tenderloin) of beef and 800g/1¾lb for a leg of lamb or medium-sized salmon.

1 Roll out the pastry to the appropriate shape – for example, a rectangle for beef, a triangle for a leg of lamb – large enough to fully enclose the meat or fish. Wrap the meat or fish in the pastry. Seal the edges with a little water, then put seam-side down on a baking sheet.

2 Use a tiny round cutter to stamp two or three steam holes out of the pastry. Bake at 200°C/400°F/Gas 6 for the first 15 minutes, then lower the temperature to 180°C/350°F/Gas 4, until cooked.

COOK'S TIP

Use a meat thermometer to check if the meat is cooked. Beef should register 60–80°C/140–176°F, while lamb should register 70–80°C/158–176°F. A whole salmon will take 30 minutes to cook after lowering the temperature. Check by flaking the flesh; it should be opaque.

Making pastry tubes

Little cannoli cylinders, 10cm/4in long, are used as moulds to shape and bake pastry. The pastry tubes can then be filled with flavoured whipped cream or, in Sicilian tradition, ricotta cheese, nuts and candied fruit, and dusted with sugar.

1 Roll out 7.5cm/3in rounds of pâte sucrée into ovals the same length as the cannoli moulds. About 350g/12oz pastry will make eight tubes. Wrap each oval lengthways around a mould, sealing the join with egg white. Chill for 30 minutes.

2 Deep-fry in sunflower oil heated to 180°C/350°F until golden brown. Drain on kitchen paper and remove from the moulds while still hot.

Making galettes

These simple round flat pastries whose name comes from the French word for a flat weather-worn pebble, are made from sweet pastries such as pâte brisée or pâte sucrée. Top with fruit and cream.

Roll out the pastry to a thickness of 5mm/¼in and stamp out 6cm/2½in rounds. Place on a baking sheet, prick all over with a fork and chill. Bake at 200°C/400°F/Gas 6 for 10 minutes, or until golden brown.

SHAPING PUFF PASTRY

Although puff pastry rises, it holds its shape well and is used for well-known pastry gâteaux such as mille-feuilles, as well as smaller sweet and savoury puff pastries, such as palmiers and mini vol-au-vents.

Making puff pastry envelopes

One of the advantages of puff pastry over shortcrust is that it is more flexible and less likely to tear when making a large parcel. It works well with partially or fully cooked fillings, such as chopped cooked chicken and vegetables in a white sauce or the traditional Russian salmon, egg and rice-filled pastry dish, known as koulibiac.

1 Roll out 350g/12oz puff pastry to a 30cm/12in square. Pile the filling into the middle to form a 14cm/5½in square at right angles to the pastry (so that it looks like a diamond).

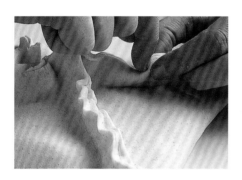

2 Bring the corners of the dough to the centre and gently crimp the edges together. Make a small steam hole. Chill for 30 minutes before brushing with beaten egg. Bake in a preheated oven at 230°C/450°F/Gas 8 for 15 minutes then reduce the temperature to 190°C/375°F/Gas 5 for 15 minutes more until crisp and golden.

> **Planning ahead**
> Puff pastry cases are best eaten on the day they are baked, but they can be made up to a day ahead and stored in an airtight container. Fill as close to serving time as possible.

Making puff pastry cases

Known as vol-au-vents, these cases can be made in many different sizes and can be stuffed with all sorts of fillings, from hot garlic mushrooms to prawns in mayonnaise. When baked, the scored inner circle makes a lid that can be lifted out and the outer circle forms the walls of the vol-au-vent.

1 Roll out 500g/1¼lb puff pastry to a 23cm/9in round. Put a dinner plate on top and cut around with a knife. Lift the pastry round on to a baking sheet.

2 Put a side plate in the middle of the round and, holding it firmly in place, score the pastry around it, but do not cut all the way through.

3 Knock up the pastry edges with the back of a knife. Chill for 30 minutes, then bake in a preheated oven at 230°C/450°F/Gas 8 for 25 minutes.

4 Cut around the pastry lid with a small sharp knife, and carefully lift the lid out in one piece. Set the lid aside. Scrape any soft pastry out of the middle of the vol-au-vent, then return it to the oven for about 4 minutes to dry out. Spoon the chosen filling into the vol-au-vent, then replace the lid and serve.

Making bouchées

Meaning "mouthful", these vol-au-vents are made quite tiny, as their name suggests. These pastries are usually served as finger food and so they are cooked at a slightly lower temperature so that the pastry becomes really dry and crisp. This ensures that they can be picked up easily without any chance of the cases collapsing. Make fillings thick but without too much sauce, so that they can be easily picked up.

Unbaked cases can be cooked from frozen. 450g/1lb puff pastry will yield about 25 bouchées.

1 Roll out the pastry to a thickness of 5mm/¼in. Stamp out rounds using a floured 4cm/1½in plain or fluted cutter. Transfer the rounds to a baking sheet. Lightly brush the tops with beaten egg.

2 To make the lid, cut halfway through the depth of each round using a slightly smaller cutter. Chill, then bake in a preheated oven at 220°C/425°F/Gas 7 for 12–15 minutes until golden brown.

3 When cooked, ease off the lid with the point of a knife. Scoop out any soft pastry from the centre and discard. Spoon or pipe in the filling then replace the lids and serve either warm or cold.

Varying vol-au-vent depth and shape

Both large and smaller individual puff pastry cases can be made deeper by placing a ring of pastry on top of the pastry round, thus making it possible to add more filling. Rectangular, square or diamond shapes are also possible.

1 To make individual deep round vol-au-vents, roll out the pastry to 5mm/¼in thick and stamp out rounds using a floured 10cm/4in cutter. Cut rings from half the pastry rounds, using a 7.5cm/3in cutter and discard the centres.

2 Place the large rounds on a baking sheet and brush around the edges with beaten egg, then place a ring on top of each. Chill, brush the rings with beaten egg, and bake at 220°C/425°F/Gas 7 for 15–18 minutes, until golden. Remove and discard the centres, or use as lids.

To make mini rectangular cases, roll out puff pastry to 7.5 × 10cm/3½ × 4in rectangles, about 5mm/¼in thick. Cut an inner rectangle 2.5cm/1in from the pastry edge, scoring halfway through. Mark criss-cross lines on top of the inner rectangle, brush with egg and bake in a preheated oven at 220°C/425°F/Gas 7 for 12–15 minutes. Lift out the notched rectangles and use as lids.

Making a slatted-top pie

Also known as a jalousie (the French word for window shutters), a slatted-top pie was originally a simple pastry filled with jam. Today, however, a variety of sweet and savoury fillings are used.

1 Roll out 500g/1¼lb puff pastry to a 30cm/12in square. Trim the edges and cut in half to make two rectangles. Put one on a baking sheet and chill. Spread the pastry on the baking sheet with 225g/8oz/¾ cup jam, leaving a 2.5cm/1in border all round. Dampen the edges with a little water or milk.

2 Fold the second piece of pastry in half lengthways. Make cuts about 1cm/½in apart along the folded edge to within 2.5cm/1in of the outer edge.

3 Without unfolding, carefully place the folded piece of pastry on top of one side of the jam-covered pastry, so that the corners and edges match, then unfold the slatted pastry to cover the other half.

4 Press the edges to seal, then knock them up with the back of a knife. Chill for 30 minutes before baking in a preheated oven at 230°C/450°F/Gas 8 for 25 minutes. Cut the jalousie in crossways slices to serve.

Gâteau Pithiviers

This scored-top pastry originates from the town of the same name, near Paris. It has a rum-flavoured almond filling and is recognized by the spiral pattern on the pastry lid.

1 Roll out two 25cm/10in rounds from 500g/1¼lb puff pastry. Place one on a baking sheet. Mix 50g/2oz/¼ cup butter, 115g/4oz/1 cup sifted icing (confectioners') sugar, 115g/4oz/1 cup ground almonds, 2 egg yolks and 30ml/2 tbsp rum in a bowl, and spread over the pastry round leaving a border of 2.5cm/1in all round.

2 Brush the border with water and top with the second pastry round, pressing to seal the edges. Knock up and scallop the edge.

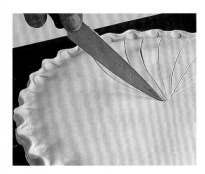

3 With a knife, mark curved lines 5mm/¼in apart, from the centre to the edge and cutting only halfway through the pastry. Cover with clear film (plastic wrap) and chill for 30 minutes. Glaze, then bake in a preheated oven at 230°C/450°F/Gas 8 for 25 minutes.

Making puff pastry layers

Mille-feuille is the classic example of a layered puff pastry dessert and means a thousand leaves. After baking, the rectangles of pastry are sandwiched together, usually with fruit and cream.

1 Roll out 500g/1¼lb puff pastry to a 30 × 20cm/12 × 8in rectangle. Cut into three pieces, each 10 × 20cm/4 × 8in.

2 Place on a baking sheet, cover and chill for 30 minutes. Brush with beaten egg, prick each piece, then bake in a preheated oven at 230°C/450°F/Gas 8 for 8–10 minutes. Cool and sandwich the layers together with the filling.

Making feuilletées

These are a simple form of mille-feuille, usually made as single servings. Small rectangles of puff pastry are baked then split in half horizontally to form two layers. A filling such as whipped cream and fruit is added, then the layers are sandwiched back together.

Roll out 350g/12oz puff pastry and cut into four 10 × 6cm/4 × 2½in rectangles, 1cm/½in thick. Chill for 20 minutes, then brush with beaten egg and bake in a preheated oven at 220°C/425°F/Gas 7 for 12–15 minutes.

Shaping palmiers

These pastries are a Parisian speciality. They are often simply rolled in sugar, or may have a nut filling of finely chopped almonds, walnuts or hazelnuts mixed with ground cinnamon and sugar.

1 Lightly sprinkle the work surface with caster (superfine) sugar and roll out 225g/8oz puff or rough puff pastry to a 50 × 20cm/20 × 8in rectangle.

2 Brush with beaten egg, then sprinkle evenly with half the nut mixture.

3 Fold in the long edges of the pastry to meet in the centre and flatten with the rolling pin. Brush the top with egg and sprinkle with three-quarters of the nut mixture. Fold in the edges again to meet in the centre, brush with egg and sprinkle with the remaining nut mixture. Fold half the pastry over the other.

4 Cut crossways into 2cm/¾in thick slices and place, cut-side down, about 2.5cm/1in apart on greased baking sheets. Slightly open up the pastries.

5 Bake in a preheated oven at 220°C/425°F/Gas 7 for 8–10 minutes until golden, carefully turning the palmiers over halfway through the cooking time.

Making coiled puff pastry cones

Strips of puff pastry are easily coiled around metal cornet moulds then baked to make cones ready to be filled with flavoured whipped cream. To make a rich savoury version, prepare the cones without the sugar coating, and fill with a piped mixture of pâté and butter.

1 Roll out 225g/8oz puff pastry to a 56 × 15cm/22 × 6in rectangle. Starting at one short end, roll up tightly. Cut the roll into 1cm/½in coiled slices.

2 Unroll each coil and dampen the ends of each strip with water. Wrap the pastry around a lightly greased metal cornet mould in a spiral, starting at the pointed end and overlapping it slightly. At the wide end, press the strip firmly to secure.

3 Chill on a baking sheet, with the finished ends underneath, for about 30 minutes. Brush with beaten egg and sprinkle with caster (superfine) sugar. Bake in a preheated oven at 220°C/425°F/Gas 7 for 8–10 minutes.

4 Cool the pastries on the baking sheet for 5 minutes, then remove from the moulds. Cool completely, before piping in flavoured whipped cream.

SHAPING FILO PASTRY

This paper-thin pastry is incredibly easy to shape into parcels and can be simply cut to the required size with a pair of scissors. It is also perfect for making large strudels, layered bakes and cooking en croûte, and can be used to make dainty baskets, purses and coils.

Making a filo pastry roll

This is an easy and excellent way to use filo pastry and combines well with sweet and spicy fruit fillings. Use 675g/1½lb of mixed chopped eating apples, dried fruit, sugar and spices.

1 Carefully separate six sheets from a large packet of filo pastry. Lay one sheet of filo on a dishtowel, lightly brush it with melted butter, then place a second sheet on top. Continue to layer the filo, brushing butter between each layer.

2 Spoon the filling over the filo pastry leaving a 2.5cm/1in margin around the edges. Turn in the short pastry edges.

3 With the help of the dishtowel, roll up from a long edge to completely enclose the filling. Transfer to a greased baking sheet and brush with butter before baking in a preheated oven at 180°C/ 350°F/Gas 4 for 30–40 minutes.

Making layered filo pastries

In the Middle East, Turkey and Greece, layered filo pastries are very popular. All these countries have their own version of baklava, where layers of buttery filo are filled with nuts, sugar and spices, and sometimes slices of fruit such as figs, before being baked and then coated in a syrup. Lemon, cinnamon or cardamom and scents such as rose water or orange flower water may be used in the syrup. This very sweet and sticky pastry is usually cut into small diamonds and served with cups of strong black coffee.

1 Cut sixteen sheets of filo to snugly fit a 18 × 25cm/10 × 7in baking tin. Put a sheet of filo pastry in the base of the tin. Brush with melted butter and top with another sheet of filo. Repeat this until there are eight layered sheets.

2 Sprinkle half of the filling over, then place two sheets of filo on top, brushing each with more melted butter as before. Sprinkle over the rest of the filling.

Making a spiced sugar syrup
This sweet spicy syrup is ideal for pouring over baklava or drizzling over fruit in baskets. To make, put the pared rind and juice of ½ lemon in a pan with 150g/ 5oz/¾ cup caster (superfine) sugar, 60ml/4 tbsp water and a cinnamon stick. Heat until the sugar dissolves then simmer for about 2 minutes. Cover and infuse (steep) for 10 minutes. Strain and stir in 10ml/2 tsp rose water or orange flower water.

3 Layer the remaining sheets of filo on top, buttering each one, including the final layer. Mark a diamond pattern, cutting through to the base. Bake in a preheated oven at 160°C/325°F/Gas 3 for about 50 minutes until golden.

4 Remove the baklava from the oven, and pour over a spicy sugar syrup. Leave in the tin until cold, then serve cut into diamonds. Store in an airtight container and eat within three days.

Making filo baskets

Crisp filo cups can be made by simply layering up buttered squares of pastry on top of small metal moulds, then baking. Fresh summer berry fruits make a delicious filling, and rich seafood is a good savoury option. When cool, they can be stored in an airtight container for up to two days, but once filled, they should be served within an hour or so.

Invert ramekins on a baking sheet and grease with a little unsalted butter. Cut filo pastry into 13cm/5in squares, brush each square with melted butter and drape four or five at different angles over each mould. Bake in a preheated oven at 180°C/350°F/Gas 4 for about 12 minutes until golden. Cool, then lift the baskets off the moulds and fill.

Making braided filo parcels

These little parcels are an attractive way of presenting individual portions. Use for savoury or sweet fillings such as cooked fruit with added dried fruit to absorb excess juices or dryish spicy minced (ground) lamb or beef mixtures.

1 Use sheets of filo about 30 × 18cm/ 12 × 7in and fold in half widthways. Put the filling in the middle and fold the sides over to make a neat parcel. This will stop the mixture from seeping out through the braided filo during cooking.

2 Brush a second sheet of folded filo with cooled melted butter and place the parcel, seam-side down, in its centre. Make six cuts in the pastry, an equal distance apart, on either side of the parcel, stopping just short of the parcel. Fold the top and bottom edges of the pastry over the ends of the parcel.

3 Fold the pastry strips over the parcel, alternating sides to achieve a braided effect. Place the parcel on a baking tray and brush with cooled melted butter, particularly over the braided ends, to fix securely in place. Bake in a preheated oven at 190°C/350°F/Gas 5 for about 20 minutes, or until the pastry is lightly browned and crisp.

Making filo cocktail snacks

Filo pastry can be stacked in layers with a filling and baked before being cut to the required shape and size. Strong flavours, such as sun-dried tomatoes, goat's cheese and olives work well.

As these are meant to be eaten with the fingers, it's important that the filling holds together when the pastries are picked up. Chop the ingredients finely before mixing together and spread them thinly; this will help to make the pastries easier to cut when baked.

1 Layer three sheets of filo, brushing each layer with a little cooled melted butter or oil. Thinly spread with full-fat cream cheese blended with plenty of chopped fresh herbs. Top with three more layers of filo, each brushed with a little melted butter or oil. If you like, add flavourings to the butter or oil – chopped fresh herbs such as parsley, mint or oregano would all work well, or try chopped red and green chillies.

2 With a sharp knife, mark squares across the pastry. Bake in a preheated oven at 180°C/350°F/Gas 4 for about 20 minutes until lightly browned and crisp. Remove from the oven, cut into bitesize pieces along the already scored lines and serve hot or cold.

Making filo purses

Sometimes called money bags or swag bags, these parcels are simply made by drawing the pastry edges together and gently pinching the neck. Choose a richly flavoured filling to contrast with the generous serving of filo pastry. A mixture of lightly cooked leeks with Roquefort cheese would be delicious, as would a rich tomato filling, given a fillip with the addition of anchovies. The more robust the filling, the better.

1 Cut filo pastry into 13cm/5in squares. Lay three squares on top of each other, each at a slight angle to the other to make a 12-pointed star, brushing each layer with a little melted butter or oil. Flavoured oils such as garlic, chilli or sesame may be used, first blended with a milder oil such as sunflower so that the flavour isn't overpowering.

2 Spoon in the filling – a heaped teaspoon will be plenty – then pull the corners of the pastry up round it and pinch firmly to seal and make a neat purse shape.

3 Place on a baking sheet and brush with melted butter or oil. Bake in a preheated oven at 190°C/375°F/Gas 5 for 15 minutes until golden brown.

Making coiled filo pastries

In Morocco and the Middle East coiled filo pastries often contain a sweet rather than savoury filling, and rich-scented almond paste is a popular choice. These coiled pastries are simple to make: you will need about 200g/7oz almond paste.

1 Use eight sheets of filo, each measuring 30 × 18cm/12 × 7in. Place two of them on a clean work surface, overlapping them slightly to form a 56 × 18cm/22 × 7in rectangle. Brush the overlapping pastry with melted butter to secure, then brush the whole sheet sparingly with more melted butter.

2 Shape one-fourth of the almond paste into a long, thin sausage, place along the edge of the filo sheet and roll up tightly. Repeat with the remaining paste and filo to make four lengths.

3 Shape the first roll into a coil, then attach the remaining rolls by brushing with melted butter to make a large coil. Place on a baking sheet and brush with melted butter. Bake in a preheated oven at 180°C/350°F/Gas 4 for 25 minutes. Invert on to another baking sheet, brush again with butter, and bake the coil for 5–10 minutes more to brown the other side. Cut in wedges and serve warm.

Making filo triangles

Traditional Indian pasties, or samosas, consist of small deep-fried or baked filo triangles, which are usually filled with a pre-cooked spiced minced (ground) meat or potato and vegetable filling. These triangles can be used to enclose other fillings, however, such as chopped spring onions softened in butter and mixed with cooked prawns, or chopped feta, or cream cheese with chocolate. Six sheets of filo will make twelve triangles.

1 Fold the filo sheets, each measuring 30 × 18cm/12 × 7in, in half lengthways. Cut in half widthways. Brush with a little melted butter if baking in the oven; if deep-frying, this step is not necessary.

2 Place a teaspoon of the filling on to the filo, 5cm/2in from the end. Turn one corner over, to make a triangle. Fold the triangle over on itself, down the length of the filo, to fully enclose the filling. Seal the ends with melted butter or oil.

3 Deep-fry the triangles in vegetable or sunflower oil heated to 190°C/375°F for 4–5 minutes, turning them so that they brown evenly. Drain on kitchen paper. Alternatively, place them on a baking sheet and bake in a preheated oven at 190°C/375°F/Gas 5 for 20 minutes.

Making filo spring rolls

Spring roll wrappers are usually used, but filo works very well, and is more readily available. Brushing the edges with a little beaten egg stops the rolls from unravelling during frying. Keep the wrapping thin, so that you can just see the filling inside. Suitable fillings include ingredients such as beansprouts, water chestnuts, bamboo shoots and soaked dried mushrooms, with chopped prawns (shrimp) or finely minced (ground) pork.

1 Cut filo pastry into 13cm/5in squares and brush lightly with oil. Place the filling in a strip about 2.5cm/1in from one side, leaving a 2cm/¾in margin at both ends.

2 Fold the sides over the filling, then roll up the pastry to enclose the filling, sealing the loose edge with beaten egg.

3 Deep-fry the spring rolls, a few at a time, in oil heated to 180°C/350°F, for 4–5 minutes. Drain on kitchen paper and serve warm.

COOK'S TIP
Deep-frying small filo parcels gives them a wonderfully crisp, bubbled texture and golden colour, which is more difficult to achieve with baking.

SAVOURY FILLINGS

A tasty savoury pie or quiche is hard to beat and, with so many different fillings to choose from, it really is possible to please all tastes. The following pages provide essential information for using fillings successfully and includes egg-set fillings, vegetable, meat and poultry fillings, and fish and shellfish fillings.

EGG-SET FILLINGS

Very moist fillings are combined with eggs to prevent them from spoiling a crisp, dry pastry base. When whisked with egg, milk and cream can be poured over other ingredients and will set on cooking to create a filling that holds together when the pie or flan is sliced. The quiche, an open flan with a savoury filling combined with eggs, is probably the best-known example of this technique.

Recipes for savoury egg-set flans and quiches vary, but as a general rule, use 2 large (US extra large) eggs for every 150ml/¼ pint/⅔ cup liquid; this can be milk, cream, Greek (US strained plain) yogurt or a creamy, soft cheese such as mascarpone. The amount of the egg mixture needed will depend on how much filling you have and how tightly it is packed into the pastry case. If you are adding ingredients that may exude some liquid during cooking, such as certain vegetables, you need to increase the proportion of egg to milk – but not too much or the filling will become too solid and unpleasantly rubbery.

Use metal flan tins (quiche pans) only, preferably made of dull metal as shiny metal reflects heat, and keep china and glass quiche dishes for the display cabinet only. Both china and glass absorb heat, so stop the pastry from cooking properly. Loose-based flan tins make turning out quiches and tarts easier. Most have fluted sides, which make the pastry shells stronger.

Shortcrust and rich shortcrust pastry are the traditional choices when making a quiche. To ensure that the pastry base is well cooked, put a heavy baking sheet in the oven when preheating and place the flan tin on this. Use heavy sheets, as flimsy ones tend to buckle, causing the filling to set unevenly.

Using egg-set fillings in open pies

There are only a few things to be aware of when making quiches and, if followed, will allow you to choose the ingredients with confidence.

Sealing the pastry Before adding an egg filling, the pastry case will need to be pre-baked, and then sealed, to prevent it becoming soggy. Brush the base and sides, but not the top edge of the partly baked pastry case, with beaten egg and return it to the oven for 3–4 minutes.

Adding the filling Scatter the sealed base with some grated cheese to give further protection against any moisture. Top with the solid ingredients, but don't press them down, or they will be stodgy when cooked. Add more cheese.

Double-crust pies

Egg-set fillings can be used in double-crust pies, but in this case it is essential to tightly pack the filling and to place the pie on a preheated baking sheet, so that the pastry starts to cook as soon as it is put in the oven and before any egg mixture can seep into it and make it soggy.

Adding the custard Mix the egg and milk mixture in a jug (pitcher) rather than a bowl, as it will be easier to pour in an even, steady stream. Fill almost to the top of the pastry case. If you have more liquid than space in the flan case, avoid the temptation to squeeze the last few drops in – it is better to throw a little away than to risk the filling overflowing and burning on the pastry crust or baking sheet. Tuck in any filling that sticks out, or it will burn.

Baking Depending on the filling, most quiches need to be cooked for about 30 minutes at 190°C/375°F/Gas 5. When cooked, the filling should still be slightly wobbly in the centre as it will continue to cook when removed from the oven.

Removing from a loose-based tin Place the baked quiche on a wire rack and leave for a few minutes to settle. If serving hot, set the tin on a sturdy bowl or wide glass and allow the side to drop down, leaving the quiche on the base of the tin. If any filling has leaked out, the quiche may stick to the tin in places and will need to be loosened with a knife before it can be removed. Slide on to a serving plate. If serving cold, leave the quiche to cool, still in its tin, on the wire rack. Remove when ready.

VEGETABLE FILLINGS

When vegetables are used in single- or double-crust pies, they are almost always pre-cooked to ensure that they are tender and so that the pastry is not affected by the moisture released from raw vegetables as they cook. The high water content of many vegetables would also otherwise dilute the filling. In addition, as raw vegetables lose water, they will contract, leaving gaps in an egg-set filling. You can, however, use raw starchy vegetables such as potatoes that don't release much moisture, or use raw vegetables in fillings, such as sauces, that will absorb excess moisture.

Using vegetables in open pies

When using vegetables in open pies, you need to ensure that, as the pie cooks, the vegetables are protected from the oven's heat, and do not dry out.

Setting the filling with eggs In flans and open pies, such as quiches, eggs are used to protect the filling from the dry heat and also to prevent the pastry from becoming soggy. Most vegetables work well in egg-set fillings such as sautéed mushrooms, grilled and sliced (bell) peppers, root vegetables such as diced waxy potatoes and sliced carrots, or canned ones like sweetcorn. Pre-cook the vegetables before using as raw ones will contract, leaving gaps in the filling.

Providing a covering Vegetables can be protected from the heat of the oven by scattering ingredients such as cheese or a savoury crumble over the top. The inverted pastry base can also be used.

Sprinkle over grated cheeses such as Cheddar, Parmesan or mozzarella in a thin, even layer. Don't add too much, or it will melt to a solid, oily mass.

A savoury crumble also makes a good protective covering for vegetables, as well as adding a contrasting texture. Use a mixture of plain or wholemeal (whole-wheat) flour, a little salt, finely chopped nuts such as walnuts and grated Cheddar. Sprinkle over vegetable fillings such as leeks and onions.

Cooking a dish upside-down, with the pastry base on top and the vegetables underneath, ensures that the pastry cooks to a perfect crispness, and the filling is protected from the oven's heat. Sauté vegetables such as onions and shallots with garlic and fresh herbs until soft in an ovenproof omelette pan, cover with a layer of rich shortcrust or puff pastry and bake. Invert to serve.

Pre-cooking the pastry When you want to use tender vegetables such as asparagus, it is best to completely bake the pastry case first then fill it with a pre-cooked vegetable mixture. This is particularly suitable when filling shallow flans, small tartlets and pastry canapés.

Using vegetables in closed pies

When using vegetables in closed pies, it is important to ensure excess moisture doesn't spoil the texture of the pastry.

Minimizing moisture with eggs When making a pie with an egg-set filling, tightly pack pre-cooked or partially cooked vegetables into the pastry case, then cover with a pastry crust. Make a hole in the pastry and pour in the egg mixture through a funnel. The pie can then be baked immediately on a hot baking sheet in a preheated oven so that the mixture begins to cook straight away. This works well with mixtures such as broccoli and blue cheese or layered root vegetables.

Eggs can also be used to thicken the filling without setting it completely, so that the juices from partially cooked vegetables are turned into a rich sauce. In particular, vegetables such as baby new potatoes, Jerusalem artichokes, carrots, asparagus, broad (fava) beans and chestnut mushrooms would benefit from cooking this way. Beaten eggs are blended with cream or curd (farmer's) cheese and double (heavy) cream to enrich the mixture. The vegetables are then carefully stirred into the egg mixture before being spooned into the pie case and covered with a pastry lid to make a double-crust pie.

Minimizing moisture with a sauce A béchamel-type sauce is an ideal base for vegetables that release a lot of water during cooking, such as mushrooms. If the sauce is fairly thick, lightly sautéed or raw vegetables will dilute the sauce to the correct consistency as they cook.

Fillings with a lot of sauce are usually made with a single top crust. Always pierce two or three steam holes in the lid of the pie to allow steam to escape, or use a pie funnel to ensure that the pastry doesn't dip and become soggy.

Using vegetables with little moisture

Certain vegetables, especially starchy ones such as potatoes, release only a small amount of water during cooking and so can be packed tightly together in a pie and will hold firm when cut. A potato terrine is a good example of this and is often made in a deep loaf tin or pie tin using puff pastry. After cooking, hot double cream is poured through the steam holes made in the pastry. This combines with the starch in the potatoes and thickens to a quiche-like consistency to fill any gaps.

MEAT AND POULTRY FILLINGS

All manner of pies and parcels combine well with meat and poultry fillings and these can be either raw or pre-cooked. When making, you need to ensure that the filling cooks through properly while being protected from the oven's dry heat, and that the texture of the pastry is unharmed by any excess moisture.

When you buy meat for pie-making, consider the type of pie and length of cooking time involved. Pies that are baked for less than an hour, such as single-crust pies and small parcels, normally contain a pre-cooked filling or one that is made with tender cuts of meat that need a shorter cooking time.

Using meat in single-crust pies

Meat and poultry fillings that have lots of rich gravy or sauce are best made in a single-crust rather than in a double-crust pie, as the base would become soggy during cooking. Shortcrust or puff pastry and their variations all work well as single-crust pies, as does filo pastry.

Ensuring a crisp pastry Always make one or more steam holes in the top of the pastry. It is a good idea to use a pie funnel in larger pies to properly support the pastry. Make sure that the top pokes through the pastry lid to let out all the steam. Choose one with semi-circular holes cut out of its base to allow the sauce to mingle freely in the dish.
Choosing the filling Single crust-pies are usually made with a pre-cooked filling or tender cuts of raw meat such as beef steak, pork fillet (tenderloin), chicken or turkey breast that will take the same time to cook as the pastry. They are cut into chunks about 2.5cm/1in as they will shrink slightly during cooking.

Using meat in double-crust pies or parcels

The key when making a meat-filled double-crust pie or parcel is to keep the base from becoming soggy as it cooks.

Fillings usually contain only a small amount of gravy or a fairly thick, often flour-based, sauce that will be thinned by the meat's juices. Alternatively, the meat can be cooked first in a gravy, then added to the pie with a slotted spoon and the gravy served separately.

Minimizing moisture Raw meat can be used in double-crust pies. Toss the raw cubes of meat in seasoned flour; this helps to thicken the juices, turning them into a flavoursome sauce.

Other absorbent ingredients may be used – undercooked macaroni, mixed together with eggs and cream, goes well with beef and pork. As the pie cooks, the pasta absorbs the meat juices and swells as the pieces of meat shrink and, when the filling reaches the required temperature, the egg mixture lightly sets the filling and holds it together.

Using meat in open pies

Cooked meat and poultry fillings are often spooned into ready-baked pastry cases. This is a good way of ensuring that both the pastry case and the filling are fully cooked, and works especially well with poultry. Cooked chicken pieces can be coated in a creamy sauce and used in a cooked shortcrust pastry case, puff pastry vol-au-vent or a filo basket.

When open pies are filled, then baked further, the pastry cases are first partially blind-baked and the meat is protected from the oven's heat by a topping. This may be a pastry lattice, a savoury crumble, or breadcrumbs.

Using meat in hot-water crust pies

Raised game pies made with raw meat need a long cooking time to make the meat tender and succulent. They are made with hot water crust pastry, as it can withstand long, slow cooking times, rather than shortcrust or puff pastry, which would overcook. Hot water crust pastry hardens as it cooks so that the pie holds its shape when unmoulded and doesn't collapse. No other pastries are as robust. As the pie cooks, juices and fat from the meat seep into the pastry and flavour it.
Preparing the filling The filling for meat or game pies is usually a mixture of diced lean game or meat and fattier meats such as streaky bacon to keep the filling really moist. It's a good idea to marinate stronger-flavoured meats such as game overnight in a mixture of wine and spices to tenderize them. To check the seasoning and flavour of a raw pie filling, dry-fry a spoonful in a non-stick pan, until cooked, then taste.

Adding the filling As the filling is raw and some shrinkage will occur, it should be tightly packed into the pastry case, pressing down well and shaping into a neat mound. Always place the pie on a baking tray to catch any leakages.
Baking Generally, the pie is baked at a high temperature for an hour, then the oven temperature reduced for the rest of the cooking time. Cover the pastry with foil if it starts to brown too early.

The filling contracts as it cooks, leaving a gap between the pie crust and the filling. This can be filled with a meat jelly or aspic. After baking, cool the pie, then pour the jelly through the hole in the pastry top, until it is level with the top of the pie. Cover and chill for 3 hours.

FISH AND SHELLFISH FILLINGS

These fillings are usually added raw to pies as they need a short cooking time.

Using fish in open pies

When using fish in open pies, you need to make sure that it is cooked through but protected from drying out.

Choosing the right fish If you want to add canned fish such as tuna or salmon to an open pie, those canned in oil are preferable to ones in brine. They need to be drained well before adding to the filling, but the light coating of oil that will remain will keep the fish succulent.

Smoked cooked salmon, trout or mackerel can be baked in open pies, but do so for the briefest amount of time possible, as they need only heating.

A number of fish fillings benefit from being pre-cooked, such as raw smoked haddock in a hot white sauce, or flaked poached or roasted salmon fillet mixed with Greek (US strained plain) yogurt and lemon mayonnaise. In these cases, the fillings are best added to flan and tartlet pastry cases that have been first fully blind-baked. Shortcrust and filo pastry work well with these types of pre-cooked fish fillings.

Cut the fish into 2.5cm/1in chunks; if they are too small they will overcook; and if too large, you may find gaps in the filling after cooking.

Using fish in an egg-set filling Raw or canned fish will give out some juices during cooking, and so should not be put directly on the pastry base in an open pie. Instead, scatter ingredients, such as sautéed chopped spring onions (scallions) or sliced or grated cheese over the base, then rest the fish on top before pouring over the egg mixture.

Providing a covering When you don't want to cook fish in a quiche-type filling, a topping is another good way to protect the fish from dry heat. One of the simplest ways is to sprinkle grated cheese over any exposed pieces of fish.

Alternatively, and this is really only used for deep and not shallow flans (where there wouldn't be room for both a filling and a topping), you can spread a thin layer of mashed potato over the filling. This works well when well-flavoured fish such as fresh raw salmon or smoked haddock is cooked in a white or creamy sauce. The potato can be mashed with butter and cream or olive oil, and with other root vegetables such as swede or carrots. It can also be flavoured with herbs or grated hard or soft cheese.

Fish fillings can also be cooked with a dry topping such as a crumble, made with plain or wholemeal (whole-wheat) flour with added cheese or nuts or oat flakes, or a breadcrumb mixture. Either sprinkle this very thinly or use cooked fish in the filling, so that any steam escaping from the fish doesn't make the topping soggy. These toppings will brown quickly and shouldn't be cooked for longer than 30 minutes. They are particularly good for partially blind-baked, shallow pastry cases, or can be sprinkled over the top of a deep open pie towards the end of cooking time.

Using fish in closed pies

Fish can be used in both single- and double-crust pies made with shortcrust, puff or filo pastry. As they generally don't take long to cook, fish fillings work best in shallow pies and those with a thin pastry crust rather than deep pies and thick pastry crusts.

Combine cubes of raw fish with moist vegetables such as spinach or a thick sauce. The pastry will brown in the same time that it takes the vegetables or sauce and fish to be cooked through.

Using whole fish in closed parcels

A whole fish wrapped in pastry will cook through and be tender and moist in the time it takes the pastry to cook. This is a good way to cook thick, oily fish such as salmon and trout, which need longer cooking time than white or flat fish.

Whole fish will release a lot of moisture, so you need to counteract this by using a pastry that benefits from the juices. Puff pastry is excellent as the steam produced helps the pastry to rise.

Using shellfish in pies and pastry cases

Shellfish takes little time to cook, so avoid adding it to pies that require long cooking, as it will become tough. Some shellfish such as scallops and prawns (shrimp) release moisture during cooking so don't add in large amounts if raw.

Shellfish such as crabmeat and cooked prawns are often added to pre-baked pastry cases. They are sometimes also mixed with other ingredients that will keep them moist during cooking, such as cream and egg fillings.

SWEET FILLINGS

Although the range of sweet pie and tart fillings is enormous, it can be sorted into three main groups: fruit, custard and cream. However, it isn't unusual to find all of these in the same tart.

FRUIT FILLINGS

There are innumerable recipes for fruit flans and pies, and every country has its own speciality. Depending on the type of pastry used and the cooking time involved, fruit can be raw, lightly cooked or fully cooked. It can also be puréed and used to make a set tart.

Most fruits can be used to make pie fillings. Fresh fruit is best with pastry, but canned, bottled or thawed frozen fruit can also be used. Fruits such as strawberries, raspberries, mango and kiwi fruit are best used fresh, usually as toppings for ready-baked pastry cases.

Whether raw or cooked, fruits can be enhanced through the addition of spices and nuts, either in the filling or in the pastry. Cinnamon goes particularly well with apples, and ginger with pears and tropical fruit such as pineapples.

Using fresh fruit in tarts and tartlets

Fresh fruit is often used as a filling for tarts and tartlets. The pastry cases are usually made from pâte sucrée, rich shortcrust or almond pastry as these cook to a crisp, almost biscuity texture. However, you can also make individual fruit tarts with puff or filo pastry.

Rather than completely fill the pastry case with fruit, it is normally partly filled with a rich custard or cream before the fresh fruit is added. Crème pâtissière works best with shortcrust, while puff and filo pastry cases are better filled with crème chantilly.

Choosing the fruit All sorts of fruits can be used in tarts and tartlets. It needs to be small, or cut into small pieces. Fresh fruit such as sliced plums, stoned and halved cherries, halved strawberries, raspberries or halved grapes work best. Fruit such as apples and pears are usually cooked, rather than used raw, as they discolour once cut. Thinly sliced bananas may be used, but need to be tossed in lemon or orange juice to prevent them from browning.

Using raw fruit in single- and double-crust pies

Double-crust pies are usually made with shortcrust pastry or its variations as the weight of the filling would prevent puff and flaky pastry from rising properly. Single-crust pies, however, can be made from any of these pastries. Uncooked fruits are used for both types of pies.

All fruits contain some juice, so will generate steam as they bake. Use a pie funnel, or make steam holes, so that the pastry will become crisp.

Choosing and preparing fruit Use fruit that is just ripe but still firm, for the best texture and sweetest flavour. When making double-crust pies, the most suitable fruits are robust ones such as apples, pears, plums and cherries. The fruit is usually tossed in sugar, which can be caster (superfine) sugar or a soft brown sugar for a more caramel-like flavour. The sugar dissolves as the fruit cooks and makes a juicy syrup.

When making a single-crust pie, you can take advantage of juicier fruits, such as rhubarb, as there is no need to worry about a soggy pastry base.

Fruits such as peaches, nectarines and apricots work wonderfully well in both single- and double-crust pies.

Protecting the pastry base Toss prepared fruit such as sliced apples, pears and plums in plain (all-purpose) flour or cornflour (cornstarch) before adding to the pie. This absorbs any excess juice from the fruit and, as the pie cooks, thickens it to make a syrup.

Another way to avoid a soggy pastry base is to sprinkle it with ground almonds or finely grated marzipan.

Never add more sugar than is specified in the recipe even if the fruit is slightly sharp, as this will draw out the juice from the fruit. If necessary, counteract the tartness of the fruit by sprinkling the cooked pastry crust with sugar or by serving the pie with custard or whipped cream.

Using cooked fruit in closed pies

Some fruits produce too much liquid during cooking to be used raw in double-crust pies. Rhubarb and black-currants are good examples of this and should be gently cooked in a pan with sugar until barely tender, then drained and cooled before adding to the pie. The juices can be reduced by boiling until thick – a few spoonfuls can then be added to the pie, or can be served separately as a sauce. Alternatively, the juices can be thickened with arrowroot and used in the pie or as a sauce.

Some fruit, such as gooseberries, must be cooked to soften them and to reduce their acidity. Fruit may also be cooked first when a pre-baked pastry case is being used, or in cases where the pastry topping would be cooked before the fruit was tender, such as pies with a scrunched filo pastry topping.

Sometimes a smooth purée of cooked fruit is desirable, particularly in flans and tartlets. Where chunkier pieces of fruit are required, it should be added to the pie still slightly under-cooked.

Using fruit in a free-form tart

This is one of the easiest ways of using fruit with pastry. The fruit is placed in the middle of a large round of pastry, then the edges are simply folded up and over the fruit to create a free-form open-topped tart. Leave a 10cm/4in border around the pastry edge when arranging the fruit on top. Fold and crimp the edge over the fruit towards the centre. Choose one of the more pliable types of shortcrust such as pâte sucrée for these types of tarts.

Choosing fruit Raw or cooked fruits may be used in this type of pie. Try stoned (pitted) and quartered ripe plums or apricots, stoned cherries, or chopped rhubarb that has been gently poached in butter and granulated sugar for about 5 minutes, then drained.

Protecting the pastry base Sprinkle the rolled-out pastry with dried breadcrumbs or stale cake crumbs. These will absorb any juices which might otherwise spoil the crisp texture of the pastry. Add the fruit to the pastry, then sprinkle, rather than mix, the fruit with a little caster (superfine) sugar before baking. This will add a crunchy, caramelized topping.

Using fruit in filo rolls

Spicy sliced apples are often used, but pear and raspberry, plum, rum and raisin, and dried fruits also make good fillings. Mix soft fruit together gently.

Absorbing moisture If using fruit with a high water content, or when using a combination of fruit and alcohol, mix the fruit with soft brown sugar and dried white breadcrumbs or ground nuts to absorb any moisture. Alternately, reduce the amount of sugar that is added to the fruit and sprinkle grated almond paste or hazelnut paste over the pastry.

Using dry ingredients When filling filo rolls with mixtures of dried fruits and nuts, chop them very finely to ensure the ingredients do not break the filo pastry. To make a moist filling, mix the dried fruit with alcohol or fruit juice in a bowl, cover and leave to soak overnight. The liquid will be absorbed and will enrich the fruit.

Using dried fruit with pastry

Dried fruit is used in individual mince pies and shoofly pie where the fruit is combined with sugar and often alcohol to make a rich and sticky filling. It is often mixed with moister fruits such as apples where it not only adds flavour

Glazes for fruit pastries

Open fruit tarts can be given a gloss by brushing the fruit with a glaze of warmed sieved jam or melted jelly. Use apricot jam for stone fruits such as apricots and peaches; red jam or red- or blackcurrant jelly for soft fruits such as raspberries, strawberries, blueberries and blackberries; and a jelly-type marmalade for citrus fruits and bananas. Apple jelly goes well with apple and pear tarts.

Put 150g/5oz/generous ½ cup good quality seedless jam, jelly or conserve in a pan. Add 10ml/ 2 tsp water, lemon juice or liqueur, such as Kirsch or Grand Marnier. Heat gently, stirring often, until the sauce is melted and smooth. Sieve, if necessary. This makes enough to glaze a 20cm/8in flan.

and texture but also absorbs excess juices. Slightly sharp dried fruit such as apricot can be made into a smooth purée and spread over the base of a partially baked shortcrust pastry case to provide a contrast to a sweet filling such as frangipane.

CUSTARD FILLINGS

Baked custard tarts filled with "proper" custard are a favourite tea-time treat. The filling is made with eggs beaten with milk or cream and sometimes a little flour to help thicken and stabilize. It is gently cooked until smooth and slightly thickened, then the mixture may either be poured into a pastry case and baked until set, or may be cooked, then cooled before spooning into a ready-baked pastry case. This rich, thick custard is known as crème pâtissière or pastry cream. Its smooth texture and rich flavour complements the crisp pastry. It is usually topped with other ingredients such as fruit.

Making a baked custard filling

In this recipe, the egg custard is cooked until set and can be made with single (light) cream, as here, with double (heavy) cream for a slightly creamier mixture, or with milk for a less rich custard. The custard is added to a partly cooked pastry case, made from pâte sucrée or rich shortcrust pastry.

After blind-baking, the pastry case should be sealed by brushing lightly inside with beaten egg, so that when the custard is added it does not seep into the pastry base. Return the pastry case to the oven for a few minutes to seal the egg. The pastry case may be scattered with other ingredients such as fruit before the custard is added. Fresh raspberries are delicious as are dried fruits such as stoned (pitted) prunes that have been soaked first in liqueur, but don't add too much fruit or the juices may dilute the custard and make the pastry soggy.

When making the custard, hot cream is whisked into the beaten egg – this starts the cooking process and ensures that, when the mixture is poured into the hot pastry case, it begins to set straight away. In this way the crispness of the pastry is not affected. The custard-filled case is baked at a low temperature of 150°C/300°F/Gas 2 so that the custard cooks gently and evenly; it should only be softly set with a velvety texture. If the oven is too hot, the custard will be rubbery.

1 Whisk together 2 eggs, 2 egg yolks and 40g/1½oz/3 tbsp caster (superfine) sugar in a bowl. Heat 450ml/¾ pint/scant 2 cups single (light) cream or milk with 1 split vanilla pod (bean) in a small pan over a gentle heat until the cream just comes to the boil. Remove the vanilla pod, then pour over the egg mixture, whisking constantly. Strain the custard into a jug (pitcher) or bowl.

2 Slowly and evenly pour the custard into a partly baked and sealed 20cm/8in shortcrust pastry case and return the case to a hot baking sheet in the oven. Bake at 150°C/300°F/Gas 2 for 45 minutes, or until the centre is softly set – the custard will continue to cook as it cools. Remove from the tin when cool and serve at room temperature.

Baking custard tartlets

Line fluted brioche tins that measure 7.5cm/3in in diameter with pastry. Bake blind for about 15 minutes, then lower the temperature to 150°C/300°F/Gas 2, fill with the custard and bake for about 20 minutes more. The pastry may be plain or rich shortcrust. Small custard tarts are traditionally sprinkled with freshly grated nutmeg before baking, or you could infuse the cream or milk with cinnamon or crushed cardamom pods.

Adding a caramelized topping

You can give a baked custard filling a thin topping of caramel, but the pastry edges must be protected from the fierce heat of the grill.

After baking, chill the custard tart for at least 2 hours. Sprinkle the top thickly with 50g/2oz/½ cup caster (superfine) sugar. Protect the pastry edges with strips of foil and place the tart under a hot grill (broiler) for 1–2 minutes or until the sugar melts and caramelizes; do not leave it under the heat for too long or the custard may curdle. Chill for 30 minutes to harden the caramel, then serve.

Flavouring baked custards

Honey custard Instead of sugar, whisk the eggs and yolks with 20ml/4 tbsp fragrant honey such as lavender. Infuse the cream with a bay leaf instead of vanilla.

Spicy custard Instead of vanilla, add a cinnamon stick to the cream and sprinkle the custard with grated nutmeg before baking.

Making crème pâtissière

This sweet custard or pastry cream is made thicker with the addition of flour. It is the classic filling for pastry tarts topped with fresh fruit but may also be used as a filling for profiteroles, éclairs and small pastries.

It is best to make the custard the day before you need it, so that it can be chilled. If a firmer set is required a little soaked gelatine can be dissolved in the hot custard. The quantity below makes about 300ml/½ pint/1¼ cups, which is enough to fill a 20cm/8in pastry case.

1 In a bowl, whisk 3 egg yolks and 50g/2oz/¼ cup caster (superfine) sugar. Sift over 40g/1½oz/6 tbsp plain (all-purpose) flour, then whisk it in. Pour 250ml/8fl oz/1 cup milk into a pan. Split a vanilla pod (bean) lengthways and add it to the pan. Bring to the boil. Remove the vanilla, then pour the milk over the egg mixture, whisking all the time.

2 Pour the mixture into a pan and return the vanilla pod. Bring to the boil, simmer for 2 minutes until thickened. Transfer to a bowl, cover the surface with cling film (plastic wrap) and cool.

3 When the crème pâtissière is cold, spread it into a baked pastry case.

Making crème mousseline

Here, butter is gradually beaten into crème pâtissière to give it a lighter and fluffier texture. It is ideal as a filling for choux pastries such as puffs and éclairs, and it is also a good alternative to whipped cream as a topping or filling for puff pastries. It retains its texture and will keep for several days in the refrigerator. Crème mousseline is also less likely to soak into the pastry, so filled pastries will last for longer before being served. It is best made several hours ahead and chilled to the desired consistency. Crème mousseline can also be made from flavoured crème pâtissière or, for a light caramel flavour and colour, soft light brown sugar may be used instead of caster sugar. The following quantity makes about 475ml/16fl oz/2 cups.

1 Make the crème pâtissière and beat in 50g/2oz/¼ cup caster (superfine) sugar and 25g/1oz/2 tbsp unsalted (sweet) butter. Cover the surface with clear film (plastic wrap) and cool.

2 In a bowl, beat 75g/3oz/6 tbsp unsalted butter until pale and fluffy, then gradually beat in the cold crème pâtissière mixture, a spoonful at a time, until the mixture is light and fluffy.

Flavouring crème pâtissière
Try any of the following for a richly flavoured crème pâtissière.

Chocolate Break up 50g/2oz dark (bittersweet) chocolate into small pieces, then stir them into the hot custard until melted.
Alcohol Omit the vanilla pod and stir in 30ml/2 tbsp brandy or rum.
Coffee Mix 10ml/2 tsp instant coffee granules with 15ml/1 tbsp hot milk or water. Stir into the hot custard with 15ml/1 tbsp coffee liqueur, if you like.

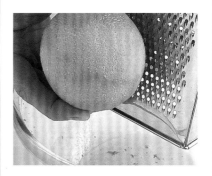

Orange, lemon or lime Whisk the grated rind of 1 orange, lemon or lime with the egg yolks and sugar.
Fresh berry Allow the custard to cool a little. Purée 75g/3oz/½ cup fresh raspberries or blueberries, and stir into the custard.
Ginger Stir 30ml/2 tbsp ginger syrup and 10ml/2 tsp finely chopped stem (preserved) ginger into the custard. Reduce the sugar to 75g/3oz/6 tbsp.
Cinnamon Infuse (steep) the milk with a stick of cinnamon instead of the vanilla pod.

NON-CREAM BASED CUSTARDS

Other types of egg-set custard fillings include a lemon filling, which is made with lemon juice and water rather than milk or cream, and gently simmered with a combination of egg yolks and cornflour (cornstarch) before being poured into the pastry case and baked briefly. Lemon meringue pie is a classic example of this type of filling.

The filling for a key lime pie is similar, but is lightly set with egg yolks alone as the lime juice and condensed milk mixture is already very thick. Egg custard may also be used to set a fruit or vegetable purée mixture. Pumpkin pie is an example of this.

Making a lemon meringue pie filling

Water is used instead of milk in this custard because the high acidity of the lemon juice would cause a milk-based mixture to curdle. The filling has a jelly-like texture as cornflour is used with egg yolks as a thickening agent. The following is enough to fill a 20cm/8in shortcrust or pâte sucrée pastry case.

1 Add the grated rind of 2 lemons to 300ml/½ pint/1¼ cups boiling water to infuse (steep). Squeeze 3 lemons and blend some of the juice with 45ml/3 tbsp cornflour in a pan, then add the rest of the juice, the water and lemon rind mixture, and simmer until thick.

2 Remove the pan from the heat and thoroughly beat in 75g/3oz/6 tbsp caster (superfine) sugar, 2 egg yolks and 15ml/1 tbsp butter. Pour or spoon the custard filling into the partially blind-baked pastry case, then top with meringue (see right) before baking at 150°C/300°F/Gas 2 for 35–40 minutes.

Making a key lime pie filling

This is a much sweeter and simpler pie filling than lemon meringue filling. It is sometimes made in a case of crushed biscuits mixed with butter, but can also be made in a partially blind-baked plain shortcrust or French flan pastry case to contrast with the sweetness of both the filling and the meringue topping.

1 To make, stir together 3 egg yolks and 400ml/14fl oz/1½ cups condensed milk in a bowl, then add 120ml/4fl oz/½ cup lime juice and the grated rind of 1 lime. This will thicken the mixture.

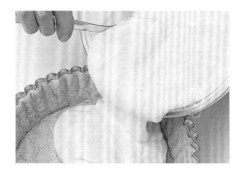

2 Spoon or pour into a partially blind-baked deep 21cm/8½ in pastry case before topping with meringue and bake at 180°C/350°F/Gas 4 for 20 minutes.

Making a puréed fruit or vegetable custard filling

Fruit such as apples and firm pears and vegetables such as pumpkin can be cooked, then puréed and stirred into a custard before baking. The following makes enough to fill a 23cm/9in shortcrust pastry case.

1 Blend cooled fruit or vegetable purée made from 450g/1lb apples, pears or pumpkin with 90g/3½oz/½ cup soft brown or caster (superfine) sugar, 150ml/¼ pint/⅔ cup double (heavy) cream, 2 beaten eggs and ground spices such as nutmeg, cinnamon or ginger to taste. Lighten the mixture with a little whisked egg white, if you like.

2 Pour the filling into the partially blind-baked pastry case, then bake at 190°C/375°F/Gas 5 for 45–55 minutes, or until lightly set.

Adding meringue toppings

Crisp on the outside and soft on the inside, meringue is an ideal topping for open pies and tarts. Its sweetness complements sharp fruits such as gooseberries and red- or blackcurrants.

Making meringue cuite

Meringue is made by whisking egg whites with caster (superfine) sugar, but meringue cuite (cooked meringue) is less likely to seep sugary liquid if left to stand. The filling must always be pre-cooked before adding the meringue.

1 Whisk 4 egg whites in a heatproof bowl until peaks form, then set the bowl over a pan of simmering water. Add 225g/8oz/2 cups sifted icing (confectioners') sugar and 2.5ml/½ tsp vanilla essence (extract). Whisk until thick. Remove the bowl from the pan and whisk for 1–2 minutes more until the meringue is cool.

2 Add the meringue to a filled pie and swirl with a palette knife (metal spatula). Bake until golden.

MOUSSE FILLINGS

These fillings owe their light texture to air, captured when eggs or cream are whisked. They are often custard-based with whipped cream or stiffly beaten egg whites folded in, and are poured into pre-baked pastry cases – those made of French flan pastry and pâte sucrée are most suitable – and chilled until set. Setting the mousse filling not only allows the pie to be sliced neatly, but also enables the pie to be kept for longer as there is less moisture to seep into and soften the pastry.

Making a gelatine-set mousse

Gelatine is often used to set mousse fillings made of fruit purées and thin custards. The gelatine may be either stirred into a custard, then the custard thinned with whipped cream or whisked egg whites, or it can be blended with a whisked egg and sugar mixture. The gelatine should always be soaked or "sponged" first.

Sprinkle over liquid, using 15ml/1 tbsp liquid for every teaspoon of powdered gelatine. Leave to soak for 5 minutes, then dissolve. Use 15ml/1 tbsp of gelatine to set a 600ml/1 pint mousse.

Soak 10ml/2 tsp gelatine in 30ml/ 2 tbsp water, then stir into 200ml/7fl oz hot, thick custard, until dissolved. Allow to cool. When it is just beginning to set, add 150ml/¼ pint double (heavy) cream, whipped until peaks have formed. Use to fill a 23cm/9in pre-baked pastry case. If you wish, cool the custard and stir in sieved or crushed soft fruits or stir some chopped plain (semisweet) chocolate into the hot custard. You can also add vanilla essence (extract), grated lemon or orange rind, or coffee essence.

Making a lemon mousse filling

This filling is a simple mixture of sugar, cream and lemon juice. Gelatine is not needed, as the filling will be set by the action of the citrus acid on the cream.

1 Gently heat 115g/4oz/1 cup caster (superfine) sugar with 120ml/4fl oz/ ½ cup lemon juice and 450ml/¾ pint/ scant 2 cups double (heavy) cream until the sugar dissolves. Bring to the boil and simmer for 1 minute. Pour into a bowl, cover and leave until cool.

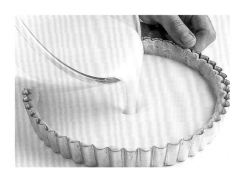

2 Pour the filling into a pre-baked 23cm/9in pastry case. Chill for 2 hours.

Making a whisked-egg mousse filling

The lightest mousse fillings are made by whisking eggs and caster (superfine) sugar together until very pale and thick, trapping countless air bubbles.

Soak 10ml/2 tsp powdered gelatine in 30ml/2 tbsp water in a heatproof bowl, then place the bowl in a pan of hot water to dissolve the gelatine. Stir into 150ml/¼ pint/1 cup fruit purée and leave until the mixture is just beginning to set. Whisk together 2 eggs and 50g/2oz/¼ cup caster sugar until thick. Fold in the fruit purée using a metal spoon, then pour into a 23cm/9in pre-baked pastry case and chill until set.

Making a chocolate mousse filling

In this filling, melted chocolate is mixed with egg yolks, then whisked egg whites are folded in. As the chocolate cools and solidifies, it sets the mousse.

Melt 115g/4oz plain (semisweet) chocolate in a heatproof bowl over a pan of hot water. Remove the bowl from the heat and beat in 2 egg yolks. Cool at room temperature for 15 minutes, then fold in 2 whisked egg whites. Pour the mixture into a 23cm/9in pre-baked pastry case and chill for 2 hours.

CREAM FILLINGS

Some of the most delectable pastries are filled with nothing more elaborate than whipped cream. It is especially good when sweetened with a little sugar and flavoured with vanilla.

Making crème chantilly

This cream filling can be spooned or piped into tartlets and used to fill pastries such as cream horns. As an alternative to vanilla, use a liqueur such as Grand Marnier. Always make crème chantilly in a well-chilled bowl, which gives lighter results. When whipping, stop often and check the consistency; it is very easy to overbeat it. The following makes 475ml/16fl oz/2 cups, enough to fill six 10cm/4in tartlet cases.

1 Pour 300ml/½ pint/1¼ cups double cream into a well-chilled mixing bowl. Add 2.5ml/½ tsp vanilla essence (extract) and 15ml/1 tbsp sifted icing (confectioners') sugar and stir to mix.

2 Whip the mixture until the cream forms soft peaks, or allow it to become slightly firmer if needed for piping.

CREAM CHEESE FILLINGS

Fresh cream cheeses such as medium- and full-fat cream cheese, mascarpone, curd (farmer's) cheese and ricotta are excellent filling bases to which other flavours can be added. Mascarpone is suitable for piping and can be softened by beating in single (light) cream to achieve the correct consistency. Cream cheese is mixed with sugar and eggs and then baked to make cheesecakes.

Making an unbaked cream cheese filling

In the simplest cream cheese fillings, the cheese is sweetened with sugar or honey then flavoured with nuts or dried fruits. The mixture is thick enough to spoon and spread into a pastry case.

Nut cream cheese filling To fill a 20cm/ 8in plain shortcrust, French flan or pâte sucrée pastry case, mix 225g/8oz/1 cup cream cheese or mascarpone with 30ml/ 2 tbsp sifted icing (confectioners') sugar and 75g/3oz/¾ cup chopped toasted almonds, hazelnuts, walnuts or pecans.

Dried fruit cream cheese filling This makes a delicious strudel filling. Mix chopped dried fruits such as figs, dates, apricots, peaches and sultanas, and glacé (candied) fruit such as pineapple and ginger with the cream cheese.

Making a baked cream cheese filling

This classic cheesecake filling is very easy to make. Modern versions of this dessert often have a case made from crushed biscuits (cookies) mixed with butter and are set using gelatine, but traditional cheesecakes are made in a partially cooked pastry case and baked.

1 In a bowl, mix 675g/1½lb/3 cups cream cheese or curd (farmer's) cheese with 200g/7oz/1 cup caster (superfine) sugar, 3 lightly beaten eggs and the finely grated rind of 1 lemon or 5ml/ 1 tsp vanilla essence (extract). Beat with a hand-held electric whisk until smooth. To mix the ingredients by hand, add the beaten eggs gradually to the flavoured cheese mixture.

2 Pour the mixture into a partly blind-baked 23cm/9in rich shortcrust pastry case that is about 5cm/2in deep. Bake in a preheated oven at 150°C/300°F/ Gas 2 for 30 minutes. The filling will be slightly wobbly, but will firm as it cools.

3 Switch off the oven but do not remove the cheesecake until it has cooled completely. When it is cold, transfer it to the refrigerator and chill for 2 hours. Shortly before serving, top the cheesecake with fresh fruit, if you like.

Baked cream cheese fillings for tartlets

Baked cream cheese fillings are equally good in individual tartlet cases as in large flans. These recipes make enough to fill eight 9cm/3½in blind-baked pastry tartlets or 12 filo pastry cases in a muffin pan or deep bun tin. Bake in a preheated oven at 200°C/ 400°F/Gas 6 for 7–8 minutes until just set. When cold, decorate the filled pastries with fresh fruit or a few curls of chocolate.

Lemon mascarpone filling Mix 250g/9oz/1 cup mascarpone cheese with the grated rind of 1 lemon, 15ml/1 tbsp lemon juice, 30ml/2 tbsp caster (superfine) sugar and 1 lightly beaten egg.

Vanilla cream cheese filling Put 115g/4oz/½ cup medium fat soft cheese in a mixing bowl. Stir with a spoon or mix with a spatula until softened, then add 90ml/6 tbsp single (light) cream, 1 egg yolk, 30ml/2 tbsp caster (superfine) sugar and 5ml/1 tsp vanilla essence (extract). Mix well.

FRANGIPANE AND SPONGE FILLNGS

Both frangipane, sometimes known as frangipani, and sponge mixtures can be used as fillings for sweet flans and tarts.

Frangipane is a thick mixture of ground almonds together with sugar, butter, egg and flour and, like sponge mixture, can be used to hold other ingredients such as fruit firmly in place.

Plain and flavoured sponge fillings are mixtures of sugar, butter, eggs and self-raising (self-rising) flour. The raising agent in sponge fillings makes the mixture less dense, ensuring a lighter, less rich filling.

The frangipane or sponge mixture is spread in the base of a partially baked pastry case. They can then be simply sprinkled with almonds or used as a base for fanned-out pear, apricot or apple halves. The frangipane or sponge rises very slightly to surround, but not completely enclose, the fruit. Because sponge mixtures rise, they should only half-fill the pastry case and have a level surface. Fruit can be pressed into it before baking or set on top afterwards.

Perhaps the most well-known tart that incorporates frangipane is Bakewell tart. In this simple recipe, the pastry base is spread with a fruit jam, such as apricot, then topped with frangipane and baked.

Soft fruit such as blueberries can also be used if protected sufficiently from the oven's heat. Spread the pastry case with the frangipane mixture and evenly scatter the blueberries over the surface, pushing them down slightly into the mixture. Alternatively, spread half the frangipane mixture over the pastry base, top with the fruit, then spread the remaining frangipane over the fruit.

Making a frangipane tart

The following is enough for a 20cm/8in shortcrust pastry case.

1 Cream 25g/1oz/2 tbsp unsalted (sweet) butter with 30ml/2 tbsp caster (superfine) sugar until pale.

2 Beat in 30ml/2 tbsp beaten egg, then fold in 25g/1oz/¼ cup ground almonds and 15ml/1 tbsp plain (all-purpose) flour.

3 Spoon the mixture into the pastry case. Top with sliced apples or pears, fanning them out on top and pressing down slightly. Alternatively sprinkle with 25g/1oz/¼ cup flaked (sliced) almonds.

4 Bake the tart in a preheated oven at 190°C/375°F/Gas 5 for 35–45 minutes. If you've used fresh fruit, brush the top with an apricot glaze. Serve warm.

Making a sponge filling

This type of filling is an excellent way to prevent moisture from a topping, such as juicy fruit, soaking into the pastry. It also adds height to a flan when very thinly sliced fruits are to be used. The following amount is sufficient for a 20cm/8in pastry case.

1 Cream 50g/2oz softened butter and 50g/2oz caster (superfine) sugar together until pale. Whisk in 1 beaten egg. Sift 50g/2oz self-raising (self-rising) flour and gently fold into the mixture with 15ml/1 tbsp milk mixed with 2.5ml/½ tsp vanilla essence (extract).

2 Spoon into a partially baked pastry case, level the top and bake in a preheated oven at 180°C/375°F/Gas 4 for 12–15 minutes until risen, golden-brown and springy to the touch. Leave to cool before topping with raw or poached fruit and glazing.

Flavouring sponge fillings

Vanilla sponge goes especially well with peaches or apricots. A chocolate sponge, which would go well with berry fruits such as raspberries and strawberries, is made with 15g/½oz/1 tbsp (unsweetened) cocoa powder instead of the same amount of flour. For a coffee sponge to go with fruit such as poached pear slices, add 10ml/2 tsp coffee essence (extract) and 15ml/1 tbsp coffee liqueur instead of the milk. The sponge may also be flavoured with brandy or rum instead of the milk and vanilla essence.

SAUCES FOR SAVOURY PASTRIES

The secret of serving savoury sauces with pies and pastries is to choose one that enhances and complements the main filling ingredient and the pastry. There are many sauces to choose from, including white sauces, velouté sauces, and butter, oil and egg-based sauces.

WHITE SAUCES

This infinitely versatile sauce forms the basis of many other flavoured sauces, all of which go particularly well with shortcrust pastry pies.

Making a basic white sauce

To make a white sauce, equal quantities of butter and flour are cooked together – this mixture is known as a roux – and bubbled for a minute or so before the milk is added. Other ingredients may be stirred into the sauce; chicken, ham and smoked fish all work well, as do mushrooms. The following recipe makes 450ml/¾ pint/scant 2 cups.

1 Melt 20g/¾oz/1½ tbsp butter in a heavy pan. Stir in 20g/¾oz/scant ¼ cup plain (all-purpose) flour to make a roux. Cook gently, stirring over a very low heat for about 1 minute.

2 Remove the pan from the heat and whisk in 400ml/14fl oz/1⅔ cups milk.

3 Set the pan over a medium heat and whisk until the mixture comes to the boil. Reduce the heat so that the sauce barely simmers, then cook for 5 minutes, stirring frequently. Season with salt, pepper and a little grated nutmeg.

COOK'S TIPS

• Take care to cook the sauce gently on a low heat, and stir frequently to prevent the sauce sticking to the base of the pan as milk can scorch easily, which will produce a burnt flavour.
• If there are any lumps in the sauce, whisk vigorously; if this doesn't solve the problem, strain it through a fine sieve or process briefly in a blender until smooth.

Other white sauces

Béchamel sauce This French white sauce goes well with chicken and hearty vegetable pies. The milk is first infused (steeped) with flavouring ingredients, such as spices and herbs.

Pour the milk into a large pan and add 4 black peppercorns, 1 bay leaf, 1 blade of mace, a few parsley stalks and half a peeled onion. Slowly bring to the boil, then turn off the heat. Cover the pan and leave to infuse for 20 minutes. Strain the milk before using to make the sauce as before.

Mornay sauce This sauce goes very well with vegetable pies. Stir 45ml/3 tbsp double (heavy) cream into white or béchamel sauce along with 115g/4oz/ 1 cup grated Cheddar, Emmenthal or Gruyère cheese. As soon as the cheese is added, remove the pan from the heat and stir until the cheese has melted.

Alternatively, use a strong flavoured blue cheese such as gorgonzola and serve with subtly flavoured vegetable pies such as broccoli and cauliflower.

Mushroom sauce This sauce is delicious with poultry and vegetarian pies. Sauté 115g/4oz finely sliced button (white) mushrooms in 25g/1oz/2 tbsp butter until tender, then stir into a white sauce with 5ml/1 tsp lemon juice.

Parsley sauce This is good with ham and bacon pies – other herbs such as coriander and dill may be used instead of the parsley. Follow the recipe for white sauce and stir in 30ml/2 tbsp chopped fresh parsley at the end.

Soubise sauce A smooth onion sauce, this is ideal with lamb and game pies.

Gently fry 1 finely chopped onion in 25g/1oz/2 tbsp butter for 10 minutes until very soft. Stir into white sauce and simmer for 5 minutes. Serve as is or sieve or purée until smooth.

VELOUTE SAUCES

This sauce is made in exactly the same way as white sauce, but uses stock instead of milk. This gives the sauce a lighter texture and a slightly more translucent appearance. Choose a good quality stock and match it to the pie filling. A little cream is often whisked into the sauce once it has thickened to enrich the flavour, enhance the texture and give it a glossy sheen.

Making a basic velouté sauce

Velouté, meaning velvety, describes the texture of the sauce that is achieved after simmering for about 10 minutes. The following makes 400ml/14fl oz/ 1⅔ cups.

1 Melt 20g/¾oz/1½ tbsp butter in a pan. Stir in 20g/¾oz/scant ¼ cup plain (all-purpose) flour and cook, stirring, over a low heat for a minute.

2 Remove the pan from the heat and whisk in 400ml/14fl oz/1⅔ cups stock. Bring the mixture to the boil, whisking continuously. Turn the heat to very low and simmer for about 10 minutes.

3 Whisk in 60ml/4 tbsp double (heavy) cream, then strain the sauce through a sieve and season with salt and pepper.

COULIS

These are simple, cooked or raw vegetable purées, sometimes thinned to a pourable consistency with stock or wine. They can be served hot or cold and go well with meat and vegetable pies. Tomato, pea, watercress and carrot coulis are just a few examples.

Making a tomato coulis

This simple tomato sauce adds a fresh flavour to vegetable- or fish-filled pies and pastries and looks stunning drizzled on the plate and over and around an individual pie serving or tartlet. The following recipe makes about 600ml/ 1 pint/2½ cups.

1 Heat 25ml/1½ tbsp olive oil in a pan then add 3 finely chopped shallots and 2 crushed garlic cloves. Sauté until soft and translucent. Add 900g/2lb roughly chopped fresh tomatoes such as plum or beefsteak, a few sprigs of fresh thyme and 1 bay leaf and stir well.

2 Cover and simmer gently for about 20 minutes, then uncover and simmer for a further 20 minutes until very thick. Purée and press through a fine sieve. Add salt and pepper to taste and stir in chopped fresh herbs if liked. Serve the sauce hot or cold.

Flavouring velouté sauces
Caper sauce Traditionally served with lamb pies, this quick and easy variation is also good with fish. Stir 30ml/2 tbsp drained, chopped capers into a velouté sauce made with lamb, fish or vegetable stock.

Mustard and dill sauce Serve with ham or red meat pies. Stir in 45ml/3 tbsp chopped fresh dill with 5ml/1 tsp English (hot) or 15ml/1 tbsp Dijon mustard.

Onion gravy This sauce is great with substantial beef or sausage pies. Sauté 2 finely sliced onions in 40g/1½oz/3 tbsp butter until soft. Sprinkle over 15ml/1 tbsp plain (all-purpose) flour and stir in. Gradually add 300ml/½ pint/ 1¼ cups brown meat stock and bring to the boil, stirring all the time. Simmer for a few minutes, then season with salt and pepper.
Red wine sauce To enrich the basic velouté sauce, use red wine in place of some of the stock, or you can stir in a few tablespoons of port or Madeira.

EMULSION SAUCES

There are three types of these thick, creamy sauces: hot sauces, such as hollandaise and béarnaise, which are emulsified mixtures of butter and egg yolks; mayonnaise, which is a cold emulsion sauce, made with oil rather than melted butter; and beurre blanc, which is a butter emulsion that is not thickened with egg yolks.

Making hollandaise sauce

This sauce is believed to have been created by French exiles in Holland, hence the name. Its rich and subtle flavour goes well with elegant fish and shellfish pies and those containing eggs or vegetables such as asparagus.

The secret of success with this sauce is patience: the butter must be worked in slowly or the sauce can curdle. Always use a non-aluminium pan to prevent the sauce from discolouring. Purists make it with clarified butter, but this makes only a slight difference to the finished result. The following makes about 300ml/½ pint/1¼ cups.

1 Put 60ml/4 tbsp white wine vinegar in a pan with 4 black peppercorns, 1 blade of mace and 1 bay leaf. Bring to the boil and reduce to 15ml/1 tbsp. Remove from the heat and immediately dip the base of the pan into cold water to prevent further evaporation. Set the pan aside to cool slightly.

2 Beat 3 egg yolks in a heatproof bowl with 15g/½oz/1 tbsp unsalted (sweet) butter and a pinch of salt. Strain in the reduced vinegar. Place the bowl over a pan of barely simmering water and whisk for 2–3 minutes until beginning to thicken.

3 Beat in a further 150g/5oz/10 tbsp unsalted butter at room temperature. Add the butter in very small amounts, making sure each addition of butter is completely incorporated before adding the next.

4 The mixture will slowly thicken and emulsify. Season with salt and pepper to taste then use.

COOK'S TIPS

• If the heat is too high or the butter is added too quickly, the sauce may separate. If there are signs of curdling, add an ice cube and whisk; the sauce should combine again. If this doesn't work, start again by whisking 1 egg yolk with 15ml/1 tbsp water. Gradually whisk in the separated mixture.
• To make hollandaise sauce in a food processor, melt the butter in a small pan and leave until tepid. Put the egg yolks and strained vinegar in a food processor and blend for a few seconds until smooth. With the motor running, add the melted butter in a thin, steady stream, taking care not to overprocess. When thick, season to taste.
• Hollandaise cannot be reheated, but can be kept warm in a bain marie or bowl set over a pan of hot water.

Making béarnaise sauce

Béarnaise is a more robust sauce than hollandaise, and is delicious served with strongly-flavoured pies containing red meat, such as boeuf en croûte.

1 Make in the same way as hollandaise but omit the mace and add 2 chopped shallots and a few sprigs of fresh tarragon to the vinegar reduction along with the peppercorns and bay leaf. Simmer until reduced to 30ml/2 tbsp. Strain through a sieve.

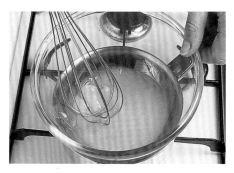

2 Beat the egg yolks in a heatproof bowl, set over a pan of very gently simmering water. Beat in the strained vinegar mixture, then the diced butter, piece by piece. Stir 30ml/2 tbsp finely chopped fresh tarragon into the sauce and serve at once.

Hollandaise variation
Maltaise This orange-flavoured hollandaise is good with fish pies containing white fish, salmon or trout. Simmer 120ml/4fl oz/½ cup orange juice, preferably from blood oranges, and the grated rind of 1 orange until reduced by half. Stir into hollandaise sauce.

Making mayonnaise

This emulsion sauce is excellent with cold pies and pastries, particularly those containing eggs, fish and shellfish or chicken. It is not difficult to make, but it is important to ensure that all the ingredients are at room temperature before you start. The following makes about 300ml/12fl oz/1½ cups.

1 Put 2 egg yolks, 10ml/2 tsp lemon juice, 5ml/1 tsp Dijon mustard, salt, pepper and a pinch of sugar in a bowl. Whisk together until combined.

2 Start adding 300ml/½ pint/1¼ cups sunflower or olive oil, one drop at a time, whisking until about a third has been added and the mixture begins to thicken, then pour in the rest of the oil in a thin, slow steady stream, whisking constantly until the mayonnaise is thick and glossy.

COOK'S TIP

To make mayonnaise in a food processor, place all the ingredients except the sunflower or olive oil in the processor and blend briefly until pale and creamy. With the motor running, very slowly add the oil in a steady, even stream until the mayonnaise is thick and glossy.

Making beurre blanc

Usually served with fish pies, this sauce is also delicious with subtly flavoured pastries, such as poultry or asparagus. It is very rich, so just a small amount is needed. The following makes about 300ml/½ pint/1¼ cups.

Mix together 45ml/3 tbsp white wine and 45ml/3 tbsp white wine vinegar. Put 2 chopped shallots and some herbs, such as tarragon, in a pan. Pour over the liquid, bring to the boil and reduce to 15ml/1 tbsp. Over a low heat, whisk in 225g/8oz/1 cup chilled diced butter, adding piece by piece. Once the sauce thickens, season to taste and serve.

SABAYON

This light, frothy sauce is thickened with egg. Serve with dainty seafood pies made with filo and puff pastry.

Making a classic sabayon

Egg yolks, vinegar and wine or stock are whisked together over a gentle heat to produce a light, airy sauce. The following makes 300ml/½ pint/1¼ cups.

1 Whisk together 4 egg yolks and 15ml/1 tbsp white wine vinegar until slightly pale. Add 90ml/6 tbsp red or white wine or stock and whisk again.

2 Place the bowl over a pan of barely simmering water, making sure that the bowl does not touch the water.

3 Continue whisking until the sauce is thick and frothy. Season to taste and serve immediately.

Mayonnaise and sabayon variations
Herb mayonnaise Stir in 30ml/ 2 tbsp chopped fresh herbs such as chives, chervil or tarragon.
Tartare sauce Add 15ml/1 tbsp capers or chopped gherkins, 15ml/1 tbsp chopped parsley and 10ml/2 tsp chopped chives to a basic mayonnaise.
Avgolemono This classic Greek variation on sabayon has a sharp lemony flavour. It is good with pies made with oily fish or vegetables. Blend 10ml/2 tsp arrowroot with the grated rind and strained juice of 1 large lemon in a small pan. Add 120ml/4fl oz/½ cup vegetable or fish stock and bring to the boil, whisking until thickened. Pour in 3 beaten egg yolks in a steady stream, whisking constantly. Pour it back into the pan and cook for 1 minute. Serve immediately.

SAUCES FOR SWEET PASTRIES

A delectable sauce adds the finishing touch to any sweet pastry dish. A frothy sabayon can transform a simple fruit tart into a really special dessert, and profiteroles without a rich chocolate sauce just wouldn't be the same.

FRUIT SAUCES

Fresh sauces made with sweet ripe fruit complement many pies and pastries. Use just enough sugar to bring out the flavour of the fruit, remembering that the pastries already contain sugar.

Making a fresh fruit coulis

This sauce is made by puréeing fruit with icing (confectioners') sugar. Use soft fruit, but do not mix different fruits. This makes 250ml/8fl oz/1 cup.

1 Put 225g/8oz/about 2 cups prepared fresh fruit, such as raspberries, strawberries or kiwi fruit, in a food processor. Add 5ml/1 tsp lemon juice and, if you like, 30ml/2 tbsp liqueur such as Kirsch, framboise or Grand Marnier. Blend to a smooth purée.

2 Press the purée through a very fine sieve placed over a bowl, then discard the seeds. Stir in 15–30ml/1–2 tbsp sifted icing sugar. Cover and chill until required. A coulis will keep for two to three days in the refrigerator.

COOK'S TIP

Professional chefs use a sugar syrup instead of icing (confectioners') sugar, but this is really only worthwhile if you are making a very large quantity. To make, dissolve 200g/7oz/1 cup caster (superfine) sugar in 200ml/7fl oz/scant 1 cup water over a low heat. Increase the heat and boil for 3 minutes, then cool.

Making a cooked fruit coulis

Coulis can also be made using harder fruits, such as plums, cherries, apricots and peaches, if they are cooked before puréeing. Sharp tasting soft fruits need to be cooked before being puréed to improve both their colour and flavour. Gooseberries, blackberries, blueberries and blackcurrants all make good cooked coulis. The following makes about 350ml/12fl oz/1½ cups.

1 Put 350g/12oz/3 cups prepared fruit in a pan with 60ml/4 tbsp water. Stir in sugar to taste and a dash of lemon juice. Gently simmer for 5–20 minutes, depending on the type of fruit used, until it is very soft.

2 Remove the pan from the heat, taste the fruit and stir in a little more sugar, if needed. If the sauce is too sweet, add a few drops of lemon juice. Cool slightly, then purée in a food processor or blender until smooth.

3 Press the purée through a sieve to remove any seeds or skins. Cover tightly and chill until required. If you like, stir in 45ml/3 tbsp liqueur such as Kirsch or framboise just before serving. Keep the coulis for up to one week in the refrigerator, well covered.

Fruit compôte

These may be made with either fresh or frozen fruits and can be served hot or cold. They are always made with whole fruit and are sometimes known as a slump because of the way the fruit softens during cooking. They differ from coulis in that they aren't puréed after cooking. Although often cooked with a little liquid and sugar, jam may be used with the fruit for added flavour. Serve with plain fruit pies or cheesecakes. This makes 250ml/8fl oz/1 cup.

Red fruit compôte You will need 225g/8oz/1⅓ cups mixed fresh red fruits such as strawberries, raspberries, red- and blackcurrants and pitted cherries. Place fruit that need longer cooking, such as cherries and currants, in a pan. Add 45–60ml/3–4 tbsp sugar and 30ml/2 tbsp water or liqueur such as crème de cassis and cook for about 3 minutes. Add the remaining softer fruits. Simmer for 5–7 minutes until tender.

Pineapple compôte Simmer 225g/8oz/1½ cups chopped fresh pineapple with 115g/4oz/scant ½ cup pineapple jam and 15ml/1 tbsp lemon juice for about 3 minutes. Stir in 30ml/2 tbsp orange liqueur. This makes about 350ml/12fl oz/1½ cups.

THICKENED FRUIT SAUCES

Sometimes you may want to thicken a sauce either because you want a larger amount of sauce with fewer fruit pieces, or because the fruit you have chosen has produced a lot of juice. There are two easy ways of thickening sauces; by removing the fruit and simmering the juices until reduced and thick, or by using a thickening agent such as cornflour (cornstarch) or arrowroot.

Making a rhubarb sauce by reduction

Fruits such as rhubarb produce a lot of juices and letting them bubble until reduced concentrates the colour, flavour and sweetness. Take care not to add too much sugar or the syrup will taste too sweet. If it does, add a few drops of strained lemon juice. The following makes 750ml/1¼ pints/3 cups.

1 Heat 90g/3½oz/½ cup granulated sugar with 120ml/4fl oz/½ cup water in a wide shallow pan until dissolved. Add 20g/¾oz sliced fresh root ginger and simmer for 3 minutes.

2 Add 675g/1½lb rhubarb, cut into 5cm/2in pieces, cover and cook for 5 minutes until tender. Lift the rhubarb into a serving dish using a slotted spoon. Boil the syrup for 7 minutes, or until well reduced. Strain over the rhubarb and serve warm or cold.

COOK'S TIP

Making a sauce in this way also works well for fruits that require a long cooking time to tenderize them, such as kumquats. Slice 450g/1lb of the fruit and add to the syrup. Cook for 20 minutes, then transfer the fruit to a bowl and reduce the syrup as before.

Making a hot orange and red wine sauce with cornflour

Cornflour (cornstarch) is used for thickening sauces when an opaque appearance is needed, and this vibrant, tangy sauce is a good example. Serve with deep-dish pies, such as apple or cherry. Always blend the cornflour with a small amount of cold liquid before adding to the hot liquid. The following makes about 350ml/12fl oz/1½ cups.

1 Thinly pare the rind from half an orange using a zester. Squeeze four oranges well and strain the juice into a small pan.

2 Add the pared orange rind to the pan, along with 250ml/8fl oz/1 cup fruity red wine, 25g/1oz/2 tbsp soft light brown sugar, 1 cinnamon stick and 2 whole cloves. Gently simmer for about 15 minutes until reduced.

3 Mix 5ml/1 tsp cornflour with 15ml/1 tbsp cold water or orange liqueur in a small cup. Add to the red wine mixture in the pan and simmer for 1 minute, until the syrup is slightly thickened. Remove the cloves and cinnamon stick and slowly whisk in 25g/1oz/2 tbsp unsalted (sweet) butter to make a smooth, glossy sauce.

Making a passionfruit sauce with arrowroot

Arrowroot is a very useful thickening agent as, unlike cornflour, it becomes transparent when it simmers making beautifully clear sauces. This is handy when making sauces with fruit such as passionfruit and you want the seeds to be seen. The following makes about 175ml/6fl oz/¾ cup.

1 Squeeze the juice from 2 oranges, then strain it into a bowl. Spoon 15ml/1 tbsp of the juice into a cup and stir in 5ml/1 tsp arrowroot, then set aside. Put the remaining orange juice in a small pan with 45ml/3 tbsp caster (superfine) sugar and heat gently until dissolved, stirring frequently.

2 Scoop the pulp out of 6 ripe passionfruits. Add to the pan and simmer for 1 minute. Stir in the blended arrowroot and simmer until thickened and clear. Stir in 15g/½oz/1 tbsp unsalted (sweet) butter a little at a time. Cool and chill until required. This sauce will keep for four to five days in the refrigerator.

Making a sauce with dried fruit

Dried fruits such as apricots and mangoes can be made into sauces by soaking overnight in water or fruit juice, then puréeing. Their sharp fresh flavour goes well with sticky flans and tarts such as treacle tart, and rich chocolate-flavoured filled pies. The following makes 600ml/1 pint/scant 2½ cups.

Soak 175g/6oz dried apricots or mangoes overnight in 750ml/1¼ pints/3 cups cold water, orange juice or apple juice. Gently simmer for 15 minutes until tender. Purée and serve cold, poured over a flan or tart.

SWEET EGG AND MILK SAUCES

From rich and creamy crème Anglaise, to a frothy sabayon or rich brandy sauce, egg- and milk-based sauces can add just the right finish to pastries.

Making a crème Anglaise

This is a "proper" custard, rich and creamy and made with all milk or a mixture of cream and milk and slightly thickened with egg yolks. Serve hot or chilled with traditional fruit pies such as apple or cherry or drizzle in a pool on a plate and top with a crispy filo basket filled with fruit. Crème Anglaise can also be set with gelatine to make a sweet pie filling. The quantity below makes about 600ml/1 pint/2½ cups.

1 Mix 250ml/8fl oz/1 cup each milk and cream in a heavy pan. Split a vanilla pod (bean) lengthways and add it to the pan. Gently heat to just below boiling point. Meanwhile, whisk 5 egg yolks and 90g/3½oz/scant ½ cup caster (superfine) sugar in a bowl until the mixture is pale and thick.

2 Remove the vanilla pod and pour the hot milk and cream over the egg yolk mixture, whisking all the time.

3 Pour the mixture back into the pan and stir constantly over a very low heat until slightly thickened. Do not allow the custard to boil or it may curdle. When ready, it should be thick enough to coat the back of a wooden spoon.

COOK'S TIP
Crème Anglaise can be kept in the refrigerator for up to two days. Cover the surface with cling film (plastic wrap) to prevent a skin from forming.

Brandy Sauce

This is a traditional sweet white sauce, less rich than crème Anglaise. It is excellent with Christmas pudding and rich pastries, especially those filled with dried fruit, such as mince pies. The following makes 600ml/1 pint/2½ cups.

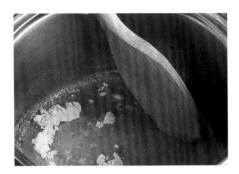

Melt 40g/1½oz/3 tbsp unsalted (sweet) butter in a pan. Stir in 30ml/2 tbsp plain (all-purpose) flour and whisk in 450ml/¾ pint/scant 2 cups milk. Add 15ml/1 tbsp caster (superfine) sugar and slowly bring to the boil, whisking all the time, until the sauce thickens and is smooth. Reduce the heat and simmer for 5 minutes, stirring occasionally. Stir in 45ml/3 tbsp brandy before serving.

Making a warm sabayon sauce

This light, frothy sauce goes well with all sorts of sweet pies and tarts, in particular delicate pastries. The following makes 450ml/¾ pint/scant 2 cups.

1 Put 4 egg yolks and 50g/2oz/¼ cup caster (superfine) sugar in a heatproof bowl and beat well until the mixture becomes slightly paler. Set the bowl over a pan of barely simmering water, making sure that the bowl does not touch the water. Whisk in 100ml/ 3½fl oz/generous ½ cup sweet wine.

2 Continue whisking the sauce over the heat for 10 minutes until it becomes very thick and frothy. Serve the sauce hot or cold.

Making a chilled sabayon sauce

This cold sabayon is best prepared ahead of time so it can be well chilled before serving. The following makes 400ml/14fl oz/1⅔ cups.

1 Put 75g/3oz/6 tbsp caster (superfine) sugar in a pan with 120ml/4fl oz/½ cup water. Heat gently until the sugar has dissolved. Increase the heat and boil for 4 minutes until the syrup registers 105°C/225°F on a sugar thermometer. Meanwhile, whisk 3 egg yolks in a bowl until pale. Gradually pour on the hot syrup in a thin stream, whisking all the time. Whisk until very thick.

2 Whip 150ml/¼ pint/⅔ cup double (heavy) cream to soft peaks. Add the finely grated rind and juice of 1 lemon and whisk again to soft peaks. Fold into the sabayon. Cover the surface with clear film (plastic wrap) and chill until needed. Whisk well before serving.

COOK'S TIP
To make a lighter version, use 1 egg yolk and 1 whole egg.

CARAMEL SAUCES

These sauces thicken as they cool, and are very rich, so serve in small portions.

Creamy caramel sauce

This rich, thick sauce looks superb pooled around small tartlets and pastries with fruit, chocolate or coffee fillings. The sweetness of the sauce depends on the degree to which the sugar is allowed to caramelize. Cook until a light golden colour for a sweeter sauce or to dark golden for a richer, less sweet flavour, but take care that it does not darken too much or it will have an unpleasant burnt flavour.

1 Put 50g/2oz/¼ cup caster (superfine) sugar in a small heavy pan with 60ml/4 tbsp cold water and heat gently until the sugar has dissolved. Bring to the boil and cook, until the sauce is a rich golden brown.

2 Remove the pan from the heat and immediately add 150ml/¼ pint/⅔ cup double (heavy) cream in a slow steady stream, taking care as you do so, as the mixture will splutter. Stir over a gentle heat until the caramel dissolves and the sauce is smooth. Serve warm or cold.

Making a dark toffee sauce

In this caramel sauce, the sugar isn't caramelized, rather the colour of the sauce comes from the use of soft dark brown sugar.

Gently heat 25g/1oz/2 tbsp unsalted (sweet) butter with 75g/3oz/6 tbsp soft dark brown sugar in a pan, stirring until the sugar has all dissolved. Stir in 150ml/¼ pint/⅔ cup double (heavy) cream, then simmer for 2 minutes until smooth. Serve warm or cold.

Making a butterscotch sauce

This is much sweeter than the creamy caramel or dark toffee sauces, and has a lovely buttery flavour, so don't serve it with overly sweet pastries.

Melt 50g/2oz/¼ cup unsalted (sweet) butter, 75g/3oz/6 tbsp soft light brown sugar, 50g/2oz/¼ cup caster (superfine) sugar and 150g/5oz/scant ½ cup golden (light corn) syrup in a heavy pan over a low heat. Cook gently, stirring, for 3–4 minutes. Remove from the heat and gradually add 150ml/¼ pint/⅔ cup double (heavy) cream, a dash of lemon juice and 5ml/1 tsp vanilla essence (extract). Serve warm or cold.

CHOCOLATE SAUCES

Always rich, chocolate sauces can vary in their sweetness, from slightly bitter to sweet and sticky.

Making a simple chocolate sauce

This is a dark and rich sauce, very good with sweet and plain shortcrust tarts.

Heat 200ml/7fl oz/scant 1 cup double (heavy) cream with 60ml/4 tbsp milk until boiling. Remove from the heat, add 150g/5oz dark (bittersweet) chocolate and whisk until the chocolate has melted. Serve warm.

Making a glossy hot chocolate sauce

This is ideal for pouring over profiteroles and similar pastries.

Heat 115g/4oz plain (semisweet) chocolate, 75g/3oz/⅓ cup golden (light corn) syrup and 30ml/2 tbsp liqueur in a heatproof bowl set over a pan of hot water. Stir until smooth. Serve warm.

Making a chocolate fudge sauce

This sauce is thick and sticky. Serve with less sweet pies and pastries.

Gently melt 50g/2oz plain (semisweet) chocolate in 120ml/4fl oz/½ cup condensed milk in a heatproof bowl set over a pan of simmering water. Stir in 60ml/4 tbsp milk and 25g/1oz/2 tbsp unsalted (sweet) butter. Serve warm.

Making a white chocolate sauce

This very sweet sauce is a good contrast to dark chocolate and coffee pie fillings.

Melt 200g/7oz white chocolate with 30ml/2 tbsp double (heavy) cream in a heatproof bowl set over very hot, but not boiling, water. Stir until smooth. Add a further 60ml/4 tbsp double cream and add 60ml/4 tbsp milk. Gently heat until it just reaches boiling point. Remove the pan from the heat and whisk until smooth. Serve warm.

THE PASTRY KITCHEN

What could be more appealing than a double-crust fruit pie with crisp golden crust, packed with tender juicy fruit, a light-as-air eclair thickly covered with rich chocolate and oozing with whipped cream or a fragile filo basket brimming with a creamy seafood filling? Whatever your pastry fancy, sweet or savoury, great or small, you'll find it among the contemporary and classic creations here, from stunningly simple starters to divine desserts, all with foolproof step-by-step instructions to ensure you attain pastry perfection every time.

SMALL SAVOURY PASTRIES

Individual pastries brimming with tasty fillings are ideal for serving

as appetizers. Delicate pastries like Cheese Scrolls and Moroccan

Prawn Packages are made from melt-in-the-mouth filo and are just

right to whet the appetite at the beginning of a meal, while more

substantial first courses such as Egg and Salmon Puff Parcels will

please those with larger appetites. This chapter also contains numerous

tempting recipes perfect for light lunches or for serving as snacks.

ALSACE LEEK AND ONION TARTLETS

THE SAVOURY FILLING IN THESE TARTLETS IS TRADITIONAL TO NORTH-EASTERN FRANCE, WHERE MANY TYPES OF QUICHE ARE POPULAR. BAKING THE TARTS IN INDIVIDUAL TINS MAKES FOR EASIER SERVING — AND THEY LOOK ATTRACTIVE ON THE PLATE, ACCOMPANIED WITH A SALAD GARNISH.

SERVES SIX

INGREDIENTS

  25g/1oz/2 tbsp butter
  1 onion, thinly sliced
  2.5ml/½ tsp dried thyme
  450g/1lb leeks, thinly sliced
  50g/2oz/½ cup grated Gruyère or
    Emmenthal cheese
  3 eggs
  300ml/½ pint/1¼ cups single
    (light) cream
  pinch of freshly grated nutmeg
  salt and ground black pepper
  salad, to serve
For the pastry
  175g/6oz/1½ cups plain
    (all-purpose) flour
  75g/3oz/6 tbsp cold butter, diced
  1 egg yolk
  30–45m/2–3 tbsp chilled water
  2.5m/½ tsp salt

1 To make the pastry, sift the flour into a bowl and add the butter. Cut in the butter using a pastry blender or rub in the flour with your fingertips until the mixture resembles fine breadcrumbs.

2 Make a well in the centre of the flour mixture. Beat together the egg yolk, chilled water and salt in a small bowl. Pour into the well in the dry ingredients and, using a fork, mix the flour and liquid until they begin to stick together and a soft, pliable dough is formed. Shape into a flattened ball. Wrap the dough in clear film (plastic wrap) and chill for about 30 minutes.

3 Lightly butter six 10cm/4in tartlet tins (mini quiche pans). Roll out the dough on a lightly floured surface until about 3mm/⅛in thick, then, using a 12.5cm/5in plain cutter, cut as many rounds as possible. Gently ease the pastry rounds into the tins, pressing the pastry firmly along the base and sides. Re-roll the trimmings and line the remaining tins. Prick the bases. Chill for 30 minutes.

4 Preheat the oven to 190°C/375°F/Gas 5. Line the pastry cases with foil and fill with baking beans, making sure they are evenly distributed over the pastry bases. Place the pastry cases on a baking sheet.

5 Bake for 6–8 minutes until the edges of the pastry are golden. Lift out the foil and beans and return the partially baked pastry cases to the oven. Bake for 2 minutes more or until the bases are dry. Transfer the pastry cases in their tins to a wire rack to cool. Reduce the oven temperature to 180°C/350°F/Gas 4.

6 Place the butter in a large frying pan, and melt over a medium heat, then add the onion and thyme and cook for about 5 minutes until the onion is soft and translucent, stirring often.

7 Add the sliced leeks and cook for about 10 minutes until they are soft and tender. Divide the mixture evenly among the pastry cases and sprinkle each with cheese, dividing it evenly.

8 Beat the eggs, cream, nutmeg and salt and pepper together in a small mixing bowl until well mixed. Place the pastry cases in their tins on a baking sheet and pour in the egg mixture, evenly covering the leek filling. Bake the tartlets for 15–20 minutes until set and golden.

9 Transfer the tartlet tins to a wire rack to cool slightly and allow the pastry to firm up a little. Remove the tartlets from the tins and lift them on to individual plates. Serve warm or at room temperature with a salad garnish.

WILD MUSHROOM AND FONTINA TARTLETS

THE NUTTINESS OF WALNUT PASTRY GOES BEAUTIFULLY WITH THE CREAMY FLAVOUR OF ITALIAN FONTINA CHEESE IN THESE DELECTABLE TARTS. SERVE THEM AS A SUMMER FIRST COURSE.

SERVES FOUR

INGREDIENTS
    25g/1oz/½ cup dried wild mushrooms
    30ml/2 tbsp olive oil
    1 red onion, chopped
    2 garlic cloves, chopped
    30ml/2 tbsp medium-dry sherry
    1 egg
    120ml/4fl oz/½ cup single
      (light) cream
    25g/1oz Fontina cheese, thinly sliced
    salt and ground black pepper
    rocket (arugula) leaves, to serve
For the pastry
    115g/4oz/1 cup wholemeal
      (whole-wheat) flour
    50g/2oz/¼ cup butter, diced
    25g/1oz/¼ cup walnuts, roasted
      and ground
    1 egg, lightly beaten

1 To make the wholemeal pastry, sift the flour into a large mixing bowl, and tip the bran back in. Rub or cut in the butter into the flour until the mixture resembles fine breadcrumbs, then stir in the ground walnuts. Add the egg and mix to form a soft dough. Wrap the pastry in clear film (plastic wrap). Chill for 30 minutes.

2 Meanwhile, soak the dried wild mushrooms in 300ml/½ pint/1¼ cups boiling water for 30 minutes. Drain through a fine sieve and reserve the liquid. Heat the oil in a large frying pan. Add the onion and fry for 5 minutes, until softened, then add the garlic and fry for 2 minutes.

3 Add the soaked mushrooms to the pan and cook for 7 minutes over a high heat. Add the sherry and the reserved liquid. Cook until the liquid evaporates. Season and set aside in a bowl to cool.

4 Preheat the oven to 200°C/400°F/ Gas 6. Grease four 10cm/4in tartlet tins (mini quiche pans). Roll out the pastry on a lightly floured work surface and use to line the tins.

5 Prick the pastry bases all over with a fork, line with foil and baking beans and bake blind for 10 minutes. Remove the foil and beans.

6 Lightly whisk the egg and cream, add to the mushrooms, then season to taste. Spoon into the pastry cases, top with the cheese slices and bake for about 20 minutes until the filling is set. Serve warm, with the rocket leaves.

LEEK, SAFFRON AND MUSSEL TARTS

SERVE THESE VIVIDLY COLOURED TARTLETS AS A FIRST COURSE, WITH A FEW SALAD LEAVES, SUCH AS WATERCRESS, ROCKET AND FRISÉE.

SERVES SIX

INGREDIENTS
  large pinch of saffron threads
  15ml/1 tbsp hot water
  30ml/2 tbsp olive oil
  2 large leeks, sliced
  2 large yellow (bell) peppers, halved,
    seeded, grilled (broiled) and peeled,
    then cut into strips
  900g/2lb mussels, scrubbed and
    beards removed
  2 large eggs
  300ml/½ pint/1¼ cups single
    (light) cream
  30ml/2 tbsp finely chopped
    fresh parsley
  salt and ground black pepper
  salad leaves, to serve
For the pastry
  225g/8oz/2 cups plain
    (all-purpose) flour
  pinch of salt
  115g/4oz/½ cup butter, diced
  45–60ml/3–4 tbsp chilled water

1 To make the pastry, sift the flour and salt into a large bowl. Rub or cut in the butter. Sprinkle over 45ml/3 tbsp of the water and mix to a dough, adding a little more water if needed. Wrap and chill for 30 minutes.

2 Preheat the oven to 190°C/375°F/ Gas 5. Roll out the pastry on a floured surface and use to line six 10cm/4in tartlet tins (mini quiche pans). Chill for about 10 minutes. Prick the bases all over with a fork and line the sides with strips of foil.

3 Bake the pastry cases for 10 minutes. Remove the foil and bake for a further 5–8 minutes. Remove from the oven. Reduce the oven temperature to 180°C/ 350°F/Gas 4.

4 Soak the saffron in the hot water for 15 minutes. Heat the oil in a large pan, add the leeks and fry over a medium heat for 6–8 minutes until softened and beginning to brown. Add the yellow pepper strips and cook for 2 minutes.

5 Bring 2.5cm/1in depth of water to a rolling boil in a large pan and add 10ml/ 2 tsp salt. Discard any open mussels that do not shut when tapped sharply, then add the rest to the pan. Cover and cook over a high heat, shaking the pan occasionally, for 3–4 minutes, or until the mussels open. Discard any mussels that do not open at this stage. Shell the remaining mussels.

6 Strain the saffron liquid into a bowl and add the eggs and cream. Beat well. Season with salt and black pepper and whisk in the parsley.

7 Arrange the leeks, peppers and mussels in the pastry cases, pour the egg mixture over the top and bake for 20–25 minutes, or until risen and just firm. Serve the tarts immediately with salad leaves.

PROSCIUTTO AND MOZZARELLA PARCELS

IN THESE TASTY LITTLE PARCELS, THE MOZZARELLA IS ADDED AS MUCH FOR ITS TEXTURE AS FOR ITS FLAVOUR. BITE INTO THESE CRISP FILO PARCELS TO REVEAL A CREAMY MELTED CHEESE AND HAM FILLING.

SERVES SIX

INGREDIENTS
  a little hot chilli sauce
  6 prosciutto slices, such as
    Parma ham
  200g/7oz mozzarella cheese, cut into
    6 slices
  6 sheets of filo pastry, each
    measuring 45 × 28cm/18 × 11in,
    thawed if frozen
  50g/2oz/¼ cup butter, melted

COOK'S TIP
Parma ham is readily available, usually along with at least one other type of prosciutto. Visit a good Italian deli and you will find a choice of regional hams.

1 Preheat the oven to 200°C/400°F/ Gas 6. Sprinkle a little of the hot chilli sauce over each slice of prosciutto. Place a slice of mozzarella in the centre of each piece of prosciutto, then fold the ends of the ham around the cheese to meet neatly in the middle.

2 Brush a sheet of filo pastry with a little melted butter. Fold in half lengthways and brush the top with butter. Wrap a ham and mozzarella parcel in the pastry to make a package, tucking the edges in neatly as you go. Place on a baking sheet, seam side down, and brush with a little more butter. Repeat with the remaining ham and cheese parcels and pastry sheets.

3 Bake the filo parcels for 15 minutes, or until the pastry is crisp and evenly golden. Serve all together or arrange on individual plates, with a frisée salad, if you wish. Serve immediately.

SMOKED CHICKEN WITH PEACH MAYONNAISE IN FILO TARTLETS

THE FILLING FOR THESE CHICKEN TARTLETS CAN BE PREPARED A DAY IN ADVANCE AND CHILLED, BUT DO NOT FILL THE PASTRY CASES UNTIL YOU ARE READY TO SERVE THEM OR THEY WILL BECOME SOGGY.

MAKES TWELVE

INGREDIENTS
  25g/1oz/2 tbsp butter
  3 sheets of filo pastry, each
    measuring 45 × 28cm/18 × 11in,
    thawed if frozen
  2 skinless, boneless smoked chicken
    breast portions, finely sliced
  150ml/¼ pint/⅔ cup mayonnaise
  grated rind of 1 lime
  30ml/2 tbsp lime juice
  2 ripe peaches, peeled, stoned
    (pitted) and chopped
  salt and ground black pepper
  fresh tarragon sprigs, lime slices
    and salad leaves, to garnish

1 Preheat the oven to 200°C/400°F/ Gas 6. Place the butter in a small pan and heat gently until melted. Lightly brush 12 mini flan rings with a little melted butter.

2 Cut each sheet of filo pastry into 12 equal rounds large enough to line the tins and stand above the rims. Place a round of pastry in each tin and brush with a little butter, then add another round of pastry. Brush each with more butter and add a third round of pastry.

3 Bake the tartlets for 5 minutes. Leave in the tins for a few moments before transferring to a wire rack to cool.

4 Mix together the chicken, mayonnaise, lime rind, peaches and seasoning. Chill for at least 30 minutes, but preferably overnight. When ready to serve, spoon the chicken mixture into the filo pastry cases and garnish with tarragon sprigs, lime slices and salad leaves.

COOK'S TIP
Use small tartlet tins (mini quiche pans) if you don't have mini flan rings.

CHEESE SCROLLS

THESE TRADITIONAL EAST EUROPEAN CHEESE SAVOURIES ARE EATEN IN CAFÉS, RESTAURANTS AND HOMES AT ANY TIME OF THE DAY AND ARE DELICIOUS EATEN BOTH WARM AND COLD.

2 Fit a piping (pastry) bag with a large 1cm/½in plain round nozzle and fill with half of the cheese mixture.

3 Fold one sheet of filo pastry into a 30 × 20cm/12 × 8in rectangle and brush with a little melted butter. Pipe a strip of feta cheese mixture along one long edge, leaving a margin of about 10mm/½in.

4 Fold in each end to prevent the filling from escaping, then roll up the pastry to form a sausage shape. Brush with more melted butter.

5 Gently twist the "sausage" into an "S" or a crescent shape. Repeat with the remaining ingredients, refilling the piping bag as necessary.

MAKES FOURTEEN TO SIXTEEN

INGREDIENTS
    450g/1lb feta cheese, well drained
      and finely crumbled
    90ml/6 tbsp Greek (US strained
      plain) yogurt
    2 eggs, beaten
    14–16 sheets of filo pastry, each
      measuring 40 × 30cm/16 × 12in,
      thawed if frozen
    225g/8oz/1 cup butter, melted
    sea salt and chopped spring onions
      (scallions), to garnish

1 Preheat the oven to 200°C/400°F/ Gas 6. Mix together the feta cheese, yogurt and eggs in a large bowl, beating well until the mixture is smooth.

6 Arrange the filo pastry shapes on a buttered baking sheet and brush with a little melted butter. Sprinkle with sea salt and chopped spring onion. Bake the pastries for 20 minutes until golden brown and crisp. Cool them on a wire rack before serving.

MOROCCAN PRAWN PACKAGES

THESE ELEGANT ROLLS ARE TRADITIONALLY MADE USING A LOCAL PASTRY, BUT FILO IS AN EXCELLENT SUBSTITUTE. THE FILLING IS LIGHTLY SPICED WITH PAPRIKA.

MAKES ABOUT TWENTY-FOUR

INGREDIENTS
175g/6oz filo pastry, thawed if frozen
40g/1½oz/3 tbsp butter, melted
sunflower oil, for frying
ground cinnamon and icing
  (confectioners') sugar, for
  dusting (optional)
spring onions (scallions) and
  coriander (cilantro) leaves, to garnish
For the filling
15ml/1 tbsp olive oil
15g/½oz/1 tbsp butter
2–3 spring onions (scallions)
15g/½oz/2 tbsp plain
  (all-purpose) flour
300ml/½ pint/1¼ cups milk
2.5ml/½ tsp paprika
350g/12oz cooked peeled prawns
  (shrimp), chopped
salt and ground white pepper

1 To make the filling, heat the olive oil and butter in a pan. Chop the spring onions finely and add them to the oil and butter mixture, and fry over a very gentle heat for 2–3 minutes until soft.

2 Stir in the flour, then slowly pour in the milk, stirring constantly, until the mixture boils and thickens to make a smooth sauce.

3 Season the sauce with paprika, salt and white pepper. Stir well, then add the prawns and fold them in.

4 Take a sheet of pastry and cut it in half widthways to make an 18 × 14cm/ 7 × 5½in rectangle. Cover the remaining filo pastry with clear film (plastic wrap) or a damp dishtowel to prevent it from drying out.

5 Brush the pastry with melted butter and then place a heaped teaspoon of filling at one end of the pastry. Roll it up like a cigar, tucking in the sides as you go. Set the package aside, keeping it covered with clear film. Continue to make more pastry rolls in the same way until you have used all the pastry and filling.

6 Heat about 1cm/½in oil in a heavy pan and fry the filo packages, in batches if necessary, for 2–3 minutes until golden. Drain on kitchen paper. To serve, dust the pastry with cinnamon and icing sugar, if you like, and garnish with spring onions and a few fresh coriander leaves.

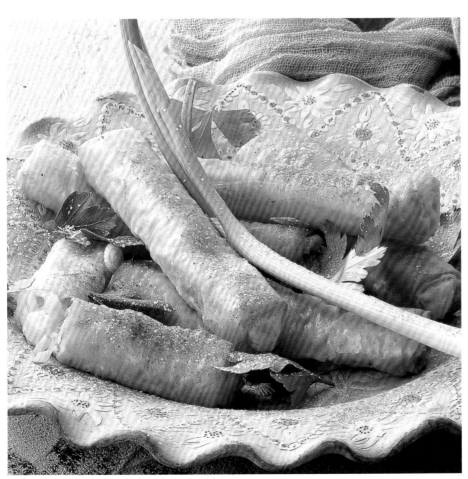

TURKEY AND CRANBERRY PURSES

THESE DELICIOUS FILO PASTRY PARCELS ARE AN EXCELLENT WAY OF USING UP SMALL PIECES OF COOKED TURKEY — A USEFUL IDEA IF YOU HAVE LOTS OF TURKEY LEFTOVERS.

SERVES SIX

INGREDIENTS

450g/1lb cooked turkey, cut
    into chunks
115g/4oz/1 cup diced Brie cheese
30ml/2 tbsp cranberry sauce
30ml/2 tbsp chopped fresh parsley
9 sheets of filo pastry, each
    measuring 45 × 28cm/18 × 11in,
    thawed if frozen
50g/2oz/¼ cup butter, melted
salt and ground black pepper

1 Preheat the oven to 200°C/400°F/ Gas 6. Place the turkey, Brie, cranberry sauce and chopped parsley in a small mixing bowl and mix well. Season with salt and pepper.

2 Cut the sheets of filo in half widthways and trim to make 18 squares. Keeping the remaining filo covered with clear film (plastic wrap), to prevent it from drying out, layer three pieces of pastry together, brushing each layer with a little melted butter. Repeat with the remaining filo squares to give six stacks.

3 Divide the turkey mixture evenly among the pastry stacks, making neat piles in the centre of each piece. Gather up the pastry to enclose the filling in neat bundles. Place on a baking sheet, brush with melted butter and bake for about 20 minutes, or until the pastry is crisp and golden.

VARIATIONS
These little parcels can be made with a variety of fillings and are great for using up left-over cooked meats.
Ham and Cheddar Purses Replace the turkey with ham and use Cheddar cheese in place of the Brie. A fruit chutney would make a good alternative to the cranberry sauce.
Chicken and Stilton Purses Use cooked, diced chicken breast portions in place of the turkey and white Stilton cheese instead of Brie. Replace the cranberry sauce with mango chutney.
Goat's Cheese and Celery Purses Use chopped celery and almonds, sautéed in a little butter, instead of the turkey. Replace the Brie with goat's cheese. Chopped fresh figs can be used in place of the cranberry sauce.

TUNISIAN BRIK

YOU CAN MAKE THESE LITTLE PARCELS INTO ANY SHAPE YOU LIKE, BUT THE IMPORTANT THING IS TO ENCASE THE EGG COMPLETELY TO PREVENT IT FROM RUNNING OUT.

SERVES SIX

INGREDIENTS

  40g/1½oz/3 tbsp butter, melted
  1 small red onion, finely chopped
  150g/5oz skinless, boneless chicken
    or turkey, minced (ground)
  1 large garlic clove, crushed
  juice of ½ lemon
  30ml/2 tbsp chopped fresh parsley
  12 sheets of filo pastry, each
    measuring 25 × 15cm/10 × 6in,
    thawed if frozen
  6 small eggs, such as bantam,
    pheasant or guinea fowl
  oil, for deep-frying
  salt and ground black pepper

1 Heat half the butter in a pan. Sauté the onion for about 3 minutes until soft. Add the minced meat, garlic, lemon juice, parsley and seasoning. Cook, stirring with chopsticks, for 2–3 minutes until the meat is just cooked. Set aside to cool.

2 Place one sheet of pastry lengthways on the work surface and brush with melted butter; top with a second sheet. Brush the edges with butter and place one-sixth of the meat mixture on the lower left side of the pastry sheet, about 2.5cm/1in from the base. Flatten the filling, making a slight hollow in it.

COOK'S TIP
If you prefer to cook these pastries in the oven, preheat it to 220°C/425°F/Gas 7. Brush the pastries with butter and cook for 8–10 minutes.

3 Carefully crack an egg into the hollow and be ready to fold up the pastry immediately so that the egg white does not run out. Lift the right-hand edge of the pastry and fold it over to the left edge to enclose the filling. Seal quickly, fold the bottom edge straight up to seal, then fold the bottom left corner across to the right corner, forming a triangle.

4 Use the remaining pastry sheets and filling to make another five parcels in the same way. Heat the oil in a wok until a cube of bread added to it turns golden in about 1½ minutes. Cook the pastries, two or three at a time until golden. Lift them out of the pan with a slotted spoon and drain on kitchen paper. Serve the pastries hot or cold.

EGG AND SALMON PUFF PARCELS

THESE ELEGANT PARCELS HIDE A MOUTHWATERING MIXTURE OF FLAVOURS, AND MAKE A DELICIOUS APPETIZER OR LUNCH DISH. SERVE WITH CURRY-FLAVOURED MAYONNAISE OR HOLLANDAISE SAUCE.

SERVES SIX

INGREDIENTS
    75g/3oz/scant ½ cup long grain rice
    300ml/½ pint/1¼ cups good-quality
      fish stock
    350g/12oz tail pieces of salmon
    juice of ½ lemon
    15ml/1 tbsp chopped fresh dill
    15ml/1 tbsp chopped fresh parsley
    10ml/2 tsp mild curry powder
    6 small eggs, soft-boiled
      and cooled
    425g/15oz flaky or puff pastry
    1 egg, beaten
    salt and ground black pepper

1 Place the rice in a large pan and cook according to the instructions on the packet, using fish stock instead of water, then drain, tip into a bowl and set aside to cool. Preheat the oven to 220°C/425°F/Gas 7.

2 Place the salmon in a large pan and cover with cold water. Gently heat until the water is not quite simmering and cook the fish for 8–10 minutes until it flakes easily when tested.

3 Lift the salmon out of the pan and remove the bones and skin. Flake the fish into the rice, add the lemon juice, herbs, curry powder and seasoning, and mix well. Peel the eggs.

4 Roll out the pastry and cut into six 15cm/6in squares. Brush the edges with the beaten egg. Place a spoonful of the rice mixture in the middle of each square, push an egg into the centre and top with a little more of the rice mixture.

5 Pull over the pastry corners to the middle to form a neat, square parcel, pressing the joins together with your fingers firmly to seal.

6 Brush the parcels with more beaten egg, place on a baking sheet and bake for 20 minutes, then reduce the oven temperature to 190°C/375°F/Gas 5. Cook for a further 10 minutes, or until golden and crisp underneath. Cool the pastries slightly before serving.

SPINACH TURNOVERS

THESE LITTLE PASTRY PARCELS HAVE A RICH SPINACH FILLING SPIKED WITH INGREDIENTS THAT HAVE A STRONG SPANISH INFLUENCE — PINE NUTS AND RAISINS.

MAKES TWENTY

INGREDIENTS
    25g/1oz/3 tbsp raisins
    25ml/1½ tbsp olive oil
    450g/1lb fresh spinach, washed
      and chopped
    6 canned anchovies, drained
      and chopped
    2 garlic cloves, finely chopped
    25g/1oz/⅓ cup pine nuts, chopped
    350g/12oz puff pastry
    1 egg, beaten
    salt and ground black pepper

4 Using a 7.5cm/3in plain pastry cutter, cut out 20 rounds, re-rolling the dough as necessary. Place two teaspoons of the filling in the middle of each, then brush the edges with a little water.

5 Bring up the sides of the pastry and press the edges together to seal. Brush with some beaten egg. Place on a lightly greased baking sheet and bake for about 15 minutes, or until golden.

1 To make the filling, soak the raisins in a little warm water for 10 minutes. Drain, then chop them roughly. Heat the oil in a large pan or wok and add the spinach, stir, then cover and cook over a low heat for about 2 minutes.

2 Remove the lid from the pan or wok, slightly raise the heat and let any liquid evaporate. Add the anchovies, garlic and salt and pepper. Cook, stirring, for 1 minute more. Remove the pan or wok from the heat, stir in the raisins and pine nuts, and set aside to cool.

3 Preheat the oven to 180°C/350°F/ Gas 4. Roll out the puff pastry on a lightly floured surface to a thickness of about 3mm/⅛in.

COOK'S TIP
Serve the turnovers warm, with a home-made tomato sauce, if you like.

SHELLFISH IN PUFF PASTRY

WITH A COASTLINE BORDERING TWO SEAS AND A VAST NETWORK OF RIVERS, FISH AND SHELLFISH PLAY A LEADING ROLE IN FRENCH CUISINE. THIS CLASSIC COMBINATION OF SHELLFISH IN A CREAMY SAUCE SERVED IN A PUFF PASTRY CASE IS FOUND ON THE MENUS OF MANY ELEGANT RESTAURANTS IN FRANCE.

SERVES SIX

INGREDIENTS

350g/12oz rough puff or
  puff pastry
1 egg beaten with 15ml/1 tbsp water
60ml/4 tbsp dry white wine
2 shallots, finely chopped
450g/1lb mussels, scrubbed and
  beards removed
15g/½oz/1 tbsp butter
450g/1lb shelled scallops,
  halved crossways
450g/1lb raw prawns (shrimp), peeled
225g/8oz/1 cup butter, diced
2 shallots, finely chopped
250ml/8fl oz/1 cup fish stock
90ml/6 tbsp dry white wine
15–30ml/1–2 tbsp single
  (light) cream
lemon juice
175g/6oz cooked lobster meat, sliced
salt and ground white pepper
fresh dill sprigs, to garnish

1 Lightly grease a large baking sheet and sprinkle it with a little water. Roll out the pastry on a lightly floured surface into a rectangle slightly less than 5mm/¼in thick. Using a sharp knife, cut into six diamond shapes about 13cm/5in long. Transfer to the baking sheet, spacing them well.

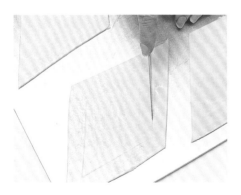

2 Brush each diamond with the egg and water mixture to glaze. Using the tip of a knife, score a line around each diamond 1cm/½in from the edge, then lightly cross hatch. Chill for 30 minutes.

3 Preheat the oven to 220°C/425°F/ Gas 7. Bake the pastry cases for about 20 minutes until puffed and brown. Carefully remove each lid, cutting along the scored line. Scoop out and discard any uncooked dough, then leave the cases and lids to cool completely.

4 Place the white wine and shallots in a large pan and bring to the boil. Add the mussels, cover tightly and cook for about 5 minutes until the shells open, shaking the pan occasionally. Discard any mussels that do not open.

5 Reserve six mussels for the garnish. Remove the rest from their shells and set aside in a bowl covered with cling film (plastic wrap). Strain the cooking liquid through a muslin- (cheesecloth-) lined sieve and reserve for the sauce.

6 Melt the butter in a heavy frying pan. Add the scallops and prawns, cover tightly and cook for 3–4 minutes until they feel just firm to the touch; take care you do not overcook them.

7 Using a slotted spoon, transfer the scallops and prawns to the bowl with the mussels and add any cooking juices to the mussel liquid.

8 Melt half the butter in a heavy pan and cook the shallots for 2 minutes, stirring. Pour in the fish stock and boil for about 15 minutes until it is reduced by three-quarters. Add the white wine and the reserved mussel liquid and boil for 5–7 minutes until reduced by half.

9 Lower the heat and whisk in the remaining butter, a little at a time, to make a smooth, thick sauce. Whisk in the cream and season with a little salt, if needed, white pepper and lemon juice. Keep warm over a very low heat, stirring frequently.

10 Warm the pastry cases and lids in the oven set at a low temperature for 10 minutes. Put the mussels, scallops and prawns in a large pan. Stir in a quarter of the sauce and reheat gently. Fold in the lobster meat and cook for 1 minute more.

11 Arrange the puff pastry cases on individual plates. Divide the shellfish mixture equally among them and top with the lids. Garnish each with one of the reserved mussels and a dill sprig and spoon the remaining sauce around the edges or serve separately.

MINI PORK AND BACON PIES

THESE LITTLE PIES CAN BE MADE UP TO A DAY AHEAD OF BEING SERVED. THEY ARE A GOOD CHOICE FOR A SUMMER PICNIC OR SPECIAL PACKED LUNCH FOR SCHOOL OR THE OFFICE.

MAKES TWELVE

INGREDIENTS

    10ml/2 tsp sunflower oil
    1 onion, chopped
    225g/8oz pork, coarsely chopped
    115g/4oz cooked bacon, finely diced
    45ml/3 tbsp chopped fresh herbs,
      such as sage, parsley and oregano
    6 eggs, hard-boiled and halved
    1 egg yolk, beaten
    20g/¾oz packet powdered aspic
    300ml/½ pint/1¼ cups boiling water
    salt and ground black pepper
For the hot water crust pastry
    450g/1lb/4 cups plain
      (all-purpose) flour
    115g/4oz/½ cup white vegetable fat
    275ml/9fl oz/generous 1 cup water

1 To make the pastry, sift the flour into a bowl and add a good pinch each of salt and pepper. Gently heat the fat and water in a large pan until the fat has melted. Increase the heat and bring the mixture to the boil. Pour the hot liquid into the flour, stirring constantly.

2 Press the mixture into a ball of dough using a spoon. When the dough is smooth, cover the bowl and set aside.

3 Preheat the oven to 200°C/400°F/Gas 6. Heat the oil in a frying pan, add the onion and cook until soft. Stir in the pork and bacon and cook until just brown. Remove from the heat and stir in the herbs and seasoning.

4 Roll out two-thirds of the pastry on a lightly floured surface. Use a 12cm/4½in fluted cutter to stamp out rounds and use to line 12 muffin pans. Place some of the meat mixture in each pie, then add half an egg to each and top with the remaining meat mixture.

5 Roll out the remaining pastry and use a 7.5cm/3in fluted cutter to stamp out lids for the pies. Dampen the rim of each pastry base and press a lid in place. Pinch the edges to seal. Brush with egg yolk and make a small steam hole in the top of each pie.

6 Bake for 30–35 minutes. Leave the pies to cool for 15 minutes, then place on a wire rack to cool completely.

7 Meanwhile, stir the aspic powder into the boiling water until dissolved. Shape a piece of foil into a small funnel and use this to guide a little aspic through the hole in the top of each pie.

8 Leave to cool and set, then chill the pies for up to 24 hours before serving at room temperature.

CORNISH PASTIES

*THESE TRADITIONAL PASTRIES ARE MADE WITH A RICH CRUMBLY SHORTCRUST. THE FILLING IS RAW
WHEN ENCLOSED IN THE PASTRY, SO THEY MUST BE COOKED THOROUGHLY.*

MAKES SIX

INGREDIENTS
   450g/1lb chuck steak, diced
   1 potato, about 175g/6oz, diced
   175g/6oz swede (rutabaga), diced
   1 onion, chopped
   2.5ml/½ tsp dried mixed herbs
   1 egg, beaten
   salt and ground black pepper
   salad, to garnish
For the pastry
   350g/12oz/3 cups plain
     (all-purpose) flour
   pinch of salt
   115g/4oz/½ cup butter, diced
   50g/2oz/¼ cup lard or white
     vegetable fat
   75–90ml/5–6 tbsp chilled water

1 To make the pastry, sift the flour and salt into a bowl. Using your fingertips or a pastry blender, lightly rub or cut in the butter and lard or vegetable fat, then sprinkle over most of the chilled water and mix to a soft dough, adding more water if necessary. Knead the pastry on a lightly floured surface for a few seconds until smooth. Wrap in clear film (plastic wrap) and chill for 30 minutes.

2 Preheat the oven to 220°C/425°F/Gas 7. Divide the pastry into six pieces, then roll out each piece on a lightly floured surface to a 20cm/8in round.

3 Mix together the steak, vegetables, herbs and seasoning in a bowl, then spoon an equal amount on to one half of each pastry round.

4 Brush the pastry edges with water, then fold the free half of each round over the filling. Press the edges firmly together to seal, then use your fingertips to crimp the edges.

5 Brush the pasties with the beaten egg. Bake for 15 minutes, then reduce the temperature to 160°C/325°F/Gas 3 and bake for 1 hour more. Serve the pasties hot or cold with a salad garnish.

QUICHES AND SAVOURY TARTS

An inspirational collection of savoury tarts that taste better than any you can buy. Included here are all-time classics such as Quiche Lorraine, with its crisp shortcrust pastry and egg-rich filling with smoked streaky bacon. Discover some of the wonderful variations on this recipe, with all manner of flavourful fillings. As delicious as it is, shortcrust isn't the only pastry used here; potato, walnut and cornmeal pastries all make wonderful cases, just waiting to be filled.

CHEESE AND ONION QUICHE

PERFECT FOR PICNICS, PARTIES OR FAMILY SUPPERS, THIS TASTY QUICHE CELEBRATES A TIMELESS COMBINATION: CHEESE AND ONION. FOR A VEGETARIAN VERSION, OMIT THE BACON.

SERVES SIX TO EIGHT

INGREDIENTS
  25g/1oz/2 tbsp butter
  1 large onion, thinly sliced
  4 rindless streaky (fatty) bacon
    rashers (strips), roughly
    chopped (optional)
  3 eggs
  300ml/½ pint/1¼ cups single (light)
    cream or milk
  1.5ml/¼ tsp freshly grated nutmeg
  90g/3½oz hard cheese, such
    as Cheddar or Gruyère, grated
  salt and ground black pepper
For the pastry
  200g/7oz/1¾ cups plain
    (all-purpose) flour
  2.5ml/½ tsp salt
  90g/3½oz/scant ½ cup butter, diced
  about 60ml/4 tbsp chilled water

1 To make the pastry, sift the flour and salt into a small bowl. Rub or cut in the butter until the mixture resembles fine breadcrumbs. Add 45ml/3 tbsp of the water and mix to a firm dough, adding more water if required. Knead until smooth, wrap in clear film (plastic wrap) and chill for 20 minutes.

2 Roll out the dough on a clean, lightly floured work surface and use to line a 23cm/9in loose-based flan tin (quiche pan). Press the pastry firmly into the sides and base of the tin and let it rise above the rim by about 1cm/½in to allow for a little shrinkage during cooking. Prick the pastry base all over with a fork.

3 Line the pastry case with foil and baking beans and chill again for about 15 minutes. Preheat the oven to 200°C/400°F/Gas 6 with a baking sheet placed in it. Stand the flan tin on the baking sheet and bake blind for 15 minutes.

4 Remove the foil and beans from the pastry case and return it to the oven for a further 5 minutes. Remove the pastry case from the oven and lower the oven temperature to 180°C/350°F/Gas 4.

5 To make the filling, melt the butter in a large, heavy frying pan. Add the onion and chopped bacon, if using, and sauté for about 10 minutes until the onion is soft and golden. Beat the eggs and the cream or milk together in a bowl. Add the grated nutmeg and seasoning to taste.

6 Spoon the onion mixture into the cooked pastry case and evenly sprinkle over the cheese. Pour the egg and cream mixture slowly over the filling. Bake the quiche for 35–40 minutes, or until the filling has just set. Remove from the oven, leave to cool, then gently ease the quiche out of the tin and transfer to a serving plate.

QUICHE LORRAINE

THIS CLASSIC QUICHE HAS SOME DELIGHTFUL CHARACTERISTICS THAT ARE OFTEN FORGOTTEN IN MODERN RECIPES; NAMELY VERY THIN PASTRY, A CREAMY, LIGHT FILLING AND SMOKED BACON.

SERVES FOUR TO SIX

INGREDIENTS
  6 rindless smoked streaky (fatty)
    bacon rashers (strips)
  300ml/½ pint/1¼ cups double
    (heavy) cream
  3 eggs, plus 2 yolks
  25g/1oz/2 tbsp butter
  salt and ground black pepper
For the pastry
  175g/6oz/1½ cups plain (all-purpose)
    flour, sifted
  pinch of salt
  115g/4oz/½ cup butter, at room
    temperature, diced
  1 egg yolk

1 To make the pastry, place the flour, salt, butter and egg yolk in a food processor and process until blended. Tip out on to a lightly floured surface and bring the mixture together into a ball. Leave to rest for 20 minutes.

2 Lightly flour a deep 20cm/8in round flan tin (quiche pan) and place it on a baking sheet. Roll out the pastry and use to line the flan tin, trimming off any overhanging pieces.

3 Gently press the pastry into the corners of the tin. If the pastry breaks, gently push it together again. Chill for 20 minutes. Preheat the oven to 200°C/400°F/Gas 6.

4 Meanwhile, snip the bacon into small pieces using kitchen scissors and grill (broil) until the fat runs. Arrange in the pastry case. Beat together the cream, the eggs and yolks and seasoning, and pour into the pastry case.

5 Bake the quiche for 15 minutes, then reduce the oven temperature to 180°C/350°F/Gas 4 and bake for 20 minutes more. When the filling is puffed up and golden brown and the pastry edge crisp, remove the quiche from the oven and top with small cubes of butter. Leave to stand for 5 minutes before serving. This allows the filling to settle and cool a little before serving, making it easier to cut the quiche.

COOK'S TIP
To prepare the quiche in advance, bake for 5–10 minutes less than the time stated, until the filling is just set. Reheat at 190°C/375°F/Gas 5 for 10 minutes.

SMOKED SALMON QUICHE <u>WITH</u> POTATO PASTRY

THE INGREDIENTS IN THIS LIGHT BUT RICHLY FLAVOURED QUICHE PERFECTLY COMPLEMENT THE MELT-IN-THE-MOUTH PASTRY, WHICH IS, UNUSUALLY, MADE WITH POTATOES.

SERVES SIX

INGREDIENTS
   275g/10oz smoked salmon
   6 eggs, beaten
   150ml/¼ pint/⅔ cup creamy milk
   300ml/½ pint/1¼ cups double
      (heavy) cream
   30–45ml/2–3 tbsp chopped fresh dill
   30ml/2 tbsp bottled capers, drained
      and chopped
   salt and ground black pepper
   salad leaves and chopped fresh dill,
      to serve
For the pastry
   1 floury potato, about 115g/4oz,
      roughly diced
   225g/8oz/2 cups plain (all-purpose)
      flour, sifted
   115g/4oz/½ cup butter, diced
   ½ egg, beaten
   about 10ml/2 tsp chilled water

1 To make the pastry, cook the diced potato in a pan of lightly salted boiling water for about 15 minutes, or until tender. Drain well through a colander and return the potato to the pan. Mash until smooth and set aside to cool while you make the pastry.

COOK'S TIPS
• To ensure the pastry base cooks through, it is vital to preheat a baking sheet in the oven first.
• Make the most of smoked salmon offcuts for this quiche, as they are much cheaper than sides of smoked salmon but work just as well.

2 Place the flour in a large bowl and rub or cut in the butter until the mixture resembles fine breadcrumbs. Beat in the potatoes and egg. Bring the mixture together, adding chilled water if needed.

3 Roll out the pastry on a lightly floured surface and use to line a deep 23cm/ 9in round, loose-based, fluted flan tin (quiche pan). Chill for 1 hour.

4 Preheat the oven to 200°C/400°F/ Gas 6 with a heavy baking sheet placed in it. To make the filling, roughly chop the smoked salmon into bitesize pieces and set aside.

5 Using a wooden spoon, beat the eggs, milk and cream in a bowl. Stir in the chopped dill and capers and season with pepper. Add the chopped salmon and stir to combine.

6 Remove the pastry case from the refrigerator, prick the base well with a fork and pour the salmon mixture into it. Place on the baking sheet and bake for 35–45 minutes, or until the filling is just set and the crust is golden brown. Serve warm with mixed salad leaves and some dill.

VARIATIONS
• These quantities can also be used to make six individual quiches, which are an ideal size to serve as a first course or a light lunch. Prepare them as in the main recipe, but reduce the baking time by about 15 minutes.
• For extra piquancy, sprinkle some finely grated fresh Parmesan cheese over the top of the quiche before baking.

CARAMELIZED ONION TART

THE FILLING FOR THIS TART IS RICH, DARK AND DELICIOUS. THE CARAMELIZED ONIONS ADD DEPTH AND FLAVOUR TO THIS SIMPLE, CLASSIC TART.

2 Knead the dough and gather it into a smooth ball, then wrap in clear film (plastic wrap) and chill for 30 minutes.

3 Meanwhile, make the filling. Heat the butter and oil in a large, heavy frying pan. Cook the onions over a low heat for 30 minutes until soft and translucent, stirring often. Stir in the nutmeg, sugar and seasoning, and gently cook for a further 5 minutes, or until the onions have caramelized. Cool slightly.

4 Preheat the oven to 220°C/425°F/ Gas 7. Lightly grease a loose-based 35 × 12cm/14 × 4½in fluted tranche tin. Roll out the pastry and use to line the tin. Trim, then chill for 20 minutes.

SERVES SIX

INGREDIENTS
  15g/½oz/1 tbsp butter
  15ml/1 tbsp olive oil
  500g/1¼lb onions, sliced
  large pinch of grated nutmeg
  5ml/1 tsp soft dark brown sugar
  2 eggs
  150ml/¼ pint/⅔ cup single
    (light) cream
  50g/2oz/½ cup grated
    Gruyère cheese
  salt and ground black pepper
For the pastry
  75g/3oz/⅔ cup plain
    (all-purpose) flour
  75g/3oz/⅔ cup wholemeal
    (whole-wheat) flour
  75g/3oz/6 tbsp butter, diced
  1 egg yolk

1 To make the pastry, mix the plain and wholemeal flours together in a large mixing bowl. Use your fingertips to rub in the butter or cut it in with a pastry blender until the mixture resembles fine breadcrumbs. Mix in the egg yolk and enough chilled water to form a firm dough. Transfer the dough to a lightly floured work surface.

5 Prick the pastry base, then line with foil and baking beans. Bake blind for 10 minutes. Remove the foil and beans, then spoon in the onions.

6 Beat the eggs with the cream, add the cheese and season to taste. Pour the mixture over the onions and bake for 30 minutes until set. Serve warm.

RED ONION TART WITH A CORNMEAL CRUST

THE WONDERFULLY MILD AND SWEET TASTE OF RED ONIONS WHEN COOKED GOES PERFECTLY WITH FONTINA CHEESE AND THYME IN THIS TART. CORNMEAL GIVES THE PASTRY A CRUMBLY TEXTURE.

SERVES FIVE TO SIX

INGREDIENTS
60ml/4 tbsp olive oil
1kg/2¼lb red onions, thinly sliced
2–3 garlic cloves, thinly sliced
5ml/1 tsp chopped fresh thyme, plus
 a few whole sprigs
5ml/1 tsp soft dark brown sugar
10ml/2 tsp sherry vinegar
225g/8oz Fontina cheese,
 thinly sliced
salt and ground black pepper
For the pastry
115g/4oz/1 cup plain
 (all-purpose) flour
75g/3oz/¾ cup fine yellow cornmeal
5ml/1 tsp soft dark brown sugar
5ml/1 tsp chopped fresh thyme
90g/3½oz/7 tbsp butter, diced
1 egg yolk
30–45ml/2–3 tbsp chilled water

1 To make the pastry, sift the flour and cornmeal with 5ml/1 tsp salt in a bowl. Add plenty of black pepper and stir in the sugar and thyme. Rub or cut in the butter until the mixture resembles fine breadcrumbs. Beat the egg yolk with 30ml/2 tbsp water and use to bind the pastry, adding more water if necessary. Gather into a ball, wrap in clear film (plastic wrap) and chill for 30 minutes.

2 To make the filling, heat 45ml/3 tbsp of the oil in a large, deep frying pan and add the onions. Cover and cook slowly, stirring occasionally, for 20–30 minutes.

3 Add the garlic and chopped thyme and cook, stirring occasionally, for about 10 minutes. Increase the heat slightly, then add the sugar and sherry vinegar. Cook, uncovered, for another 5 minutes until the onions start to caramelize slightly. Season and cool.

4 Preheat the oven to 190°C/375°F/ Gas 5. Roll out the pastry thinly and use to line a 25cm/10in loose-based flan tin (quiche pan). Prick the pastry all over with a fork and support the sides with foil. Bake for 12–15 minutes until the pastry is just lightly coloured.

5 Remove the foil and spread the onions in the base of the pastry case. Add the Fontina and season to taste. Drizzle over the remaining oil, then bake for 15–20 minutes until the filling is hot. Garnish with a few thyme sprigs and serve immediately.

GREEK PICNIC PIE

AUBERGINES LAYERED WITH SPINACH, FETA CHEESE AND RICE MAKE A MARVELLOUS FILLING FOR A PIE THAT IS PERFECT FOR PICNICS. IT CAN BE SERVED WARM OR COLD AND MAKES A GOOD VEGETARIAN DISH FOR A BUFFET LUNCH IN SUMMER OR AUTUMN.

SERVES SIX

INGREDIENTS
  45–60ml/3–4 tbsp olive oil
  1 large aubergine (eggplant), sliced
    into rounds
  1 onion, chopped
  1 garlic clove, crushed
  175g/6oz fresh spinach, washed
  4 eggs
  75g/3oz/½ cup crumbled feta cheese
  40g/1½oz/½ cup freshly grated
    Parmesan cheese
  60ml/4 tbsp natural (plain) yogurt
  90ml/6 tbsp creamy milk
  225g/8oz/2 cups cooked white or
    brown long grain rice
  salt and ground black pepper
For the pastry
  225g/8oz/2 cups plain
    (all-purpose) flour
  pinch of salt
  5ml/1 tsp dried basil
  115g/4oz/½ cup butter, diced
  45–60ml/3–4 tbsp chilled water

1 To make the pastry, sift the flour and salt into a mixing bowl. Stir in the basil, then rub or cut in the butter until the mixture resembles fine breadcrumbs. Sprinkle over most of the water and mix to a dough, adding more water if required. Wrap in clear film (plastic wrap) and chill for 30 minutes.

2 Roll out the pastry thinly and use to line a 25cm/10in flan ring or flan tin (quiche pan). Cover with clear film and chill for 30 minutes more. Meanwhile, preheat the oven to 180°C/350°F/Gas 4.

VARIATION
Courgettes (zucchini) make a good alternative to the aubergines (eggplant). Fry the sliced courgettes in a little oil for 3–4 minutes until golden. You will need three to four medium-size courgettes. Or, use baby courgettes and thinly slice them horizontally; these would look particularly attractive arranged on top of the pie.

3 Prick the base of the chilled pastry case all over with a fork and bake in the oven for 10–12 minutes until the pastry is just turning golden. (If you prefer, bake blind the pastry – line the pastry with baking parchment and weight it with baking beans. Remove the paper and beans for the last few minutes of baking.)

4 To make the filling, heat 45ml/3 tbsp of the oil in a frying pan and gently fry the aubergine slices for 6–8 minutes on each side until golden. You may need to add a little more oil at first, but this will be released as the flesh softens. Lift out the aubergine slices and drain on kitchen paper.

5 Add the onion and garlic to the oil remaining in the pan and fry over a gentle heat for 4–5 minutes until soft, adding a little extra oil if necessary.

6 Chop the spinach finely, by hand or in a food processor. Beat the eggs in a large mixing bowl.

7 Add the spinach, feta, Parmesan, yogurt, milk and the onion mixture to the eggs. Season well and stir thoroughly.

8 Spread the cooked rice in an even layer over the base of the pastry case. Reserve about 8 aubergine slices, and arrange the rest in an even layer over the rice.

9 Spoon the spinach and feta mixture over the aubergines and place the reserved slices of aubergine on top. Bake the pie for 30–40 minutes until lightly browned. Serve warm or cold.

COURGETTE <u>AND</u> DILL TART

THE SUBTLE FLAVOUR OF COURGETTES IS LIFTED DRAMATICALLY BY THE ADDITION OF FRESH DILL IN THIS TART. TAKE TIME TO ARRANGE THE COURGETTE LAYERS TO CREATE AN EYE-CATCHING DISH.

4 Roll out the pastry and ease it into the tin. Prick the base, trim the edges and bake blind for 10–15 minutes.

5 Meanwhile, heat the oil in a frying pan, add the courgettes and sauté for 2–3 minutes until lightly browned, turning occasionally. Mix the egg yolks, cream, garlic and dill in a small bowl. Season with salt and pepper.

6 Line the pastry case with courgettes and pour over the cream mixture. Return to the oven for 25–30 minutes and bake until firm. Cool the pie in the tin, then remove and serve.

SERVES FOUR

INGREDIENTS
15ml/1 tbsp sunflower oil
3 courgettes (zucchini), thinly sliced
2 egg yolks
150ml/¼ pint/⅔ cup double
  (heavy) cream
1 garlic clove, crushed
15ml/1 tbsp finely chopped fresh dill
salt and ground black pepper
For the pastry
115g/4oz/1 cup wholemeal
  (whole-wheat) flour
115g/4oz/1 cup self-raising
  (self-rising) flour
pinch of salt
115g/4oz/½ cup butter, chilled
  and diced
75ml/5 tbsp chilled water

1 To make the pastry, sift the flours into a bowl, tipping the bran into the bowl, then place in a food processor. Add the salt and diced butter and process using the pulse button until the mixture resembles fine breadcrumbs.

2 With the motor running, gradually add the water until the mixture forms a dough. Do not over-process. Wrap the pastry and chill for 30 minutes.

3 Preheat the oven to 200°C/400°F/ Gas 6 and grease a 20cm/8in flan tin (quiche pan).

COOK'S TIP
The smaller and skinnier courgettes are, the better they taste. Choose ones that have glossy green skins and feel firm.

ROQUEFORT TART WITH WALNUT PASTRY

MILD LEEKS GO EXCEPTIONALLY WELL WITH THE SALTY FLAVOUR OF THE ROQUEFORT CHEESE, AND THE NUTTINESS OF THE PASTRY COMPLEMENTS THE INGREDIENTS PERFECTLY IN THIS TART.

SERVES FOUR TO SIX

INGREDIENTS
    25g/1oz/2 tbsp butter
    450g/1lb leeks (trimmed
      weight), sliced
    175g/6oz Roquefort cheese, sliced
    2 large eggs
    250ml/8fl oz/1 cup double
      (heavy) cream
    10ml/2 tsp chopped fresh tarragon
    salt and ground black pepper
For the pastry
    175g/6oz/1½ cups plain
      (all-purpose) flour
    5ml/1 tsp soft dark brown sugar
    50g/2oz/¼ cup butter, diced
    75g/3oz/¾ cup walnuts, ground
    15ml/1 tbsp lemon juice
    30ml/2 tbsp chilled water

1 To make the pastry, sift the flour and 2.5ml/½ tsp salt into a bowl. Add some black pepper and the sugar. Rub or cut in the butter until the mixture resembles fine breadcrumbs, then add the ground walnuts and stir well. Add the lemon juice and chilled water and bind to form a dough. Gather the mixture into a ball, wrap in clear film (plastic wrap) and chill for 30–40 minutes.

2 Preheat the oven to 190°C/375°F/ Gas 5. Roll out the pastry and use to line a 21–23cm/8½–9in loose-based flan tin (quiche pan).

COOK'S TIP
To prepare the walnuts, mix with a little of the pastry flour and use a small food processor or clean coffee mill to grind.

3 Protect the sides of the pastry case with a thin strip of foil, prick the base all over with a fork and bake for about 15 minutes. Remove the foil and bake the pastry case for 10 minutes more until just firm to the touch. Reduce the oven temperature to 180°C/350°F/Gas 4.

4 To make the filling, melt the butter in a pan, add the leeks, then cover and cook for 10 minutes. Season and cook for a further 10 minutes until soft. Set aside to cool.

5 Spoon the leeks into the pastry case, spreading them evenly, and arrange the slices of Roquefort cheese on top. Beat the eggs with the cream in a small bowl, and season with plenty of black pepper. Beat in the tarragon and carefully pour the mixture into the pastry case, evenly covering the leek filling.

6 Bake the tart on the centre shelf of the oven for 30–40 minutes until the filling has risen and browned and become firm to the touch. Allow to cool for 10 minutes before serving.

HERBED GREEK MINI TARTS

IF YOU CAN, USE LARGE MUFFIN PANS TO MAKE THESE LITTLE PIES. THEY PROVIDE A DEEP CASE TO HOLD PLENTY OF THE DELICIOUSLY TANGY YOGURT FILLING.

MAKES EIGHT

INGREDIENTS
45–60ml/3–4 tbsp tapenade or
   sun-dried tomato paste
1 large egg
100g/3¾oz/scant ½ cup thick Greek
   (US strained plain) yogurt
90ml/6 tbsp milk
1 garlic clove, crushed
30ml/2 tbsp chopped mixed herbs,
   such as thyme, marjoram, basil
   and parsley
salt and ground black pepper
For the pastry
   115g/4oz/1 cup plain
      (all-purpose) flour
   pinch of salt
   50g/2oz/¼ cup butter, diced
   30ml/2 tbsp chilled water

1 To make the pastry, sift the flour and salt into a large bowl. Rub or cut in the butter. Sprinkle over the water and mix to a dough. Knead briefly, then wrap and chill for 20 minutes.

2 Roll out the pastry and cut out eight rounds. Use to line deep muffin pans.

3 Chill the pastry cases for 30 minutes. Meanwhile, preheat the oven to 190°C/375°F/Gas 5. Line each pastry case with a small piece of foil. Bake for about 15 minutes. Remove the foil and bake for a further 5 minutes or until the cases are crisp and dry.

4 Spread a little tapenade or tomato paste in the base of each pastry case. Whisk together the egg, yogurt, milk, garlic, herbs and seasoning.

5 Carefully spoon the egg mixture into the pastry cases and bake for about 30 minutes, or until the filling is just firm to the touch and the pastry golden. Allow the pies to cool slightly before carefully removing them from the pans and serving.

TOMATO AND BLACK OLIVE TART

THIS DELICIOUS TART HAS A FRESH, RICH MEDITERRANEAN FLAVOUR AND IS PERFECT FOR PICNICS. IF YOU ARE TAKING THIS TART ON A PICNIC, KEEP IN THE TIN FOR EASY TRANSPORTING.

SERVES EIGHT

INGREDIENTS
6 firm plum tomatoes
75g/3oz ripe Brie cheese
about 16 pitted black olives
3 eggs, beaten
300ml/½ pint/1¼ cups milk
30ml/2 tbsp chopped fresh herbs
salt and ground black pepper
For the pastry
   225g/8oz/2 cups plain
      (all-purpose) flour
   115g/4oz/½ cup butter, diced
   45–60ml/3–4 tbsp chilled water

1 To make the pastry, sift the flour into a mixing bowl and rub or cut in the butter until the mixture resembles fine breadcrumbs. Sprinkle over the water and mix to a dough. Knead lightly on a floured surface for a few seconds until smooth. Wrap and chill for 30 minutes.

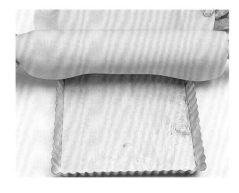

2 Preheat the oven to 190°C/375°F/Gas 5. Roll out the pastry thinly and use to line a greased 28 × 18cm/11 × 7in loose-based rectangular flan tin (quiche pan). Trim the edges.

3 Line the pastry case with some foil and baking beans, and bake blind for 15 minutes. Remove the foil and beans and bake for a further 5 minutes until the base is crisp.

4 Slice the tomatoes, cube the cheese and finely slice the olives. Place the flan case on a baking sheet and arrange the tomatoes, cheese and olives in it. Mix together the eggs, milk, seasoning and chopped herbs.

5 Pour the egg mixture into the case. Bake for about 40 minutes until just firm and turning golden. Slice hot or cool in the tin, then serve.

VEGETARIAN FESTIVE TART

THIS SOPHISTICATED FLAN MADE WITH A SPICY CHEESE PASTRY CAN BE SERVED AS A VEGETARIAN ALTERNATIVE FOR ANY CELEBRATION OR SPECIAL OCCASION.

SERVES EIGHT

INGREDIENTS
    25g/1oz/2 tbsp butter
    1 onion, finely chopped
    1–2 garlic cloves, crushed
    350g/12oz/4–5 cups mushrooms,
        roughly chopped
    10ml/2 tsp dried mixed herbs
    15ml/1 tbsp chopped fresh parsley
    50g/2oz/1 cup fresh white
        breadcrumbs
    15ml/1 tbsp Dijon mustard
    salt and ground black pepper
For the pastry
    225g/8oz/2 cups plain
        (all-purpose) flour
    175g/6oz/¾ cup butter
    10ml/2 tsp paprika
    115g/4oz Parmesan cheese, grated
    1 egg, beaten with 15ml/1 tbsp
        chilled water
For the cheese topping
    25g/1oz/2 tbsp butter
    25g/1oz/2 tbsp plain flour
    300ml/½ pint/1¼ cups milk
    25g/1oz Parmesan
        cheese, grated
    75g/3oz Cheddar cheese, grated
    1.5ml/¼ tsp English
        mustard powder
    1 egg, separated

1 To make the pastry, sift the flour into a bowl and rub or cut in the butter until it resembles fine breadcrumbs. Stir in the paprika and Parmesan cheese. Bind to a soft dough with the egg and water. Knead until smooth, wrap in clear film (plastic wrap) and chill for 30 minutes.

2 To make the filling, melt the butter in a pan, add the onion and cook until tender. Add the garlic and mushrooms and cook, uncovered, for 5 minutes, stirring occasionally. Increase the heat to evaporate any liquid in the pan. Remove the pan from the heat and stir in the herbs, white breadcrumbs and seasoning. Allow to cool. Preheat the oven to 190°C/375°F/Gas 5, with a baking sheet placed inside.

3 On a lightly floured surface, roll out the pastry and use to line a 23cm/9in loose-based flan tin (quiche pan), pressing it into the edges and making a narrow rim around the top. Chill.

4 To make the cheese topping, melt the butter in a pan, stir in the flour and cook for 2 minutes. Gradually blend in the milk. Bring to the boil, stirring constantly, and simmer for 2–3 minutes. Remove the pan from the heat and stir in the cheeses, mustard powder and egg yolk, and season. Beat vigorously until smooth. Whisk the egg white until it holds soft peaks, then fold into the cheese mixture.

5 Spread the mustard evenly over the pastry case. Spoon in the mushroom filling and then pour over the cheese topping. Bake on the hot baking sheet for 35–45 minutes until golden.

SHALLOT AND GARLIC TARTE TATIN

SAVOURY VERSIONS OF THE CELEBRATED APPLE TARTE TATIN HAVE BEEN POPULAR FOR SOME YEARS.
HERE, CARAMELIZED SHALLOTS ARE BAKED BENEATH A LAYER OF PARMESAN PASTRY.

SERVES FOUR TO SIX

INGREDIENTS
    300g/11oz puff pastry
    50g/2oz/¼ cup butter, softened
    75g/3oz/1 cup freshly grated
      Parmesan cheese
For the topping
    40g/1½oz/3 tbsp butter
    500g/1¼lb shallots
    12–16 large garlic cloves, peeled but
      left whole
    15ml/1 tbsp caster (superfine) sugar
    15ml/1 tbsp balsamic or
      sherry vinegar
    45ml/3 tbsp water
    5ml/1 tsp chopped fresh thyme
    salt and ground black pepper

1 Roll out the pastry to a rectangle on a lightly floured work surface. Spread the butter over it, leaving a 2.5cm/1in border. Sprinkle the grated Parmesan on top.

2 Fold the lower third of the pastry up to cover the middle and fold the top third down over it. Seal the edges well, give the pastry a quarter turn and roll it out to a rectangle, then fold in thirds and seal as before. Wrap in clear film (plastic wrap) and chill in the refrigerator for at least 30 minutes.

3 Preheat the oven to 190°C/375°F/ Gas 5. Melt the butter in a 23–25cm/ 9–10in round, heavy, ovenproof omelette pan. Add the shallots and garlic and cook over a low heat until lightly browned all over.

4 Sprinkle the sugar over and increase the heat a little. Cook until the sugar begins to caramelize, then stir. Add the vinegar, water, thyme and seasoning. Cook, partly covered, for 5–8 minutes until the garlic cloves are just tender. Set aside to cool.

5 Roll out the pastry to a round the same size as the omelette pan. Lay the pastry round over the shallots and garlic. Prick the pastry, then bake for 25–35 minutes until risen and golden. Cool for about 10 minutes, then invert the tart on to a serving platter.

SINGLE- AND DOUBLE-CRUST PIES

Comforting and substantial main-course pies are always welcome.

Winter chills are warded off with a classic Steak and Kidney Pie

with a contemporary Mustard Gravy, while summer specials include

a mouthwatering Chicken and Apricot Filo Pie. At Christmas or

Thanksgiving, either Turkey and Cranberry Pie or Chestnut, Stilton

and Ale Pie would make a stunning centrepiece, as would

a vegetarian Potato and Leek Filo Pie.

CHICKEN CHARTER PIE

THIS IS A TRADITIONAL RECIPE FROM CORNWALL, IN ENGLAND, AN AREA FAMOUS FOR ITS CLOTTED CREAM. IT IS NOT SURPRISING, THEREFORE, THAT THE SAUCE FOR THIS PIE IS CREAM-BASED.

SERVES FOUR

INGREDIENTS
  50g/2oz/¼ cup butter
  4 chicken legs
  1 onion, finely chopped
  150ml/¼ pint/⅔ cup milk
  150ml/¼ pint/⅔ cup sour cream
  4 spring onions (scallions),
    quartered
  20g/¾oz/¾ cup fresh parsley leaves,
    finely chopped
  225g/8oz puff pastry
  2 eggs, beaten, plus extra for glazing
  120ml/4fl oz/½ cup double
    (heavy) cream
  salt and ground black pepper

1 Melt the butter in a heavy, shallow pan, then brown the chicken legs on all sides. Transfer to a plate.

2 Add the chopped onion to the pan and cook until just softened but not browned. Stir in the milk, sour cream, spring onions, parsley and seasoning. Bring to the boil, then simmer for 2 minutes.

3 Return the chicken to the pan with any juices, cover tightly and cook very gently for about 30 minutes. Transfer the chicken and sauce mixture to a 1.2 litre/2 pint/5 cup pie dish and leave to cool.

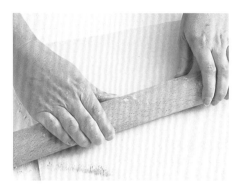

4 Meanwhile, roll out the pastry until about 2cm/¾in larger all round than the top of the pie dish. Leave the pastry to relax while the chicken is cooling.

5 Preheat the oven to 220°C/425°F/ Gas 7. Cut off a narrow strip around the edge of the pastry, then place the strip on the edge of the pie dish. Moisten the strip with a little water, then cover the dish with the pastry. Press the edges together to seal. Trim and neatly crimp the edge all round.

6 Make a hole in the centre of the pastry and insert a small funnel of foil. Brush the pastry with beaten egg, then bake for 15–20 minutes.

7 Reduce the oven temperature to 180°C/350°F/Gas 4. Mix the cream and eggs, then carefully pour into the pie through the funnel. Gently shake the pie dish to evenly distribute the cream mixture, then return the pie to the oven for a further 7 minutes. Let the pie cool for 5–10 minutes before serving warm, or serve it cold.

HARE POT PIES

*THE FULL, GAMEY FLAVOUR OF HARE IS PERFECT FOR THIS DISH; HOWEVER, BONELESS VENISON,
RABBIT, PHEASANT OR ANY OTHER GAME MEAT CAN BE USED INSTEAD.*

SERVES FOUR

INGREDIENTS
30ml/2 tbsp olive oil
1 leek, sliced
225g/8oz parsnips, sliced
225g/8oz carrots, sliced
1 fennel bulb, sliced
675g/1½lb boneless hare, diced
30ml/2 tbsp plain (all-purpose) flour
60ml/4 tbsp Madeira
300ml/½ pint/1¼ cups game or
  chicken stock
45ml/3 tbsp chopped
  fresh parsley
450g/1lb puff pastry
1 egg yolk, beaten
salt and ground black pepper

1 Heat the oil in a flameproof casserole, add the leek, parsnips, carrots and fennel and cook for 10 minutes, stirring frequently. Remove the vegetables from the casserole and set aside.

2 Add the hare to the casserole in batches and stir-fry over a high heat for 10 minutes, or until browned.

3 When all the meat has browned, return it to the pan. Sprinkle in the flour, stir well, then stir in the Madeira and stock. Return the vegetables to the casserole with the chopped parsley and seasoning. Heat until simmering, then increase the temperature slightly and cook for 20 minutes, stirring frequently.

4 Preheat the oven to 220°C/425°F/ Gas 7. Spoon the hare mixture into four individual pie dishes. Cut the pastry into quarters and roll out on a lightly floured surface to cover the pies, making the pieces 2cm/¾in larger than the dishes.

5 Trim off the excess pastry and use the pastry trimmings to line the rim of each pie dish.

6 Dampen the pastry rims with cold water and cover with pastry lids. Pinch the edges together to seal. Glaze with beaten egg yolk and make a steam hole in the top of each pie. Bake for about 25 minutes, or until the pastry is risen and golden.

CHESTNUT, STILTON AND ALE PIE

THIS HEARTY WINTER DISH HAS A RICH GRAVY AND A HERB PASTRY TOP. THE STILTON CHEESE ADDS A DELICIOUS CREAMINESS TO THE CHESTNUT AND MUSHROOM FILLING.

SERVES FOUR

INGREDIENTS
30ml/2 tbsp sunflower oil
2 large onions, chopped
500g/1¼lb/8 cups button (white)
  mushrooms, halved
3 carrots, sliced
1 parsnip, thickly sliced
15ml/1 tbsp chopped fresh thyme or
  5ml/1 tsp dried thyme
2 bay leaves
250ml/8fl oz/1 cup Guinness
  (dark ale)
120ml/4fl oz/½ cup vegetable stock
5ml/1 tsp Worcestershire sauce
5ml/1 tsp soft dark brown sugar
350g/12oz/3 cups drained canned
  chestnuts, halved
30ml/2 tbsp plain (all-purpose) flour
150g/5oz Stilton cheese, diced
1 egg, beaten, or a little milk
salt and ground black pepper
For the pastry
115g/4oz/1 cup wholemeal
  (whole-wheat) flour
pinch of salt
50g/2oz/¼ cup butter
15ml/1 tbsp chopped fresh thyme or
  5ml/1 tsp dried thyme

3 Meanwhile, to make the filling, heat the oil in a pan and fry the onions until soft. Add the mushrooms and cook for 3 minutes more. Add the carrots, parsnip and herbs, and cook for 3 minutes.

4 Pour in the Guinness, vegetable stock and Worcestershire sauce, then add the sugar and seasoning. Simmer, covered, for 5 minutes. Add the chestnuts.

5 Mix the flour with 30ml/2 tbsp water in a bowl to make a paste. Add to the vegetable mixture and cook, uncovered, for 5 minutes until the sauce thickens, stirring constantly. Stir in the cheese and heat until melted, still stirring constantly, then set aside. Preheat the oven to 220°C/425°F/Gas 7.

6 Roll out the pastry to fit the top of a 1.5 litre/2½ pint/6¼ cup deep pie dish. Spoon the chestnut mixture into the dish. Dampen the edges of the dish and cover with the pastry. Seal, trim and crimp the edges.

7 Cut a small slit in the top of the pie and use the pastry trimmings to make pastry leaves. Arrange these on the pie. Lightly brush with egg or milk to glaze and bake for 30 minutes until the pastry is golden.

1 To make the pastry, put the flour and salt in a bowl and rub or cut in the butter until the mixture resembles fine breadcrumbs. Add the chopped thyme and enough water to form a soft dough.

2 Knead the dough on a lightly floured surface for 1 minute until smooth. Wrap and chill for 30 minutes.

GUINNESS AND OYSTER PIE

BENEATH A CRUST OF CRISP YET FLAKY PUFF PASTRY, A TASTY, RICH STEW OF TENDER BEEF AND FRESH OYSTERS IS THE IDEAL ANTIDOTE TO WINTER CHILLS.

SERVES FOUR

INGREDIENTS

    450g/1lb stewing beef
    30ml/2 tbsp plain (all-purpose) flour
    15ml/1 tbsp vegetable oil
    25g/1oz/2 tbsp butter
    1 onion, sliced
    150ml/¼ pint/⅔ cup Guinness
     (dark ale)
    150ml/¼ pint/⅔ cup beef stock
    5ml/1 tsp granulated sugar
    bouquet garni
    12 oysters, opened
    350g/12oz puff pastry
    1 egg, beaten
    salt and ground black pepper
    chopped fresh parsley, to garnish

1 Preheat the oven to 180°C/350°F/ Gas 4. Trim any excess fat from the meat and cut it into 2.5cm/1in pieces. Place in a plastic bag with the flour and plenty of seasoning. Shake until the meat is well coated.

2 Heat the oil and butter in a large flameproof casserole and fry the meat for 10 minutes until browned all over. Add the onion and continue cooking for 2–3 minutes until just softened. Pour in the Guinness and stock. Add the sugar and bouquet garni. Cover and cook in the oven for 1¼ hours.

3 Remove the casserole from the oven, spoon the mixture into a large 2 litre/ 2 pint/5 cup pie dish and leave to cool for about 15 minutes. Increase the oven temperature to 200°C/400°F/Gas 6.

4 Meanwhile, use a round-bladed knife to remove the oysters from their shells. Put them in a colander and rinse them well. Drain, then dry on kitchen paper. Stir into the beef mixture.

5 Roll out the pastry until about 2cm/ ¾in larger than the top of the pie dish. Brush the edge of the dish with beaten egg and lay the pastry over the top. Trim neatly and decorate with leaves.

6 Brush with the remaining egg and bake for 25 minutes until the pastry is puffed and golden. Serve at once, garnished with a little parsley.

COOK'S TIP
Use the pastry trimmings to make small decorations for the pie. To make leaves, cut the pastry into small diamond shapes and mark veins using the point of a small knife.

CHICKEN AND MUSHROOM PIE

A CLASSIC PIE THAT GOES DOWN WELL WITH DINERS OF ALL AGES. PORCINI MUSHROOMS INTENSIFY THE FLAVOUR OF THE CHICKEN AND VEGETABLE FILLING.

SERVES SIX

INGREDIENTS

15g/½oz/¼ cup dried
  porcini mushrooms
50g/2oz/¼ cup butter
30ml/2 tbsp plain (all-purpose) flour
250ml/8fl oz/1 cup hot chicken stock
60ml/4 tbsp single (light) cream
1 onion, coarsely chopped
2 carrots, sliced
2 celery sticks, coarsely chopped
50g/2oz/¾ cup fresh mushrooms,
  quartered
450g/1lb cooked chicken
  meat, cubed
50g/2oz/½ cup fresh or frozen peas
salt and ground black pepper
beaten egg, to glaze
For the pastry
225g/8oz/2 cups plain
  (all-purpose) flour
1.5ml/¼ tsp salt
115g/4oz/½ cup cold butter, diced
65g/2½oz/⅓ cup white vegetable
  fat, diced
60–120ml/4–8 tbsp chilled water

1 To make the pastry, sift the flour and salt into a bowl. Cut or rub in the butter and white vegetable fat until the mixture resembles breadcrumbs. Sprinkle with 90ml/6 tbsp chilled water and mix until the dough holds together. If the dough is too crumbly, add a little more water, 15ml/1 tbsp at a time.

2 Gather the dough into a ball and flatten it into a round. Wrap and chill for at least 30 minutes.

3 To make the filling, place the porcini mushrooms in a bowl. Add hot water to cover and leave to soak for 30 minutes. Drain in a muslin- (cheesecloth-) lined sieve, then dry well on kitchen paper. Preheat the oven to 190°C/375°F/Gas 5.

4 Melt half of the butter in a heavy pan. Whisk in the flour and cook until bubbling, whisking constantly. Add the hot stock and whisk over a medium heat until the mixture boils. Cook for 2–3 minutes, then whisk in the cream. Season to taste, and set aside.

5 Heat the remaining butter in a large, non-stick frying pan and cook the onion and carrots over a low heat for about 5 minutes. Add the celery and fresh mushrooms and cook for 5 minutes more. Stir in the cooked chicken, peas and drained porcini mushrooms.

6 Add the chicken mixture to the hot cream sauce and stir to mix. Adjust the seasoning if necessary. Spoon the mixture into a 2.5 litre/4 pint/2½ quart oval baking dish.

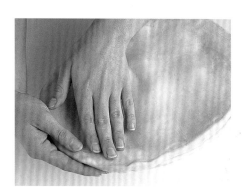

7 Roll out the pastry to a thickness of about 3mm/⅛in. Cut out an oval 2.5cm/1in larger all around than the dish. Lay the pastry over the filling. Gently press around the edge of the dish to seal, then trim off the excess pastry. Crimp the edge of the pastry by pushing the forefinger of one hand into the edge and, using the thumb and forefinger of the other hand, pinch the pastry. Continue all round the pastry edge.

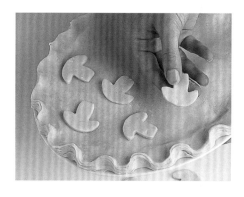

8 Press together the pastry trimmings and roll out again. Cut out mushroom shapes with a sharp knife and stick them on to the pastry lid with beaten egg. Glaze the lid with beaten egg and cut several slits in the pastry to allow the steam to escape.

9 Bake the pie for about 30 minutes, until the pastry has browned. Serve the pie hot.

COOK'S TIP

Using a combination of butter and white vegetable fat gives shortcrust pastry a lovely crumbly texture.

STEAK AND KIDNEY PIE WITH MUSTARD GRAVY

THIS IS A VARIATION OF A TRADITIONAL FAVOURITE. THE FRAGRANT MUSTARD, BAY AND PARSLEY GRAVY COMPLEMENTS THE BEEF BEAUTIFULLY.

SERVES FOUR

INGREDIENTS
   450g/1lb puff pastry
   40ml/2½ tbsp plain
   (all-purpose) flour
   675g/1½lb rump (round)
   steak, cubed
   175g/6oz lamb's kidneys
   25g/1oz/2 tbsp butter
   1 onion, chopped
   15ml/1 tbsp English (hot) mustard
   2 bay leaves
   15ml/1 tbsp chopped fresh parsley
   150ml/¼ pint/⅔ cup beef stock
   1 egg, beaten
   salt and ground black pepper

1 Roll out two-thirds of the pastry on a floured surface to a thickness of 3mm/⅛in. Use to line the base and sides of a 1.5 litre/2½ pint/6¼ cup pie dish. Place a pie funnel in the centre of the dish.

2 Put the flour, salt and pepper in a bowl and toss the steak in the mixture.

3 Remove the fat, skin and tough central core from the kidneys, and slice them thickly. Add the slices to the steak and toss well.

4 Melt the butter in a pan, add the onion and fry over a low heat, stirring occasionally, until soft and translucent. Add the mustard, bay leaves, parsley and stock and stir well.

5 Preheat the oven to 190°C/375°F/ Gas 5. Place the steak and kidney in the pie dish and add the stock mixture.

6 Roll out the remaining puff pastry to a thickness of 3mm/⅛in to use for the pie lid. Brush the edges of the pastry case with beaten egg and cover with the lid. Press the edges firmly together to seal, then trim. Use the trimmings to decorate the top with pastry leaves.

7 Brush the pie with a little beaten egg and make a small hole in the pastry lid for the funnel. Bake for about 1 hour until the pastry is well risen and golden brown. Serve the pie hot, straight from the pie dish.

COOK'S TIP
For an attractive appearance, scallop the pastry crust. Pressing down on the rim with the first two fingers of one hand, use the blunt side of a knife blade to draw the pastry towards the centre.

TURKEY AND CRANBERRY PIE

THE CRANBERRIES ADD A TART LAYER TO THIS MEATY PIE. CRANBERRY SAUCE CAN BE USED IF FRESH CRANBERRIES ARE NOT AVAILABLE. THE PIE FREEZES WELL.

SERVES EIGHT

INGREDIENTS
  450g/1lb pork sausage meat (bulk
    pork sausage)
  450g/1lb lean minced (ground) pork
  15ml/1 tbsp ground coriander
  15ml/1 tbsp dried mixed herbs
  finely grated rind of 2 large oranges
  10ml/2 tsp grated fresh root ginger or
    2.5ml/½ tsp ground ginger
  10ml/2 tsp salt
  450g/1lb turkey breast fillets
  115g/4oz/1 cup fresh cranberries
  ground black pepper
  1 egg, beaten
  300ml/½ pint/1¼ cups aspic jelly,
    made according to the instructions
    on the packet
For the pastry
  450g/1lb/4 cups plain
    (all-purpose) flour
  5ml/1 tsp salt
  150g/5oz/⅔ cup lard
  150ml/¼ pint/⅔ cup mixed milk
    and water

1 Preheat the oven to 180°C/350°F/ Gas 4. Place a baking sheet in the oven to preheat. In a bowl, mix together the sausage meat, pork, coriander, herbs, orange rind, ginger and salt. Season with black pepper to taste.

2 To make the pastry, sift the flour into a large bowl with the salt. Heat the lard in a small pan with the milk and water until just beginning to boil. Remove the pan from the heat and allow the mixture to cool slightly.

3 Quickly stir the liquid into the flour until a very stiff dough is formed. Place on a clean work surface and knead until smooth. Cut one-third off the dough for the lid, wrap in clear film (plastic wrap) and keep in a warm place.

4 Roll out the large piece of dough on a floured surface and use to line the base and sides of a greased 20cm/8in loose-based, springform cake tin. Work with the dough while it is still warm, as it will break if it becomes too cold.

5 Thinly slice the turkey breast fillets. Put them between two pieces of clear film and flatten with a rolling pin to a thickness of 3mm/⅛in. Spoon half the pork mixture into the tin, pressing it well into the edges. Cover it with half the turkey slices and then the cranberries, followed by the remaining turkey and finally the rest of the pork mixture.

6 Roll out the remaining dough and use to cover the filling, trimming off any excess and sealing the edges with a little beaten egg. Make a steam hole in the centre of the lid and decorate the top by cutting pastry trimmings into leaf shapes. Brush with some beaten egg and bake for 2 hours. Cover the pie with foil if the top gets too brown.

7 Place the pie on a wire rack to cool. When cold, use a funnel to fill the pie with liquid aspic jelly. Leave the jelly to set for a few hours or overnight, before unmoulding the pie to serve it.

BACON AND EGG PIE

WHOLE EGGS ARE BROKEN OVER SMOKED BACON AND SOFTENED ONIONS BEFORE BEING COVERED IN PASTRY IN A DOUBLE-CRUST PIE, IN THIS CELEBRATION OF THE BEST OF BREAKFAST INGREDIENTS.

SERVES FOUR

INGREDIENTS
   30ml/2 tbsp sunflower oil
   4 smoked bacon rashers (strips), cut
      into 4cm/1½in pieces
   1 small onion, finely chopped
   5 eggs
   25ml/1½ tbsp chopped fresh parsley
   salt and ground black pepper
   a little milk, to glaze
For the pastry
   350g/12oz/3 cups plain
      (all-purpose) flour
   pinch of salt
   115g/4oz/½ cup butter, diced
   50g/2oz/¼ cup lard or white
      vegetable fat
   75–90ml/5–6 tbsp chilled water

1 To make the pastry, sift the flour and salt into a large bowl and rub or cut in the fat until the mixture resembles fine breadcrumbs. Sprinkle over most of the water and mix to a pliable dough, adding more water if required. Knead until smooth, then wrap in clear film (plastic wrap) and chill for 30 minutes.

2 Butter a deep 20cm/8in flan tin (quiche pan). Roll out two-thirds of the pastry and use to line the flan tin. Cover the pastry case. Chill for 30 minutes.

3 Preheat the oven to 200°C/400°F/ Gas 6. Heat the oil in a pan, add the bacon and cook for a few minutes, then add the onion and cook until soft. Drain on kitchen paper and leave to cool.

4 Cover the base of the pastry case with the bacon mixture, spreading it evenly, then break the eggs on to the bacon, spacing them evenly apart. Carefully tilt the flan tin so the egg whites flow together. Sprinkle the eggs with the chopped parsley, a little salt and plenty of black pepper. Place a baking sheet in the oven to heat.

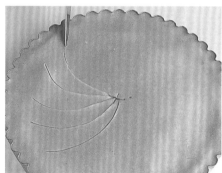

5 Roll out the remaining pastry, dampen the edges and place over the pie. Roll over the top with a rolling pin to seal the edge and remove the excess pastry. With a sharp knife, carefully cut curved lines from the centre of the lid to within 2cm/¾in of the edge. Lightly brush the pie with the milk to glaze.

6 Place the pie on the hot baking sheet and bake for 10 minutes, then lower the oven temperature to 180°C/350°F/Gas 4 and bake for a further 20 minutes. Leave to cool for a few minutes before cutting and serving.

CHEESE AND SPINACH FLAN

THE DECORATIVE PASTRY TOPPING FOR THIS FLAN IS MADE USING A LATTICE CUTTER. IF YOU DON'T HAVE ONE, CUT THE PASTRY INTO FINE STRIPS AND WEAVE THEM INTO A LATTICE.

SERVES EIGHT

INGREDIENTS
    450g/1lb frozen spinach
    1 onion, chopped
    pinch of grated nutmeg
    225g/8oz/1 cup cottage cheese
    2 large eggs
    50g/2oz Parmesan cheese, grated
    150ml/¼ pint/⅔ cup single
      (light) cream
    1 egg, beaten
    salt and ground black pepper
For the pastry
    225g/8oz/2 cups plain
      (all-purpose) flour
    115g/4oz/½ cup butter
    2.5ml/½ tsp English (hot) mustard
    2.5ml/½ tsp paprika
    115g/4oz Cheddar cheese,
      finely grated
    45–60ml/3–4 tbsp chilled water

1 To make the pastry, sift the flour into a large mixing bowl and rub or cut in the butter until the mixture resembles fine breadcrumbs. Stir in the mustard powder, paprika, salt and cheese. Bind to a soft, pliable dough with the chilled water. Knead lightly until smooth, wrap in clear film (plastic wrap) and chill for 30 minutes.

2 Put the spinach and onion in a pan, and cook until the onion has softened. Increase the heat to evaporate any liquid in the pan. Season with salt, pepper and nutmeg. Put the mixture into a bowl and add the cottage cheese, eggs, Parmesan and cream. Mix well.

3 Preheat the oven to 200°C/400°F/ Gas 6. Put a baking sheet in the oven to preheat. Roll out two-thirds of the pastry on a lightly floured surface and use to line a 23cm/9in loose-based flan tin (quiche pan). Press the pastry into the edges and make a narrow lip around the top edge. Remove the excess pastry with a rolling pin. Spoon the filling into the flan case.

4 Roll out the remaining pastry and cut it with a lattice pastry cutter. Carefully open the lattice and, with the help of a rolling pin, lay it over the flan. Lightly brush the edges with beaten egg, press together and trim off the excess pastry. Brush the top of the pastry lattice with beaten egg and bake on the hot baking sheet for 35–40 minutes, or until golden brown. Serve hot or cold.

POTATO AND LEEK FILO PIE

THIS FILO PASTRY WOULD MAKE AN ATTRACTIVE AND UNUSUAL CENTREPIECE FOR A VEGETARIAN BUFFET. THIS PIE IS BEST SERVED COLD, WITH A SELECTION OF SALADS.

SERVES EIGHT

INGREDIENTS

  800g/1¾lb new potatoes
  2 large leeks
  75g/3oz/6 tbsp butter
  15g/½oz/½ cup fresh parsley,
    finely chopped
  60ml/4 tbsp chopped mixed
    fresh herbs
  12 sheets of filo pastry, thawed
    if frozen
  150g/5oz Cheshire or Lancashire
    cheese, sliced
  2 garlic cloves, finely chopped
  250ml/8fl oz/1 cup double
    (heavy) cream
  2 large egg yolks
  salt and ground black pepper

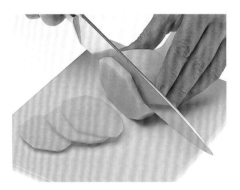

1 Preheat the oven to 190°C/375°F/Gas 5. Slice the potatoes and cook them in a pan of salted boiling water for 3–4 minutes, then drain and set aside.

2 Trim the leeks and rinse thoroughly under cold running water. Drain them well, then slice thinly.

3 Melt 25g/1oz/2 tbsp of the butter in a frying pan, add the sliced leeks and fry, stirring occasionally, until softened. Remove from the heat, season with pepper and stir in half the parsley and half the mixed herbs. Set the pan aside.

4 Melt the remaining butter in a pan. Line a deep 23cm/9in loose-based cake tin with 6–7 sheets of filo pastry, lightly brushing each layer with butter. Let the edges of the pastry overhang the tin.

5 Layer the potatoes, leek mixture and cheese in the tin, sprinkling some of the herbs and all the garlic between each of the layers. Season each with salt and plenty of pepper.

COOK'S TIPS
• Any fresh herbs can be used for this pie, but chervil, chives, tarragon and basil work particularly well. Chop them with a mezzaluna or cook's knife just before adding them to the pie.
• Most moist, crumbly, richly-flavoured cheeses will work well in this dish, such as Stilton, Cheddar and Milawa Blue.

6 Fold the overhanging pastry over the filling and cover with 2 sheets of filo, tucking in the sides to fit. Brush with melted butter. Cover the pie loosely with foil and bake for 35 minutes. (Keep the remaining sheets of filo pastry covered with clear film (plastic wrap) and a damp dishtowel.)

7 Meanwhile, in a small bowl, beat the cream, egg yolks and remaining herbs together. Remove the foil from the pie, make a hole in the centre of the pastry and gradually pour in the egg and cream mixture.

8 Lower the oven temperature to 180°C/350°F/Gas 4. Cut the remaining pastry into strips and arrange them on top of the pie, gently teasing the strips into decorative loose swirls and folds, then brush the top of the pie with melted butter.

9 Bake the pie for 25–30 minutes more until the top is golden and crisp. Allow the pie to cool before transferring it to a large platter and serving.

SPINACH FILO PIE

THIS POPULAR SPINACH AND FILO PASTRY PIE IS SOMETIMES CALLED SPANAKOPITA IN ITS NATIVE GREECE. THERE ARE SEVERAL WAYS OF MAKING IT, BUT FETA IS INEVITABLY INCLUDED.

SERVES SIX

INGREDIENTS
  1kg/2¼lb fresh spinach
  4 spring onions (scallions), chopped
  300g/11oz feta cheese, crumbled or
    coarsely grated
  2 large eggs, beaten
  30ml/2 tbsp chopped fresh parsley
  15ml/1 tbsp chopped fresh dill
  45ml/3 tbsp currants (optional)
  about 8 sheets of filo pastry, each
    measuring 30 × 18cm/12 × 7in
  150ml/¼ pint/⅔ cup olive oil
  ground black pepper

VARIATION
Any crumbly hard cheese will work well in this pie. Try English Lancashire or Vermont Cheddar for a change.

1 Break off any thick stalks from the spinach, then blanch the leaves in a very small amount of boiling water for 1–2 minutes until just wilted.

2 Drain and refresh under cold water. Drain again, squeeze the spinach dry and chop it roughly.

3 Place the spinach in a bowl with the spring onions and cheese, then pour in the eggs and stir them in thoroughly. Mix in the herbs and currants, if using. Season with pepper.

4 Preheat the oven to 190°C/375°F/ Gas 5. Brush a sheet of filo with oil and fit it into a 23cm/9in pie dish, allowing it to hang over the edges. Add 3–4 more sheets, placing them at different angles and brushing each with oil.

5 Spoon the filling into the filo pastry case, then top with all but one of the remaining filo sheets, brushing each filo sheet with oil as you go. Fold the overhanging filo pastry over the top sheets to seal. Brush the reserved filo with oil and scrunch it over the top of the pie.

6 Brush the pie with oil. Sprinkle with a little water to stop the filo edges from curling, then place on a baking sheet. Bake for about 40 minutes until golden and crisp. Allow the pie to cool for 15 minutes before serving.

CHICKEN AND APRICOT FILO PIE

THE FILLING FOR THIS UNUSUAL YET UTTERLY DELICIOUS PIE HAS A MIDDLE EASTERN FLAVOUR — CHICKEN COMBINED WITH APRICOTS, BULGUR WHEAT, NUTS AND SPICES.

SERVES SIX

INGREDIENTS

75g/3oz/½ cup bulgur wheat
75g/3oz/6 tbsp butter
1 onion, chopped
450g/1lb minced (ground) chicken
50g/2oz/¼ cup ready-to-eat dried
  apricots, finely chopped
25g/1oz/¼ cup chopped almonds
5ml/1 tsp ground cinnamon
2.5ml/½ tsp ground allspice
60ml/4 tbsp Greek (US strained
  plain) yogurt
15ml/1 tbsp chopped fresh chives
30ml/2 tbsp chopped fresh parsley
8 large sheets of filo pastry
salt and ground black pepper
chives, to garnish

1 Soak the bulgur wheat in 120ml/ 4fl oz/½ cup boiling water for about 10 minutes until the water is absorbed.

2 Heat 25g/1oz/2 tbsp of the butter in a frying pan, add the onion and chicken and gently fry until golden.

3 Stir in the apricots, almonds and bulgur wheat and cook for 2 minutes. Remove from the heat and stir in the cinnamon, allspice, yogurt, chives and parsley. Season with salt and pepper.

4 Preheat the oven to 200°C/ 400°F/ Gas 6. Melt the remaining butter. Unroll the filo pastry and cut into 25cm/10in rounds. Keep the pastry rounds covered with a damp dishtowel to prevent them from drying out.

5 Line a 23cm/9in loose-based flan tin (quiche pan) with three filo rounds, brushing each one with butter as you go. Spoon in the chicken mixture and cover with three more rounds, brushing with melted butter as before.

COOK'S TIP
Thaw frozen filo pastry well before use, following the instructions on the packet.

6 Crumple the remaining two pastry rounds and place them on top of the pie, then brush over the remaining melted butter. Bake the pie for about 30 minutes until the pastry is golden brown and crisp. Serve the pie hot or cold, cut in wedges and garnished with a few chives.

SPICED CHICKEN AND EGG FILO PIE

THIS RECIPE IS BASED ON BISTEEYA, ONE OF THE MOST ELABORATE AND INTRIGUING DISHES IN MOROCCAN CUISINE. A DELICIOUS AND UNUSUAL DISH, THIS VERSION USES CHICKEN INSTEAD OF PIGEON AND FILO PASTRY INSTEAD OF THE TRADITIONAL OUARKA.

SERVES FOUR

INGREDIENTS

30ml/2 tbsp sunflower oil, plus extra
  for brushing
25g/1oz/2 tbsp butter
3 chicken quarters, preferably
  with breasts attached
1½ Spanish onions, very
  finely chopped
generous pinch of ground ginger
generous pinch of saffron powder
10ml/2 tsp ground cinnamon, plus
  extra for dusting
40g/1½oz/⅓ cup flaked
  (sliced) almonds
1 large bunch fresh coriander
  (cilantro), finely chopped
1 large bunch fresh parsley, chopped
3 eggs, beaten
about 175g/6oz filo pastry, thawed
  if frozen
5–10ml/1–2 tsp icing (confectioners')
  sugar, plus extra for dusting
  (optional)
salt and ground black pepper

1 Heat the oil and butter in a large pan, add the chicken pieces and cook, stirring frequently, until browned. Add the onions, ginger, saffron, 2.5ml/½ tsp of the cinnamon and 300ml/½ pint/ 1¼ cups water. Season well. Bring to the boil and then cover and simmer very gently for 45–55 minutes.

2 When the chicken is cooked but still tender, transfer it to a plate. Dry-fry the almonds until golden and set aside.

3 As soon as the cooked chicken is cool enough to handle, remove the skin and bones and cut the flesh into neat, bitesize pieces.

4 Stir the coriander and parsley into the pan and simmer the sauce until well reduced and thickened. Add the beaten eggs and cook over a very gentle heat, stirring constantly, until the eggs are lightly scrambled.

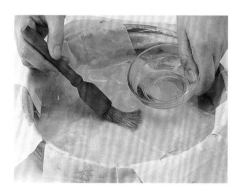

5 Preheat the oven to 180°C/350°F/ Gas 4. Oil a shallow 25cm/10in round ovenproof dish. Place 1–2 sheets of filo pastry in an even layer over the base and sides of the dish, so that it is completely covered and the edges of the pastry sheets hang over the sides. Lightly brush the pastry with oil and make two more layers of filo, brushing with oil between the layers.

6 Place the chicken in the pastry case then spoon the egg and herb mixture on top. Level the surface of the filling with the back of a spoon.

7 Place a layer of filo on top of the filling (you may need to use more than one sheet of pastry) and scatter with the dry-fried almonds. Lightly sprinkle with the remaining cinnamon and the icing sugar, if using.

8 Fold the edges of the filo over the almonds and then make four further layers of filo (using one or two sheets per layer, depending on size), brushing each layer with a little oil. Tuck the filo edges down the side of the pie and brush the top layer with oil.

9 Bake the pie for 40–45 minutes until it is golden brown. Dust the top of the pie with icing sugar and cinnamon, creating a geometric design by using a paper template if you wish. Serve the pie immediately.

Parcels and Shaped Pastry Cases

You'll find all manner of traditional and more unusual parcels and shaped pastry packages here. Pastry is amazingly versatile and can be wrapped around large or small joints of meat, rolled up for a strudel, slashed to make a jalousie, or cut and braided. In the following recipes, pastry is not only used to hold the filling, but also as a decoration, as in the elegant Salmon in Puff Pastry. These are dishes to delight the eye as well as the palate.

RICH GAME PIE

TERRIFIC FOR STYLISH PICNICS OR JUST AS SMART FOR A MORE FORMAL SPECIAL OCCASION, THIS PIE LOOKS SPECTACULAR WHEN BAKED IN A FLUTED RAISED PIE MOULD.

SERVES TEN

INGREDIENTS

25g/1oz/2 tbsp butter
1 onion, finely chopped
2 garlic cloves, finely chopped
900g/2lb mixed boneless game meat, such as skinless pheasant and/or pigeon breast, venison and rabbit, diced
30ml/2 tbsp chopped mixed fresh herbs
1 egg, beaten
salt and ground black pepper

For the pâté
50g/2oz/¼ cup butter
2 garlic cloves, finely chopped
450g/1lb chicken livers, trimmed and chopped
60ml/4 tbsp brandy
5ml/1 tsp ground mace

For the pastry
675g/1½lb/6 cups strong white bread flour
5ml/1 tsp salt
120ml/4fl oz/½ cup milk
90ml/3fl oz/6 tbsp water
115g/4oz/½ cup lard, diced
115g/4oz/½ cup butter, diced

For the jelly
300ml/½ pint/1¼ cups game or beef consommé
2.5ml/½ tsp powdered gelatine

1 Melt the butter in a small pan, then add the onion and garlic, and cook gently until softened but not coloured. Remove the pan from the heat and add the onions and garlic to the diced game meat and the chopped mixed herbs. Mix well. Season with salt and plenty of pepper, cover and chill.

2 To make the pâté, melt the butter in a frying pan, add the garlic and chicken livers and cook over a medium heat, stirring frequently, until just browned. Remove the pan from the heat and stir in the brandy and ground mace. Purée the mixture in a blender or food processor until smooth, then set aside and leave to cool.

3 To make the pastry, sift the flour and salt into a bowl and make a well in the centre. Pour the milk and water into a pan. Add the lard and butter and heat gently until melted, then bring to the boil. Immediately, pour the hot liquid into the well in the flour and beat until smooth. Cover and leave until cool enough to handle.

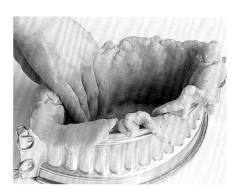

4 Preheat the oven to 200°C/400°F/ Gas 6. Roll out two-thirds of the pastry and use to line a 23cm/9in raised pie mould. Spoon in half the game mixture and press it down evenly. Add the pâté and then top with the remaining game.

5 Roll out the remaining pastry to form a lid. Brush the edge of the pastry case with a little water and cover with the pastry lid. Trim off the excess pastry from around the edge. Pinch the edges together to seal in the filling. Make two holes in the centre of the lid and brush the lid with beaten egg. Use the pastry trimmings to make small leaves to decorate the pie. Brush the leaves with a little beaten egg.

6 Bake the pie for 20 minutes, then cover with foil and cook for 10 minutes more. Reduce the oven temperature to 150°C/300°F/Gas 2. Lightly glaze the pie again with beaten egg and cook for a further 1½ hours, keeping the top covered loosely with foil.

7 Remove the pie from the oven and leave it to stand for 15 minutes to cool slightly. Increase the oven temperature to 200°C/400°F/Gas 6. Stand the tin on a baking sheet and remove the sides. Quickly glaze the sides of the pie with beaten egg and cover the top with foil. Cook the pie for a final 15 minutes to brown the sides. Leave the pie to cool completely, then chill overnight.

8 Next day, make the jelly. Heat the game or beef consommé in a small pan until just beginning to bubble, whisk in the gelatine until dissolved and leave to cool until just setting. Using a small funnel, carefully pour the jellied consommé into the holes in the pie. Chill until set. This pie will keep in the refrigerator for up to three days.

LAMB PIE WITH PEAR AND MINT SAUCE

COOKING LAMB WITH FRUIT IS AN IDEA DERIVED FROM TRADITIONAL PERSIAN CUISINE. THE GINGER AND MINT ADD A DELIGHTFUL BITE TO THE MILD FLAVOURS IN THIS DISH.

SERVES SIX

INGREDIENTS
  400g/14oz can pear halves
    in juice
  50g/2oz/¼ cup butter
  1 small onion, chopped
  grated rind of 1 lemon
  75g/3oz/1 cup coarse wholemeal
    (whole-wheat) breadcrumbs
  1.5ml/¼ tsp ground ginger
  1 small egg, beaten
  900g/2lb boned and rolled loin
    of lamb
  8 large sheets of filo pastry
  10ml/2 tsp finely chopped fresh mint
    plus a few mint sprigs, to garnish
  salt and ground black pepper

1 Preheat the oven to 180°C/350°F/ Gas 4. Drain the pears, reserving the juice. Set half the pears aside and chop the remainder.

2 Melt 15g/½oz/1 tbsp of the butter in a pan and add the onion. Cook until soft. Put in a bowl and add the lemon rind, breadcrumbs, chopped pears and ginger. Bind with egg and season well.

3 Open out the lamb, fat side down, and season. Place the pear stuffing along the middle of the lamb and roll the meat around it. Secure with skewers while you tie it up with string (twine).

4 Heat a roasting pan in the oven and brown the loin of lamb slowly on all sides. This will take 20–30 minutes. Remove from the oven, leave to cool, then chill until needed.

5 Increase the oven temperature to 200°C/400°F/Gas 6. Melt the remaining butter. Brush two sheets of filo pastry with melted butter. Overlap the sheets of filo to make a square. Place the next two sheets on top and brush with butter. Continue until all the pastry has been used.

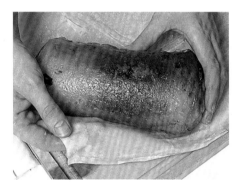

6 Place the roll of lamb diagonally across one corner of the pastry. Fold the corner over the lamb, fold in the sides, and brush the pastry well with melted butter. Roll up the lamb in the pastry, tucking in the edges as you go.

7 Place the filo-wrapped lamb, seam side down, on a buttered baking sheet and brush it all over with the remaining melted butter. Bake the lamb for about 30 minutes, or until the pastry is crisp and golden brown.

8 To make the sauce, process the reserved pears with their juice and the mint in a food processor or blender. Spoon the pear and mint sauce into a small bowl and serve with the lamb, garnished with a few mint sprigs.

BEEF WELLINGTON

This dish, a fillet of beef baked in puff pastry, is a variation of the classic French boeuf en croûte. The English name was applied in 1815 in honour of the Duke of Wellington.

SERVES SIX

INGREDIENTS
   1.6kg/3¼lb fillet (tenderloin) of beef
   45ml/3 tbsp sunflower oil
   115g/4oz/1½ cups button (white)
      mushrooms, chopped
   2 garlic cloves, crushed
   175g/6oz smooth liver pâté
   30ml/2 tbsp chopped fresh parsley
   400g/14oz puff pastry
   1 egg, beaten
   salt and ground black pepper

1 Preheat the oven to 220°C/425°F/Gas 7. Tie the beef with string (twine). Heat 30ml/2 tbsp of the oil in a frying pan, and brown the beef on all sides for 10 minutes. Put in a roasting pan and roast for 20 minutes. Remove and set aside to cool. Leave the oven on.

2 Heat the remaining oil in a frying pan and cook the mushrooms and garlic for about 5 minutes until softened. Beat the mushroom mixture into the pâté with the chopped parsley, and season well. Set aside to cool.

3 Roll out the puff pastry into a sheet large enough to enclose the beef, plus a strip to spare. Trim off the spare pastry. Spread the pâté mixture down the middle of the pastry. Untie the beef and lay it on top of the pâté mixture.

4 Brush the edges of the pastry with beaten egg and fold the pastry over the meat to enclose it in a neat parcel. Seal the edges well. Place the meat parcel on a baking sheet, seam side down. Cut decorative leaf shapes from the reserved pastry. Brush the parcel with beaten egg, decorate with the pastry leaves and brush with egg. Chill for about 10 minutes.

5 Bake the beef for 50–60 minutes, covering it loosely with foil after about 30 minutes to prevent the pastry from over-browning. Transfer to a serving platter and leave to stand for about 10 minutes. Serve in thick slices, and garnish each portion with parsley.

FILLETS OF SEA BREAM IN FILO PASTRY

ANY FIRM FISH FILLETS CAN BE USED FOR THIS DISH. EACH LITTLE PARCEL IS A MEAL IN ITSELF AND CAN BE PREPARED SEVERAL HOURS IN ADVANCE, WHICH MAKES THIS IDEAL FOR ENTERTAINING.

2 Thinly slice the potatoes lengthways. Brush a baking tray with a little oil. Lay a sheet of filo pastry on the tray, brush it with oil, then lay a second sheet crossways over the first. Repeat with two more sheets. Arrange a quarter of the sliced potatoes in the centre of the pastry, season well and add a quarter of the shredded sorrel. Lay a bream fillet on top, skin-side up. Season again.

3 Loosely fold the filo pastry up and over to make a neat parcel. Make three more parcels in the same way. Place on the baking tray and brush them with half the butter. Bake for 20 minutes until the filo has fully puffed up and is golden brown.

SERVES FOUR

INGREDIENTS
   8 small waxy salad potatoes
   200g/7oz sorrel, stalks removed
   30ml/2 tbsp olive oil
   16 sheets of filo pastry, thawed
     if frozen
   4 sea bream fillets, about 175g/6oz
     each, scaled but not skinned
   50g/2oz/¼ cup butter, melted
   120ml/4fl oz/½ cup fish stock
   250ml/8fl oz/1 cup double
     (heavy) cream
   salt and ground black pepper
   finely diced red (bell) pepper,
     to garnish

VARIATION
Use small spinach leaves or baby chard in place of the sorrel.

1 Preheat the oven to 200°C/400°F/ Gas 6. Cook the salad potatoes in lightly salted boiling water for 15–20 minutes, until just tender. Drain and set aside to cool. Shred half the sorrel leaves by piling up six or eight at a time, rolling them up like a fat cigar and slicing them with a sharp knife. Reserve the rest of the sorrel.

4 Meanwhile, make the sorrel sauce. Heat the remaining butter in a small pan, add the reserved sorrel and cook until it wilts. Stir in the fish stock and cream. Heat almost to boiling point, stirring constantly. Season and keep hot. Serve the fish parcels garnished with red pepper and offer the sauce separately, in its own bowl.

CHICKEN AND COUSCOUS PARCELS

BASED ON THE TURKISH BÖREK OR BOREG, *THESE SAVOURY RICH PASTRY PARCELS ARE SERVED AT ROOM TEMPERATURE WITH A YOGURT SAUCE, SPIKED WITH CAYENNE AND COOLED WITH MINT.*

SERVES FOUR

INGREDIENTS

- 50g/2oz/⅓ cup couscous
- 45ml/3 tbsp olive oil
- 1 onion, chopped
- 115g/4oz/1½ cups mushrooms
- 1 garlic clove, crushed
- 115g/4oz cooked chicken, diced (about 1 cup)
- 30ml/2 tbsp walnuts, chopped
- 30ml/2 tbsp raisins
- 60ml/4 tbsp chopped fresh parsley
- 5ml/1 tsp chopped fresh thyme
- 2 eggs, hard-boiled and peeled
- salt and ground black pepper

For the pastry
- 400g/14oz/3½ cups self-raising (self-rising) flour
- 1 egg, plus extra for glazing
- 150ml/¼ pint/⅔ cup natural (plain) yogurt
- 150ml/¼ pint/⅔ cup olive oil
- grated rind of ½ lemon

For the yogurt sauce
- 200ml/7fl oz/scant 1 cup natural (plain) yogurt
- 45ml/3 tbsp chopped fresh mint
- 2.5ml/½ tsp caster (superfine) sugar
- 1.5ml/¼ tsp cayenne pepper
- 1.5ml/¼ tsp celery salt
- a little milk or water (optional)

1 Preheat the oven to 190°C/375°F/ Gas 5. Place the couscous in a bowl and just cover with boiling water. Soak for 10 minutes, or until all the liquid has been absorbed.

2 Heat the oil in a frying pan, add the onion and cook over a medium heat until soft but without letting it colour. Add the mushrooms and garlic, and cook until the juices begin to run. Increase the heat to evaporate the juices.

VARIATION
Alternative fillings for these parcels include mixed cheeses and herbs; mushrooms with ground cumin and coriander; or a spicy potato and vegetable mixture.

3 Transfer the mushroom and onion mixture to a large mixing bowl, add the chicken, walnuts, raisins, parsley, thyme and couscous, and stir well. Chop the eggs roughly and stir them into the mixture with seasoning to taste.

4 To make the pastry, sift the flour and 5ml/1 tsp salt into a bowl. Make a well in the centre, add the egg, yogurt, olive oil and lemon rind, and mix together with a round-bladed knife.

5 On a floured surface, roll out the pastry to a 30cm/12in round. Pile the filling into the centre and bring the edges over to enclose the filling. Place seam side down on a baking sheet and gently flatten with your hand. Glaze with beaten egg and bake for 25 minutes.

6 Meanwhile, make the sauce. Mix together all the ingredients, adding milk or water if the mixture is too thick. Spoon a little sauce over each serving.

CHICKEN, CHEESE AND LEEK PARCEL

STRIPS OF PUFF PASTRY ARE CLEVERLY CROSSED OVER A CREAMY CHICKEN FILLING TO MAKE THIS ATTRACTIVE FAMILY-SIZE PIE, WHICH TASTES GOOD EITHER WARM OR COLD.

SERVES SIX

INGREDIENTS

1 roast chicken, about 1.6kg/3½lb
40g/1½oz/3 tbsp butter
2 large leeks, thinly sliced
2 garlic cloves, crushed
115g/4oz/1 cup button (white) mushrooms, sliced
200g/7oz/scant 1 cup low-fat cream cheese
grated rind of 1 small lemon
45ml/3 tbsp chopped fresh flat leaf parsley
500g/1¼lb puff pastry
1 egg, beaten
salt and ground black pepper
fresh herbs, to garnish

1 Strip the meat from the chicken, discarding the skin and bones. Chop or shred the meat and set it aside.

2 Melt the butter in a pan, add the leeks and garlic and cook for 10 minutes. Stir in the mushrooms and cook for 5 minutes. Leave to cool, then add the cream cheese, lemon rind, parsley and seasoning. Stir in the chicken.

VARIATION
For a richer flavour, use dolcelatte cheese instead of the cream cheese.

3 Roll out the pastry on a lightly floured work surface to a large rectangle, about 35 × 25cm/14 × 10in. Using a rolling pin to help you, lift the pastry on to a non-stick baking sheet.

4 Spoon the filling on to the pastry, leaving a generous margin at each end, and about 10cm/4in on each long side. Use a sharp knife to cut the pastry sides diagonally in strips, cutting up to the filling at 2cm/¾in intervals.

5 Brush the edges of the pastry with a little of the beaten egg. Cross the pastry strips over each other alternately to enclose the filling. Seal the edges.

6 Glaze the top with beaten egg. Leave the pie to rest while you preheat the oven to 200°C/400°F/Gas 6. Bake for about 15 minutes, then lower the oven temperature to 190°C/375°F/Gas 5 and bake for a further 15 minutes, or until the pastry is golden brown and crisp. Allow to stand for 10 minutes before sliding the parcel on to a board or platter to serve. Garnish with herbs.

MUSHROOM, NUT AND PRUNE JALOUSIE

JALOUSIE, THE FRENCH WORD FOR SHUTTER, REFERS TO THIS PIE'S SLATTED TOP. IT HAS A RICH NUTTY FILLING THAT WILL BE ENJOYED BY VEGETARIANS AND MEAT-EATERS ALIKE.

SERVES SIX

INGREDIENTS
  75g/3oz/⅓ cup green lentils, rinsed
  5ml/1 tsp vegetable bouillon powder
  15ml/1 tbsp sunflower oil
  2 large leeks, sliced
  2 garlic cloves, chopped
  200g/7oz/3 cups field (portabello)
    mushrooms, finely chopped
  10ml/2 tsp dried mixed herbs
  75g/3oz/¾ cup chopped mixed nuts
  15ml/1 tbsp pine nuts
  75g/3oz/⅓ cup ready-to-eat
    pitted prunes
  25g/1oz/½ cup fresh breadcrumbs
  2 eggs, beaten
  500g/1¼lb puff pastry
  salt and ground black pepper

1 Put the lentils in a pan and cover with cold water. Bring to the boil, then reduce the heat slightly and stir in the vegetable bouillon powder. Partly cover the pan and simmer for 20 minutes or until the lentils are tender and have absorbed the liquid. Set aside.

2 Heat the oil in a large heavy frying pan, add the leeks and garlic and fry for about 5 minutes, or until just softened. Add the mushrooms and herbs and cook for a further 5 minutes.

3 Transfer the leek and mushroom mixture to a mixing bowl using a slotted spoon. Stir in the chopped nuts, pine nuts, prunes, fresh breadcrumbs and lentils. Preheat the oven to 220°C/425°F/Gas 7.

4 Add two-thirds of the beaten egg to the mushroom mixture and season well. Set aside and leave to cool.

5 Meanwhile, roll out just under half the pastry to a 25 × 15cm/10 × 6in rectangle, then lay it on a dampened baking sheet. Roll out the remaining pastry to a 28 × 19cm/11 × 7½in rectangle, dust it with flour, then fold in half lengthways. Make a series of cuts across the fold, 1cm/½in apart, leaving a 2.5cm/1in border around the edge.

6 Spoon the mushroom mixture evenly over the pastry base, leaving a 2.5cm/1in border. Dampen the edges of the pastry with water. Open out the folded piece of pastry and carefully lay it over the filling. Press the edges of the pastry together to seal, trim off the excess then crimp the edges.

7 Brush the top of the pastry with the remaining beaten egg and bake for 25–30 minutes until golden. Leave to cool slightly before serving.

SPICY POTATO STRUDEL

Wrap up in crisp filo pastry a tasty mixture of vegetables cooked in a spicy, creamy sauce. Serve with a good selection of chutneys or a yogurt and mint sauce.

2 Add the thyme, water and seasoning. Bring to the boil, then reduce the heat and simmer for 10 minutes until tender, stirring occasionally. Set aside to cool.

3 Transfer the vegetable mixture to a large bowl, then mix in the egg, cream and cheese. Chill until you are ready to fill the filo pastry.

4 Preheat the oven to 190°C/375°F/ Gas 5. Melt the remaining butter and lay out four sheets of filo pastry, slightly overlapping them to form a fairly large rectangle. Brush with some melted butter and fit the other sheets on top. Brush with some more of the butter.

5 Spoon the filling along one long side of the pastry, then roll it up. Form it into a circle and place on a baking sheet. Brush with the remaining butter and sprinkle over the sesame seeds.

6 Bake for about 25 minutes, or until golden and crisp. Leave the strudel to stand for 5 minutes before cutting into slices and serving.

SERVES FOUR

INGREDIENTS

65g/2½oz/5 tbsp butter
1 onion, chopped
2 carrots, coarsely grated
1 courgette (zucchini), chopped
350g/12oz firm potatoes, chopped
10ml/2 tsp mild curry paste
2.5ml/½ tsp dried thyme
150ml/¼ pint/⅔ cup water
1 egg, beaten
30ml/2 tbsp single (light) cream
50g/2oz/½ cup grated
 Cheddar cheese
8 sheets of filo pastry, thawed
 if frozen
sesame seeds, for sprinkling
salt and ground black pepper

1 Melt 25g/1oz/2 tbsp of the butter in a frying pan and cook the onion, carrots, courgette and potatoes for 5 minutes, tossing them to ensure they cook evenly. Stir in the curry paste and continue to cook the vegetables for 1–2 minutes more until tender.

RATATOUILLE AND FONTINA STRUDEL

MIX A COLOURFUL JUMBLE OF RATATOUILLE VEGETABLES WITH CHUNKS OF CREAMY FONTINA CHEESE, THEN WRAP IN SHEETS OF FILO AND BAKE FOR A DELICIOUS, SUMMERY PARTY PASTRY.

SERVES SIX

INGREDIENTS

1 small aubergine (eggplant), diced
45ml/3 tbsp extra virgin olive oil
1 onion, sliced
2 garlic cloves, crushed
1 red (bell) pepper, cored and sliced
1 yellow (bell) pepper, cored
  and sliced
2 courgettes (zucchini), cut into
  small chunks
generous pinch of dried
  mixed herbs
30ml/2 tbsp pine nuts
30ml/2 tbsp raisins
8 sheets of filo pastry, each
  measuring 30 × 18cm/12 × 7in,
  thawed if frozen
50g/2oz/¼ cup butter, melted
130g/4½oz/generous 1 cup diced
  Fontina cheese
salt and ground black pepper
dressed mixed salad, to serve

1 Layer all the diced aubergine in a colander, sprinkling each layer with salt. Drain over the sink for 20 minutes, then rinse well and pat dry.

2 Heat the oil in a large, heavy frying pan, add the onion, garlic, peppers and aubergine and gently fry over a low heat, stirring occasionally, for about 10 minutes until soft and golden.

VARIATION
Try a different cheese if you like: Bel Paese, Port Salut and Caerphilly all make suitable alternatives.

3 Add the courgettes, herbs and salt and pepper. Cook for 5 minutes until softened. Cool to room temperature, then stir in the pine nuts and raisins.

4 Preheat the oven to 180°C/350°F/ Gas 4. Brush two sheets of filo pastry with a little of the melted butter. Lay the filo sheets side by side, overlapping them slightly by about 5cm/2in, to make a large rectangle.

5 Cover with the remaining filo sheets, brushing each layer with melted butter. Spoon the vegetable mixture down one long side of the filo.

6 Sprinkle the cheese on top, then roll up and transfer to a non-stick baking sheet, curling the roll round in a circle. Brush with the remaining butter. Bake for 30 minutes, cool for 10 minutes, then slice and serve with mixed salad.

SALMON IN PUFF PASTRY

THIS FUN PARTY DISH HAS A VERY TASTY RICE, EGG AND SALMON FILLING, ENCASED IN AN ATTRACTIVE PUFF PASTRY CRUST. DON'T WORRY IF THE FISH SHAPE ISN'T PERFECT — THAT'S PART OF ITS APPEAL.

SERVES SIX

INGREDIENTS

   450g/1lb puff pastry
   1 egg, beaten
   3 eggs, hard-boiled and peeled
   90ml/6 tbsp single (light) cream
   200g/7oz/1¾ cups cooked long grain
     white rice
   30ml/2 tbsp finely chopped
     fresh parsley
   10ml/2 tsp chopped
     fresh tarragon
   675g/1½lb fresh salmon fillets
   40g/1½oz/3 tbsp butter
   juice of ½ lemon
   salt and ground black pepper

1 Preheat the oven to 190°C/375°F/ Gas 5. Roll out two-thirds of the pastry into a large oval, measuring 35cm/14in in length. Cut into a curved fish shape and place on a lightly greased large baking sheet.

2 Use the trimmings to make narrow strips. Brush one side of each strip with a little beaten egg and secure in place around the rim of the pastry to make a raised edge.

3 Prick the base all over with a fork, then bake for 8–10 minutes until the sides are well risen and the pastry is lightly golden. Leave to cool.

4 Mash the hard-boiled eggs with the cream in a bowl, then stir in the cooked rice. Add the parsley and tarragon and season well. Spoon this mixture on to the prepared pastry.

5 Cut the salmon into 2cm/¾in chunks. Melt the butter in a pan until it starts to sizzle, then add the salmon. Turn the pieces over in the butter so that they colour but do not cook through.

6 Remove from the heat and arrange the salmon on top of the rice. Stir the lemon juice into the butter in the pan, then spoon the juices over the filling.

7 Roll out the remaining pastry and cut out a rough semi-circle to cover the head portion and a tail shape to cover the tail. Brush both pieces of pastry with a little beaten egg and place on top of the fish, pressing the edges down firmly to secure. Score a criss-cross pattern on the tail.

8 Cut the remaining pastry into small rounds and, starting from the tail end, arrange the rounds in overlapping lines to represent scales. Press the edges to seal. Add a smaller round for the eye. Brush the whole fish shape with the remaining beaten egg.

9 Bake for 10 minutes, then lower the oven temperature to 160°C/325°F/Gas 3 and cook for a further 15–20 minutes until the pastry is golden all over. Slide on to a serving plate and serve.

VARIATION

If time is short, simply encase the salmon filling in a rectangular puff pastry parcel, scoring the top in a decorative criss-cross pattern.

MUSHROOM AND QUAIL'S EGG GOUGÈRE

GOUGÈRE IS A POPULAR PASTRY FROM THE BURGUNDY REGION OF FRANCE. IN THIS VERSION IT IS FILLED WITH WILD MUSHROOMS AND TINY, LIGHTLY BOILED QUAIL'S EGGS.

SERVES FOUR TO SIX

INGREDIENTS
  25g/1oz/¼ cup cornflour (cornstarch)
  150ml/¼ pint/⅔ cup mixed red wine
    and water
  25g/1oz/2 tbsp butter
  1 onion, chopped
  2 celery sticks, sliced
  350g/12oz/4–5 cups mixed wild and
    cultivated mushrooms, halved
    or quartered
  150ml/¼ pint/⅔ cup stock
  dash of Worcestershire sauce
  15ml/1 tbsp chopped fresh parsley
  12 quail's eggs
For the pastry
  75g/3oz/6 tbsp butter, diced
  2.5ml/½ tsp salt
  175ml/6fl oz/¾ cup water
  100g/3¾oz/scant 1 cup plain
    (all-purpose) flour, sifted
  4 eggs
  115g/4oz/1 cup grated
    Gruyère cheese

1 Preheat the oven to 220°F/425°C/ Gas 7. To make the pastry, melt the butter in a pan with the salt and water, and bring to the boil. Remove from the heat, add all the flour and beat with a wooden spoon until it forms a ball.

2 Return the pan to the heat and cook, beating hard, for 1–2 minutes. Leave to cool slightly. Add two eggs, beating until the mixture becomes glossy. Beat in the third egg, then beat in as much of the fourth egg as you need to create glossy, soft pastry. Beat in half the cheese.

3 Place a round of baking parchment on a large baking sheet and place large spoonfuls of the choux pastry evenly in a 20cm/8in circle. Position them close together so that they will join up as they cook. Bake the choux pastry for about 30 minutes until well risen and golden all over. Remove from the oven, cut a few slits in the side to release the steam and set aside to cool slightly.

4 Mix the cornflour and wine and water in a bowl. Meanwhile, melt the butter in a pan, add the onion and celery and fry until soft. Add the mushrooms and cook gently, then add the wine mixture.

5 Add the stock to the mushrooms and gradually stir in the cornflour mixture. Cook gently until it is starting to thicken. Add the Worcestershire sauce and parsley, and cook until thick.

6 Place the quail's eggs in a pan of cold water, bring to the boil and cook for 1 minute. Cool thoroughly, then peel.

7 To serve, slice the gougère in half horizontally. Fill with the mushroom mixture and top with the eggs. Replace the pastry lid, sprinkle over the remaining cheese and return to the oven until the cheese melts.

SCALLOPS WITH WILD MUSHROOMS

FROM THE DEPTHS OF THE SEA AND THE FOREST FLOOR COME TWO FLAVOURS THAT MARRY PERFECTLY IN A SMOOTH CREAMY SAUCE. CRISP PASTRY COMPLETES THE DISH.

SERVES FOUR

INGREDIENTS
  350g/12oz puff pastry
  1 egg, beaten
  75g/3oz/6 tbsp butter
  12 scallops, trimmed and
    thickly sliced
  2 shallots, chopped
  ½ celery stick, cut into strips
  ½ carrot, cut into strips
  225g/8oz/3 cups assorted wild
    mushrooms, trimmed and sliced
  60ml/4 tbsp Noilly Prat or other
    dry vermouth
  150ml/¼ pint/⅔ cup crème fraîche
  4 egg yolks
  15ml/1 tbsp lemon juice
  salt, ground black pepper, celery salt
    and cayenne pepper

1 Roll out the puff pastry on a floured surface, then cut out four 13cm/5in shell shapes, using a paper template if you need to. Mark a shell pattern on each with a small knife then brush with a little beaten egg. Place on a baking sheet, then chill for 1 hour. Preheat the oven to 200°C/400°F/Gas 6.

2 Melt 25g/1oz/2 tbsp of the butter in a pan. Season the scallops with salt and black pepper, add them to the pan and cook for 30 seconds over a high heat. Transfer to a plate.

3 Score an inner shell 2.5cm/1in from the outer edge of each pastry shape. Bake the shapes for 20–25 minutes until golden. Set aside on a wire rack.

4 Fry the shallots, celery and carrot gently in the remaining butter. Add the mushrooms and cook until the juices begin to run. Pour in the vermouth and then increase the heat to evaporate the pan juices. Add the crème fraîche and cooked scallops and bring to a simmer (do not boil).

5 Remove the pan from the heat and blend in the egg yolks. Return the pan to a gentle heat and cook for a moment or two until the sauce has thickened to the consistency of thin cream, then remove the pan from the heat. Season with celery salt and cayenne pepper, and add the lemon juice.

6 Gently split the pastry shapes open and place the bases on four plates. Spoon in the filling and arrange the lids on top. Serve with potatoes and salad, if you like.

COOK'S TIP
Take care not to use dark mushrooms in a cream sauce as they will cause it to become an unattractive grey colour.

SEAFOOD GOUGÈRE

IN THIS RECIPE, THE CHOUX PASTRY IS BAKED AT THE SAME TIME AS ITS FILLING OF LIGHTLY SPICED HADDOCK WITH MUSHROOMS. THIS IS AN EASY-TO-PREPARE YET IMPRESSIVE SUPPER DISH.

SERVES FOUR

INGREDIENTS
130g/4½oz/1 cup plus 30ml/2 tbsp
   plain (all-purpose) flour
1.5ml/¼ tsp salt
130g/4½oz/9 tbsp butter
200ml/7fl oz/scant 1 cup water
3 eggs, beaten
150g/5oz Emmenthal or Gruyère
   cheese, grated
250g/9oz smoked haddock fillet
1 bay leaf
250ml/8fl oz/l cup milk
1 small red onion, chopped
150g/5oz/2–2½ cups white (button)
   mushrooms, sliced
5ml/1 tsp mild curry paste (optional)
fresh lemon juice
30ml/2 tbsp chopped fresh parsley
salt and ground black pepper

1 Lightly grease a shallow ovenproof dish. Sift 100g/3¾oz/scant 1 cup of the flour on to a sheet of baking parchment and add the salt. Place 75g/3oz/6 tbsp of the butter in a pan. Add the water and heat gently. As soon as the butter has melted, bring the water to the boil. tip in the flour mixture and beat well.

2 When the mixture comes away from the sides of the pan and forms a soft, smooth paste, remove the pan from the heat and leave to cool for 5 minutes.

COOK'S TIP
Choose pale yellow, traditionally smoked haddock rather than vividly dyed, bright yellow fillets.

3 Slowly work the beaten eggs into the dough, beating well, until the mixture has the consistency of creamy mashed potato. You may not need all the egg. Stir in two-thirds of the grated cheese.

4 Spoon the choux pastry around the edge of the prepared dish, making sure it comes well up the sides. Set aside.

5 Preheat the oven to 180°C/350°F/ Gas 4. Put the haddock in a baking dish with the bay leaf. Pour in the milk, cover and bake for 15 minutes until just cooked. Lift out the fish and set aside. Discard the bay leaf but retain the milk.

6 Melt the remaining butter in a frying pan. Add the onion and mushrooms and sauté for about 5 minutes. Mix in the curry paste, if using, then add the remaining flour. Gradually stir in the hot milk. Heat, stirring, until the sauce is smooth. Simmer for 2–3 minutes, then add the lemon juice, parsley, and salt and pepper to taste.

7 Increase the oven temperature to 200°C/400°F/Gas 6. Skin the haddock and flake the flesh and then spoon it into the centre of the uncooked choux pastry, along with the mushroom mixture, spreading it evenly. Sprinkle over with the rest of the cheese. Bake for 35–40 minutes until the filling is cooked and the gougère has risen and is golden brown. Serve at once.

VARIATIONS
For an alternative filling use cooked chicken in place of the haddock. Both the choux pastry and the filling can be flavoured with blue cheese instead of those listed. As the flavour will be stronger, use 115g/4oz in total.

TUNA AND EGG GALETTE

READY-ROLLED PUFF PASTRY IS USED IN THIS EASY-TO-MAKE COLOURFUL PIE. IF YOU PREFER TO MAKE YOUR OWN PASTRY, YOU WILL NEED 500G/1¼LB.

SERVES FOUR

INGREDIENTS

2 sheets of ready-rolled puff pastry
1 egg, beaten
60ml/4 tbsp olive oil
175g/6oz tuna steak
2 onions, sliced
1 red (bell) pepper, chopped
2 garlic cloves, crushed
45ml/3 tbsp capers, drained
5ml/1 tsp grated lemon rind
30ml/2 tbsp lemon juice
5 eggs
salt and ground black pepper
30ml/2 tbsp chopped flat leaf
  parsley, to garnish

1 Preheat the oven to 190°C/375°F/ Gas 5. Lay one sheet of puff pastry on a lightly floured baking sheet and cut to a 28 × 18cm/11 × 7in rectangle. Glaze the whole sheet with beaten egg.

2 Cut the second sheet of puff pastry to the same dimensions. Cut out the centre and reserve for another recipe, leaving a 2.5cm/1in border. Carefully lift the pastry border on to the first sheet. Brush the border with beaten egg and prick the base with a fork.

3 Bake the pastry case in the hot oven for about 15 minutes until golden and well risen.

4 Heat 30ml/2 tbsp of the oil in a frying pan and fry the tuna steak for about 3 minutes on each side until golden but still pale pink in the middle. Transfer to a plate and flake into small pieces.

5 Add the remaining oil to the pan and fry the onions, red pepper and garlic for 6–8 minutes until softened, stirring occasionally. Remove the pan from the heat and stir in the tuna, capers and lemon rind and juice. Season well.

6 Spoon the filling into the pastry case and level the surface with the back of a spoon. Break the eggs into the filling, cover the tart with lightly oiled foil, and return to the oven for about 10 minutes, or until the eggs have just cooked through. Garnish with chopped parsley and serve at once.

COOK'S TIP
If you are using fresh, unfrozen pastry, the rectangle of pastry you cut out can be wrapped in clear film (plastic wrap) and frozen. Thaw at room temperature for 1 hour before using.

MEDITERRANEAN ONE-CRUST PIE

THIS FREE-FORM PIE ENCASES A RICH TOMATO, AUBERGINE AND KIDNEY BEAN FILLING. IF YOUR
PASTRY CRACKS, JUST PATCH IT UP — A ROUGH APPEARANCE ADDS TO THE PIE'S RUSTIC CHARACTER.

SERVES FOUR

INGREDIENTS
   500g/1¼1b aubergine
      (eggplant), cubed
   1 red (bell) pepper
   30ml/2 tbsp olive oil
   1 large onion, finely chopped
   1 courgette (zucchini), sliced
   2 garlic cloves, crushed
   15ml/1 tbsp chopped fresh oregano
      or 5ml/1 tsp dried, plus extra fresh
      oregano to garnish
   200g/7oz can red kidney beans,
      drained and rinsed
   115g/4oz/1 cup pitted black
      olives, rinsed
   150ml/¼ pint/⅔ cup passata (bottled
      strained tomatoes)
   1 egg, beaten, or a little milk
   30ml/2 tbsp semolina
   salt and ground black pepper
For the pastry
   75g/3oz/⅔ cup plain
      (all-purpose) flour
   75g/3oz/⅔ cup wholemeal
      (whole-wheat) flour
   75g/3oz/6 tbsp vegetable margarine
   50g/2oz/⅔ cup freshly grated
      Parmesan cheese
   60–90ml/4–6 tbsp chilled water

1 Preheat the oven to 220°C/425°F/ Gas 7. To make the pastry, sift both the flours into a bowl, tipping the bran into the bowl. Rub or cut in the margarine until the mixture resembles breadcrumbs, then stir in the Parmesan. Mix in just enough chilled water to form a firm dough. Chill for 30 minutes.

2 Transfer the dough to a lightly floured surface and knead into a smooth ball. Wrap in cling film (plastic wrap) and chill for 30 minutes.

3 To make the filling, place the aubergine in a colander and sprinkle with salt, then leave for 30 minutes. Rinse and pat dry with kitchen paper. Meanwhile, place the red pepper on a baking sheet and roast in the oven for 20 minutes. Put the pepper in a plastic bag. When cool, remove, peel and seed, then dice the flesh. Set aside.

4 Heat the oil in a large frying pan. Add the onion and fry for 5 minutes until softened and translucent, stirring occasionally. Add the aubergine and fry for 5 minutes until tender.

5 Add the sliced courgettes, garlic and oregano, and cook for 5 minutes more, stirring often. Add the kidney beans and olives, stir well, then add the passata and season to taste with salt and black pepper. Cook until heated through, then set aside to cool.

6 Roll out the pastry on a lightly floured surface to a rough 30cm/12in round. Place on a lightly oiled baking sheet. Brush with beaten egg or milk, sprinkle over the semolina, leaving a 4cm/1½in border, then spoon over the filling.

7 Gather up the edges of the pastry to partly cover the filling – it should be open in the middle. Brush the pastry with the remaining egg or milk and bake for 30–35 minutes until golden.

Sweet Shortcrust and Choux Pastries

This is a tantalizing collection of small sweet pastries to suit any occasion. Chocolate Éclairs, with their rich and glossy topping, and more substantial Baked Apple Dumplings are perennial favourites, along with daintier tartlets, some made from flavoured pastries, including chocolate and coffee. Little pastries are found all around the world; try Gazelles' Horns with their orange-scented almond paste filling from Morocco or fragrant Greek Fruit and Nut Pastries.

SUMMER FRUIT BRÛLÉE TARTLETS

THIS QUANTITY OF PASTRY IS ENOUGH FOR EIGHT TARTLETS, SO FREEZE HALF FOR ANOTHER DAY. THE
BRÛLÉE TOPPING IS BEST ADDED NO MORE THAN TWO HOURS BEFORE THE TARTS ARE SERVED.

MAKES FOUR

INGREDIENTS
  4 egg yolks
  15ml/1 tbsp cornflour (cornstarch)
  50g/2oz/¼ cup caster
    (superfine) sugar
  a few drops of vanilla
    essence (extract)
  300ml/½ pint/¼ cups creamy milk
  225g/8oz/2 cups mixed
    summer fruits
  50g/2oz/½ cup icing
    (confectioners') sugar
For the pastry
  250g/9oz/2¼ cups plain
    (all-purpose) flour
  pinch of salt
  25g/1oz/¼ cup ground almonds
  15ml/1 tbsp icing
    (confectioners') sugar
  150g/5oz/⅔ cup chilled butter, diced
  1 egg yolk
  about 45ml/3 tbsp chilled water

1 To make the pastry, mix the flour,
salt, ground almonds and icing sugar in
a bowl. Cut or rub in the butter until the
mixture resembles fine breadcrumbs.
Add the egg yolk and enough chilled
water to form a soft dough. Knead the
dough gently, then cut it in half. Wrap
half in cling film (plastic wrap) and
freeze for use later.

2 Cut the remaining half of the pastry
into four equal pieces and roll them out
on a lightly floured surface. Stamp out
pastry rounds large enough to line four
tartlet tins (mini quiche pans).

3 Line the tins, using your fingers to
mould the pastry into the tin. Let the
excess pastry hang over the edges. Chill
for 30 minutes. Meanwhile, preheat the
oven to 200°C/400°F/Gas 6.

4 Line the pastry cases with baking
parchment and baking beans. Bake
blind for 10 minutes. Remove the paper
and beans, and return to the oven for
5 minutes until golden. Allow to cool,
then trim carefully.

5 To make the custard filling, beat the
egg yolks, cornflour, caster sugar and
vanilla essence together in a bowl.

6 Warm the milk in a small pan, pour
it on to the egg yolk mixture, whisking
constantly, then return the mixture to
the cleaned pan. Heat the custard until
it thickens, stirring all the time, but do
not let it boil. Remove from the heat,
press a circle of baking parchment
directly on the custard's surface and
leave to cool.

7 Sprinkle the fruits in the tartlet cases
and spoon over the custard. Chill the
tartlets for 2 hours.

8 Preheat the grill (broiler) to the
highest setting. Sift the icing sugar over
the tops of the tartlets. Place the tartlets
under the hot grill until the sugar melts
and caramelizes. Allow the topping to
cool and harden for about 10 minutes
before serving the tartlets on individual
dessert plates.

VARIATION
Instead of mixed summer fruit, such as
strawberries, raspberries, blackcurrants
and redcurrants, use a single variety, or
try these tartlets with pitted cherries.

RED GRAPE AND CHEESE TARTLETS

Fruit and cheese make a natural combination in this simple recipe. Look out for small, pale, mauve-coloured or red grapes. These are often seedless, and sweeter than large black varieties.

MAKES SIX

INGREDIENTS
    225g/8oz/1 cup curd (farmer's) cheese
    150ml/¼ pint/⅔ cup double
        (heavy) cream
    2.5ml/½ tsp vanilla essence (extract)
    30ml/2 tbsp icing
        (confectioners') sugar
    200g/7oz/2 cups red grapes, halved,
        seeded if necessary
    60ml/4 tbsp apricot conserve
    15ml/1 tbsp water
For the pastry
    200g/7oz/1¾ cups plain
        (all-purpose) flour
    15ml/1 tbsp caster (superfine) sugar
    150g/5oz/⅔ cup butter
    2 egg yolks
    15ml/1 tbsp chilled water

1 To make the pastry, sift the flour and sugar into a mixing bowl. Rub or cut in the butter until the mixture resembles fine breadcrumbs.

2 Add the egg yolks and water and mix to a dough. Knead lightly until smooth. Wrap and chill for 30 minutes.

3 Preheat the oven to 200°C/400°F/ Gas 6. Roll out the pastry and use to line six deep 10cm/4in fluted tartlet tins (mini quiche pans). Prick the bases and line with foil and baking beans. Bake for 10 minutes, remove the foil and beans, then bake for a further 5 minutes until golden. Remove the pastry cases from the tins and cool.

4 Meanwhile, beat the curd cheese, double cream, vanilla essence and icing sugar in a small bowl. Divide the mixture among the pastry cases. Smooth the surface and arrange the halved grapes attractively on top.

5 Sieve the apricot conserve into a pan. Add the water and heat, stirring constantly, until smooth and glossy. Generously spoon the apricot glaze over the grapes. Leave to cool, then chill before serving.

TIA MARIA TRUFFLE TARTLETS

SOPHISTICATED AND SERIOUSLY INDULGENT, THESE MINI COFFEE PASTRY CASES ARE FILLED WITH A
CHOCOLATE LIQUEUR TRUFFLE CENTRE AND TOPPED WITH FRESH RIPE BERRIES.

SERVES SIX

INGREDIENTS
   300ml/½ pint/1¼ cups double
     (heavy) cream
   225g/8oz/generous ¾ cup seedless
     blackberry or raspberry jam
   150g/5oz plain (semisweet)
     chocolate, broken up
   45ml/3 tbsp Tia Maria liqueur
   450g/1lb/4 cups mixed berries
For the pastry
   225g/8oz/2 cups plain
     (all-purpose) flour
   15ml/1 tbsp caster (superfine) sugar
   150g/5oz/⅔ cup butter, diced
   1 egg yolk
   30ml/2 tbsp very strong brewed
     coffee, chilled

1 Preheat the oven to 200°C/400°F/ Gas 6, placing a large baking sheet in the oven to heat. To make the pastry, sift the flour and sugar into a large bowl. Rub or cut in the butter until the mixture resembles fine breadcrumbs. Blend the egg yolk with the coffee, add to the bowl and mix to a stiff dough. Knead on a floured surface for a few seconds until smooth. Wrap in clear film (plastic wrap) and chill for 20 minutes.

2 Roll out the pastry and use to line six 10cm/4in fluted tartlet tins (mini quiche pans). Prick the bases with a fork and line with foil and baking beans. Place on the hot baking sheet and bake for 10 minutes. Remove the foil and beans, and bake for a further 8–10 minutes. Allow to cool in the tins.

3 To make the filling, slowly bring the cream and 175g/6oz/generous ½ cup of the jam to the boil, stirring constantly.

4 Remove the pan from the heat, add the chocolate and 30ml/2 tbsp of the liqueur. Stir until melted. Leave to cool, then spoon the mixture into the pastry cases, and smooth the tops. Place on a baking tray and chill for 40 minutes.

5 Heat the remaining jam and liqueur and stir until smooth. Arrange the fruit on the tarts, then brush the jam glaze over. Chill until ready to serve.

COOK'S TIP
When making the pastry, the yolk and coffee must be blended together until very well mixed to ensure that the pastry is evenly coloured.

LEMON CURD TARTS

THESE TASTY LITTLE TARTS ARE A POPULAR TEA-TIME TREAT IN THE NORTH OF ENGLAND. THEY HAVE A CURD CHEESE AND CURRANT FILLING ON A TANGY LAYER OF LEMON CURD.

MAKES TWENTY-FOUR

INGREDIENTS
    225g/8oz/1 cup curd
      (farmer's) cheese
    2 eggs, beaten
    75g/3oz/6 tbsp caster
      (superfine) sugar
    5ml/1 tsp finely grated lemon rind
    50g/2oz/¼ cup currants
    60ml/4 tbsp lemon curd
    thick cream, to serve
For the pastry
    275g/10oz/2½ cups plain
      (all-purpose) flour
    pinch of salt
    75g/3oz/6 tbsp butter, diced
    50g/2oz/¼ cup lard or white
      vegetable fat
    60ml/4 tbsp chilled water

VARIATION
For a more sophisticated flavour, add a little brandy to the filling.

1 To make the pastry, sift the flour and salt into a mixing bowl. Rub or cut in the fat until the mixture resembles fine breadcrumbs. Sprinkle the water over the dry ingredients and mix to a dough. Knead on a lightly floured surface for a few seconds until smooth. Chill.

2 Preheat the oven to 180°C/350°F/ Gas 4. Roll out the pastry thinly, stamp out 24 rounds using a 7.5cm/3in plain pastry cutter and use to line mini muffin or cupcake tins. Chill until required.

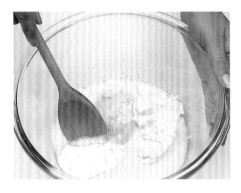

3 Cream the curd cheese with the eggs, sugar and lemon rind in a bowl. Stir in the currants. Place 2.5ml/½ tsp of the lemon curd in the base of each tartlet case. Spoon on the filling, flatten the tops and bake for 35–40 minutes until just turning golden. Serve warm or cold, topped with thick cream.

COOK'S TIP
The pastry can be made in advance and frozen. Line the tins with pastry, wrap in clear film (plastic wrap) and store.

PECAN TASSIES

CREAM CHEESE PASTRY HAS A RICH FLAVOUR THAT GOES WELL WITH THE PECAN FILLING IN THESE TINY TARTLETS, WHICH TAKE THEIR NAME FROM A SCOTTISH WORD MEANING "A SMALL CUP".

MAKES TWENTY-FOUR

INGREDIENTS
   2 eggs
   175g/6oz/¾ cup firmly packed soft
     dark brown sugar
   5ml/1 tsp vanilla essence (extract)
   large pinch of salt
   25g/1oz/2 tbsp butter, melted
   115g/4oz/1 cup pecan nuts
For the pastry
   115g/4oz/½ cup butter
   400g/14oz/1¾ cups cream cheese
   115g/4oz/1 cup plain
     (all-purpose) flour

1 Place a baking sheet in the oven and preheat to 180°C/350°F/Gas 4. Grease two 12-cup mini muffin or cupcake tins. To make the pastry, cut the butter and cream cheese into pieces and place in a mixing bowl. Sift over the flour and mix to a smooth dough.

3 To make the filling, whisk the eggs in a bowl. Whisk in the brown sugar, a few tablespoons at a time, then add the vanilla, salt and butter. Set aside.

5 Place a spoonful of chopped nuts in each mini muffin cup and cover with the filling. Set a pecan half on the top of each. Bake on the hot baking sheet for about 20 minutes, until puffed and set. Transfer to a rack to cool. Serve at room temperature.

2 Roll out the dough thinly, then, using a 6cm/2½in fluted pastry cutter, stamp out 24 rounds. Line the mini muffin cups with the rounds and chill.

4 Reserve 24 undamaged pecan halves for the decoration and chop the rest.

BAKED APPLE DUMPLINGS

*A TREAT TO TEMPT THE MOST DETERMINED DIETER. THE SHARPNESS OF THE FRUIT CONTRASTS
PERFECTLY WITH THE MAPLE SYRUP DRIZZLED OVER THIS DELIGHTFUL PASTRY PARCEL.*

4 Cut pastry rounds to cover the tops of the apples. Reserve the trimmings. Combine the sugar, cream and vanilla essence in a small bowl. Spoon into the hollow of each apple.

5 Place a pastry circle on top of each apple, then bring up the sides of the pastry square to enclose it, pleating the larger piece of pastry to make a snug fit around the apple. Moisten the joins where they overlap.

6 Make apple stalks and leaves from the pastry trimmings and decorate the dumplings. Set them in a large greased baking dish, at least 2cm/¾in apart. Bake for 30 minutes, then lower the oven temperature to 180°C/350°F/Gas 4 and continue baking for 20 minutes more until the pastry is golden brown and the apples are tender.

7 Transfer the dumplings to a serving dish. Mix the maple syrup with the juices in the baking dish and drizzle over the dumplings. Serve hot with whipped cream.

SERVES EIGHT

INGREDIENTS
    8 firm cooking apples, peeled
    1 egg white
    130g/4½oz/⅔ cup caster
      (superfine) sugar
    45ml/3 tbsp double (heavy) cream,
      plus extra whipped cream, to serve
    2.5ml/½ tsp vanilla essence (extract)
    250ml/8fl oz/1 cup maple syrup
For the pastry
    475g/1lb 2oz/4½ cups plain
      (all-purpose) flour
    2.5ml/½ tsp salt
    350g/12oz/1½ cups butter or white
      vegetable fat, diced
    175–250ml/6–8fl oz/¾–1 cup
      chilled water

1 To make the pastry, sift the flour and salt into a large bowl. Rub or cut in the butter or fat until the mixture resembles fine breadcrumbs.

2 Sprinkle over 175ml/6fl oz/¾ cup water and mix until the dough holds together, adding a little more water if necessary. Gather into a ball. Wrap the dough in clear film (plastic wrap) and chill for at least 20 minutes. Preheat the oven to 220°C/425°F/Gas 7.

3 Cutting from the stem end, core the apples without cutting through the base. Roll out the pastry thinly. Cut squares almost large enough to enclose the apples; brush with egg white and set an apple in the centre of each.

GREEK FRUIT AND NUT PASTRIES

AROMATIC SWEET PASTRY CRESCENTS, KNOWN AS MOSHOPOUNGIA *IN* GREECE, *ARE PACKED WITH CANDIED CITRUS PEEL AND WALNUTS, WHICH HAVE BEEN SOAKED IN A COFFEE SYRUP.*

MAKES SIXTEEN

INGREDIENTS
  60ml/4 tbsp clear honey
  60ml/4 tbsp strong brewed coffee
  75g/3oz/½ cup mixed candied citrus
    peel, finely chopped
  175g/6oz/1½ cups walnuts, chopped
  1.5ml/¼ tsp freshly grated nutmeg
  milk, to glaze
  caster (superfine) sugar,
    for sprinkling
For the pastry
  450g/1lb/4 cups plain
    (all purpose) flour
  2.5ml/½ tsp ground cinnamon
  2.5ml/½ tsp baking powder
  pinch of salt
  150g/5oz/⅔ cup butter
  30ml/2 tbsp caster (superfine) sugar
  1 egg
  120ml/4fl oz/½ cup chilled milk

1 Preheat the oven to 180°C/350°F/ Gas 4. To make the pastry, sift the flour, cinnamon, baking powder and salt into a bowl. Rub or cut in the butter until the mixture resembles breadcrumbs. Stir in the sugar. Make a well.

2 Beat the egg and milk together and pour into the well in the dry ingredients. Mix to a soft dough. Divide the dough into two and wrap each piece in clear film (plastic wrap). Chill for 30 minutes.

3 Meanwhile, mix the honey and coffee in a mixing bowl. Add the candied peel, walnuts and nutmeg. Stir well, cover and leave for 20 minutes.

4 Roll out one portion of the dough on a lightly floured surface to a thickness of 3mm/⅛in. Stamp out rounds, using a 10cm/4in plain pastry cutter.

5 Place a heaped teaspoonful of filling on one side of each round. Brush the edges with a little milk, then fold over and press together to seal. Repeat with the second piece of pastry until all the filling has been used.

6 Place the pastries on lightly greased baking sheets, brush with a little milk and sprinkle with caster sugar. Make a steam hole in each with a skewer. Bake for 35 minutes, or until lightly browned. Cool on a wire rack.

VARIATION
Instead of the walnuts, use pecan nuts or almonds, if you prefer.

BAKED SWEET RAVIOLI

THESE DELICIOUS SWEET RAVIOLI ARE MADE WITH A RICH PASTRY FLAVOURED WITH LEMON AND
FILLED WITH A MIXTURE OF RICOTTA CHEESE, FRUIT AND CHOCOLATE.

SERVES FOUR

INGREDIENTS
   175g/6oz/¾ cup ricotta cheese
   50g/2oz/¼ cup caster
     (superfine) sugar
   4ml/¾ tsp vanilla essence (extract)
   small egg, beaten, plus 1 egg yolk
   15ml/1 tbsp mixed candied fruits
   25g/1oz dark (bittersweet) chocolate,
     finely chopped
For the pastry
   225g/8oz/2 cups plain
     (all-purpose) flour
   65g/2½oz/⅓ cup caster
     (superfine) sugar
   90g/3½oz/scant ½ cup butter, diced
   1 egg
   5ml/1 tsp finely grated lemon rind

1 To make the pastry, place the flour and sugar in a food processor and, with the motor running at full speed, slowly add the butter until fully worked into the mixture. Keep the motor running while you add the egg and lemon rind. The mixture should form a dough that just holds together.

2 Transfer the dough to a sheet of clear film (plastic wrap), cover with another sheet of clear film and flatten into a round. Chill the pastry while you make the filling.

3 Press the ricotta through a sieve into a mixing bowl. Stir in the sugar, vanilla essence, egg yolk, candied fruits and dark chocolate.

4 Remove the pastry round from the refrigerator and allow it to come back to room temperature. Divide it in half and roll each half between sheets of clear film to make a rectangle measuring 15 × 56cm/6 × 22in. Preheat the oven to 180°C/350°F/Gas 4.

5 Arrange heaped tablespoonfuls of the filling in two rows along one of the pastry strips, leaving a 2.5cm/1in margin around each. Brush the pastry between the mounds of filling with beaten egg. Place the second strip of pastry on top and press down between each mound of filling to seal.

6 Use a 6cm/2½in plain pastry cutter to cut around each mound of filling to make small circular ravioli. Gently pinch each ravioli with your fingertips to seal the edges.

7 Place the ravioli on a greased baking sheet and bake for 15 minutes until golden brown. Serve warm, sprinkled with lemon rind, icing (confectioners') sugar and grated chocolate, if you wish.

GAZELLES' HORNS

THESE HORN-SHAPED PASTRIES, FILLED WITH ALMOND PASTE, ARE COMMONLY SERVED AT WEDDING CEREMONIES IN THEIR NATIVE MOROCCO, WHERE THEY ARE A FIRM FAVOURITE.

MAKES ABOUT SIXTEEN

INGREDIENTS
  200g/7oz/scant 2 cups ground
    almonds
  115g/4oz/1 cup icing
    (confectioners') sugar, plus
    extra for dusting
  30ml/2 tbsp orange flower water
  25g/1oz/2 tbsp butter, melted
  2 egg yolks, beaten
  2.5ml/½ tsp ground cinnamon
For the pastry
  200g/7oz/1¾ cups plain
    (all-purpose) flour
  pinch of salt
  25g/1oz/2 tbsp butter, melted
  about 30ml/2 tbsp orange
    flower water
  1 egg yolk, beaten
  60–90ml/4–6 tbsp chilled water

1 Mix the ground almonds, icing sugar, orange flower water, melted butter, egg yolks and cinnamon in a mixing bowl to make a smooth paste.

2 To make the pastry, sift the flour and salt into a large bowl, then stir in the melted butter, orange flower water and about three-quarters of the egg yolk. Stir in enough chilled water to make a fairly soft dough.

3 Quickly and lightly, knead the pastry until it is smooth and elastic, then place it on a lightly floured surface and roll it out as thinly as possible. With a sharp knife, cut the dough into long strips about 7.5cm/3in wide.

4 Preheat the oven to 180°C/350°F/ Gas 4. Roll small pieces of the almond paste into thin sausages about 7.5cm/ 3in long with tapering ends.

5 Place these in a line along one side of the strips of pastry, about 3cm/1¼in apart. Dampen the pastry edges with water, then fold the other half of the strip over the filling and press the edges together firmly.

6 Using a pastry wheel, cut around each pastry sausage to make a crescent shape. Make sure that the edges are firmly pinched together.

7 Prick the crescents with a fork and place on a buttered baking sheet. Brush with the remaining beaten egg yolk and bake for 12–16 minutes until lightly coloured. Allow to cool, then dust with icing sugar.

WHISKY-LACED MINCE PIES

MINCEMEAT GETS THE LUXURY TREATMENT WITH THE ADDITION OF GLACÉ PINEAPPLE, CHERRIES AND WHISKY TO MAKE A MARVELLOUS FILLING FOR THESE TRADITIONAL FESTIVE PIES. SERVING THEM WITH A DOLLOP OF WHISKY BUTTER IS PURE INDULGENCE.

MAKES TWELVE TO FIFTEEN

INGREDIENTS
225g/8oz/1 cup mincemeat
50g/2oz/¼ cup glacé (candied)
  pineapple, chopped
50g/2oz/¼ cup glacé (candied)
  cherries, chopped
30ml/2 tbsp whisky
1 egg, beaten or a little milk
icing (confectioners') sugar,
  for dusting
For the pastry
1 egg yolk
5ml/1 tsp grated orange rind
15ml/1 tbsp caster
  (superfine) sugar
225g/8oz/2 cups plain
  (all-purpose) flour
150g/5oz/⅔ cup butter, diced
For the whisky butter
75g/3oz/6 tbsp butter, softened
175g/6oz/1½ cups icing
  (confectioners') sugar, sifted
30ml/2 tbsp whisky
5ml/1 tsp grated orange rind

1 To make the pastry, mix the egg yolk with the orange rind, caster sugar and 10ml/2 tsp chilled water in a small bowl and set aside. Sift the flour into a separate mixing bowl.

VARIATIONS
• Use either puff or filo pastry instead of shortcrust for a change.
• Replace the whisky in both the filling and the flavoured butter with Cointreau or brandy, if you like.

2 Rub or cut in the butter into the flour until the mixture resembles fine breadcrumbs. Stir in the egg mixture and mix to a dough. Wrap in clear film (plastic wrap) and chill for 30 minutes.

3 Mix the mincemeat, glacé pineapple and cherries in a small bowl. Spoon the whisky over and leave to soak.

4 Roll out three-quarters of the pastry. Stamp out fluted rounds and use to line 12–15 patty or cupcake tins. Roll out the remaining pastry thinly and stamp out star shapes.

5 Preheat the oven to 200°C/400°F/ Gas 6. Spoon a little filling into each pastry case and top with a star shape. Brush with a little beaten egg or milk and bake for 20–25 minutes until golden. Leave to cool.

6 Meanwhile, make the whisky butter. Place the butter, icing sugar, whisky and grated orange rind in a small bowl and beat with a wooden spoon until light and fluffy.

7 To serve, lift off each pastry star, pipe a whirl of whisky butter on top of the filling, then replace the star. Dust the mince pies with a little icing sugar.

GREEK CHOCOLATE MOUSSE TARTLETS

IF YOU ARE A CHOCOLATE FAN, YOU WILL ADORE THESE TARTS, WITH THEIR DARK RICH CHOCOLATE PASTRY, CREAMY FILLING AND YET MORE CHOCOLATE DRIZZLED OVER THE TOP.

SERVES SIX

INGREDIENTS

200g/7oz white chocolate, broken up
120ml/4fl oz/½ cup milk
10ml/2 tsp powdered gelatine
30ml/2 tbsp caster (superfine) sugar
5ml/1 tsp vanilla essence (extract)
2 eggs, separated
250g/9oz/generous 1 cup Greek-style
   (US strained plain) yogurt
melted dark (bittersweet) chocolate,
   to decorate
For the pastry
115g/4oz/1 cup plain
   (all-purpose) flour
25g/1oz/¼ cup icing
   (confectioners') sugar
25g/1oz/¼ cup cocoa powder
   (unsweetened)
75g/3oz/6 tbsp butter
2 eggs
2.5ml/½ tsp vanilla essence (extract)

1 To make the pastry, sift the flour, sugar and cocoa powder into a mixing bowl. Rub or cut in the butter until the mixture resembles fine breadcrumbs.

2 Mix together the eggs and vanilla essence in a small bowl, then add to the dry ingredients and mix to a soft dough. Tip out on to a lightly floured surface and knead lightly until smooth. Wrap in clear film (plastic wrap) and chill for 20 minutes.

3 Roll out the pastry and use to line six deep 10cm/4in loose-based tartlet tins (mini quiche pans). Cover and chill for a further 20 minutes. Meanwhile, preheat the oven to 190°C/375°F/Gas 5.

4 Prick the base of each pastry case all over using a fork, then line with baking parchment, fill with baking beans and bake blind for 10 minutes.

5 Remove the paper and beans, return the cases to the oven and bake for a further 15 minutes, or until the pastry is firm. Cool completely in the tins.

6 To make the filling, melt the white chocolate in a heatproof bowl set over a pan of hot water. Pour the milk into a pan, sprinkle over the gelatine and heat gently, stirring, until the gelatine has all dissolved. Remove from the heat and stir in the chocolate.

7 Whisk together the sugar, vanilla essence and egg yolks in a large bowl, then beat in the chocolate mixture. Beat in the yogurt until evenly mixed. Chill until beginning to set.

8 Whisk the egg whites in a grease-free bowl until stiff, then gently fold into the mixture. Divide among the pastry cases and leave to set. Drizzle the melted dark chocolate over the tartlets in a random pattern to decorate.

COFFEE CREAM PROFITEROLES

CRISP-TEXTURED COFFEE CHOUX PASTRY PUFFS ARE FILLED WITH CREAM AND DRIZZLED WITH A WHITE CHOCOLATE SAUCE. FOR THOSE WITH A SWEET TOOTH, THERE IS PLENTY OF EXTRA SAUCE.

SERVES SIX

INGREDIENTS
   50g/2oz/¼ cup granulated sugar
   100ml/3¾fl oz/scant ½ cup water
   150g/5oz good quality white
      chocolate, broken up
   25g/1oz/2 tbsp butter
   300ml/½ pint/1¼ cups double
      (heavy) cream
   30ml/2 tbsp coffee liqueur, such as
      Tia Maria or Kahlúa
For the pastry
   65g/2½oz/9 tbsp plain
      (all-purpose) flour
   pinch of salt
   50g/2oz/¼ cup butter, diced
   150ml/¼ pint/⅔ cup freshly
      brewed coffee
   2 eggs, lightly beaten

1 Preheat the oven to 220°C/425°F/ Gas 7. To make the pastry, sift the flour and salt on to a sheet of baking parchment and set aside. Put the butter into a pan with the coffee. Bring to a rolling boil, then remove the pan from the heat and tip in all the flour. Beat vigorously with a wooden spoon until the mixture forms a ball and comes away from the sides of the pan. Leave to cool for 2 minutes.

2 Gradually add the beaten eggs to the flour mixture, beating thoroughly after each addition, until they are fully incorporated and you have a smooth consistency. Spoon the mixture into a piping (pastry) bag fitted with a 1cm/ ½in plain nozzle.

3 Pipe about 24 small buns on to a dampened baking sheet. Bake for about 20 minutes, then transfer to a wire rack. Pierce each bun with a knife to let out the steam. Leave the buns to cool.

4 To make the sauce, put the sugar and water in a pan and heat gently until the sugar has dissolved. Bring to the boil, then simmer for about 3 minutes. Remove the pan from the heat and add the chocolate and butter, stirring until smooth. Stir in 45ml/3 tbsp of the cream and the coffee liqueur. Keep warm or cool to room temperature.

5 To assemble, whip the remaining cream in a small bowl until soft peaks form. Spoon the cream into a piping bag and use to fill the buns through the slits in the sides. Pile on a large plate and pour a little sauce over. Serve the remaining sauce separately.

CHOCOLATE ECLAIRS

MANY OF THE ÉCLAIRS SOLD IN FRENCH CAKE SHOPS ARE FILLED WITH CRÈME PÂTISSIÈRE. HERE, THE CRISP CHOUX PASTRY FINGERS ARE FILLED WITH FRESH CREAM, SLIGHTLY SWEETENED AND FLAVOURED WITH VANILLA, AND THE ÉCLAIRS ARE THICKLY COATED IN DARK CHOCOLATE.

MAKES TWELVE

INGREDIENTS
300ml/½ pint/1¼ cups double
  (heavy) cream
10ml/2 tsp icing (confectioners')
  sugar, sifted
1.5ml/¼ tsp vanilla essence (extract)
115g/4oz plain (semisweet)
  chocolate
30ml/2 tbsp water
25g/1oz/2 tbsp butter
For the pastry
65g/2½oz/9 tbsp plain
  (all-purpose) flour
pinch of salt
50g/2oz/¼ cup butter, diced
150ml/¼ pint/⅔ cup water
2 eggs, lightly beaten

3 Return the pan to a low heat, then beat the mixture until it leaves the sides of the pan and forms a ball. Set the pan aside and allow to cool for 2–3 minutes.

4 Add the beaten eggs, a little at a time, beating well after each addition, until you have a smooth, shiny paste, which is thick enough to hold its shape.

1 Preheat the oven to 200°C/400°F/Gas 6. Grease a large baking sheet and line with baking parchment. To make the pastry, sift the flour and salt on to a small sheet of baking parchment. Heat the butter and water in a pan very gently until the butter melts.

2 Increase the heat and bring to a rolling boil. Remove the pan from the heat and immediately tip in all the flour. Beat vigorously with a wooden spoon until the flour is mixed into the liquid.

COOK'S TIP
When melting the chocolate, ensure that the bowl does not touch the hot water and keep the heat low. If the chocolate gets too hot, it will become unworkable.

5 Spoon the choux pastry into a piping (pastry) bag fitted with a 2.5cm/1in plain nozzle. Pipe 10cm/4in lengths on to the prepared baking sheet. Use a wet knife to cut off the pastry at the nozzle.

6 Bake for 25–30 minutes, or until the pastries are well risen and golden brown. Remove from the oven and make a neat slit along the side of each to release the steam. Lower the oven temperature to 180°C/350°F/Gas 4 and bake for a further 5 minutes. Cool on a wire rack.

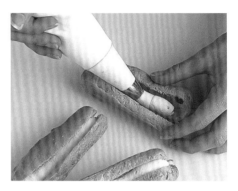

7 To make the filling, whip the cream with the icing sugar and vanilla essence until it just holds its shape. Spoon into a piping bag fitted with a 1cm/½in plain nozzle and use to fill the éclairs.

8 Place the chocolate and water in a small bowl set over a pan of hot water. Melt, stirring until smooth. Remove from the heat and gradually stir in the butter.

9 Carefully dip the top of each éclair in the melted chocolate, then place on a wire rack. Leave in a cool place until the chocolate is set. The éclairs are best served within 2 hours of being made, but they can be stored in the refrigerator for up to 24 hours.

SWEET PUFF AND FILO PASTRIES

Crisp puff pastry and light-as-a-feather filo make some of the most memorable pastries. They rise to airy heights and often need just the simplest of fillings, such as whipped cream and fresh fruit, to create a tempting treat for afternoon tea or a dessert that will have everyone eager for second helpings. Try the delicate flavours of Almond Cream Puffs, Peach and Redcurrant Tartlets or sweet and sticky Baklava. These pastries may be small, but they are difficult to resist.

DANISH PASTRIES

THESE WORLD-FAMOUS SWEET PUFF PASTRIES ARE TIME-CONSUMING TO MAKE, BUT WELL WORTH THE EFFORT. THE COFFEE ADDS A NEW DEPTH AND FLAVOUR TO THESE PERENNIAL FAVOURITES.

MAKES SIXTEEN

INGREDIENTS
  45ml/3 tbsp near-boiling water
  30ml/2 tbsp ground coffee
  40g/1½ oz/3 tbsp butter
  115g/4oz/½ cup caster
    (superfine) sugar
  1 egg yolk
  115g/4oz/1 cup ground almonds
  1 egg, beaten
  275g/10oz/1 cup apricot jam
  30ml/2 tbsp water
  175g/6oz/1½ cups icing
    (confectioners') sugar
  50g/2oz/½ cup flaked (sliced)
    almonds, toasted
  50g/2oz/¼ cup glacé
    (candied) cherries
For the pastry
  275g/10oz/2½ cups plain
    (all-purpose) flour
  1.5ml/¼ tsp salt
  15g/½oz/1 tbsp caster
    (superfine) sugar
  225g/8oz/1 cup butter, softened
  10ml/2 tsp easy-blend (rapid-rise)
    dried yeast
  1 egg, beaten
  100ml/3½fl oz/scant ½ cup chilled
    water

1 To make the pastry, sift the flour, salt and sugar into a bowl. Rub in 25g/1oz/ 2 tbsp butter. Stir in the yeast. In a separate bowl, mix the egg and water together, add to the flour mixture and mix to a soft dough. Lightly knead for 4–5 minutes. Place in a plastic bag, seal and chill for 15 minutes.

2 Put the remaining butter for the pastry between two sheets of baking parchment and beat with a rolling pin to make an 18cm/7in square. Chill.

3 Roll out the dough on a floured surface to a square about 25 × 25cm/ 10 × 10in. Put the butter in the middle of the dough square, angled like a diamond, then bring up each corner of the dough to enclose it fully.

4 Roll out the pastry thinly to measure about 35cm/14in in length. Turn up the bottom third of the pastry, then gently fold down the top third. Seal the edges together with a rolling pin. Wrap the pastry in clear film (plastic wrap) and chill for 15 minutes.

5 Repeat the rolling and folding three more times, turning the pastry after folding over so that the short ends are at the top and bottom. Allow the pastry a 15-minute rest between each turn.

6 To make the filling, pour the hot water over the coffee and infuse for 4 minutes. Strain through a fine sieve. Cream the butter and sugar together. Beat in the egg yolk, ground almonds and 15ml/1 tbsp of the coffee.

7 Divide the dough and filling equally into three. Roll one dough portion to an 18 × 35cm/7 × 14in rectangle. Spread with filling and roll up from a short end. Cut into six equal slices. Roll another portion into a 25cm/10in round, and cut into six equal segments.

8 Put a spoonful of filling at the widest end of each segment. Roll the pastry towards its point to form a crescent.

9 Roll out the remaining dough into a 20cm/8in square; cut into four. Place some filling in the centre of each piece, and shape by making cuts from each corner almost to the centre, then fold four alternate points to the centre.

10 Preheat the oven to 220°C/425°F/ Gas 7. Space the pastries well apart on greased baking sheets. Cover loosely with oiled clear film and leave to rise for about 20 minutes, until almost doubled in size. Brush with the egg and bake for 15–20 minutes until lightly browned and crisp. Cool on wire racks.

11 Put the jam in a pan with the water; bring to the boil, then sieve. Brush the jam over the warm pastries. Mix the icing sugar with the remaining coffee to make a thick icing. Drizzle the icing over some of the pastries and decorate some with almonds or chopped glacé cherries. Leave to set before serving.

MANGO <u>and</u> TAMARILLO PASTRIES

THESE FRUIT-TOPPED PASTRY SLICES ARE THE PERFECT COMPANION FOR A CUP OF AFTERNOON TEA.
USE READY-ROLLED PUFF PASTRY IF YOU ARE SHORT OF TIME.

<u>MAKES EIGHT</u>

INGREDIENTS
   225g/8oz puff pastry
   1 egg yolk, lightly beaten
   115g/4oz white marzipan
   40ml/2½ tbsp ginger or
    apricot conserve
   1 mango, peeled and thinly sliced
   2 tamarillos, halved and sliced
   caster (superfine) sugar, for sprinkling

1 Preheat the oven to 200°C/400°F/
Gas 6. Roll out the pastry thinly and
trim it to a 30 × 25cm/12 × 10in
rectangle. Cut this into eight rectangles
and place on baking sheets.

VARIATION
Use apricot slices instead of tamarillos.

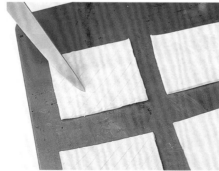

2 Using the point of a small sharp
knife, score the surface of each piece of
pastry in a diamond pattern, then brush
lightly with the egg yolk to glaze. Cut the
marzipan into eight thin slices and lay
one slice on each pastry rectangle. Top
each with a teaspoonful of the ginger or
apricot conserve and spread evenly.

3 Top the pastries with alternate slices
of mango and tamarillo. Sprinkle with a
little caster sugar, then bake for about
20 minutes until the pastry is puffed up
and golden. Transfer the pastries to a
wire rack to cool then place on dessert
plates. Sprinkle with more caster sugar
before serving.

NECTARINE PUFF PASTRY TARTS

THESE SIMPLE, FRESH FRUIT PASTRIES ARE EASY TO PUT TOGETHER, BUT THE PUFF PASTRY GIVES THEM AN ELEGANT LOOK. YOU COULD USE PEACHES, APPLES OR PEARS INSTEAD OF NECTARINES.

SERVES SIX

INGREDIENTS
  15g/½oz/1 tbsp butter
  225g/8oz rough puff or puff pastry
  450g/1lb nectarines
  30ml/2 tbsp caster (superfine) sugar
  freshly grated nutmeg
  crème fraîche or lightly whipped
    cream, to serve (optional)

1 Lightly butter a large baking sheet and sprinkle very lightly with water.

2 On a lightly floured surface, roll out the puff pastry to a large rectangle, measuring about 40 × 25cm/15 × 10in and cut into six smaller rectangles.

3 Transfer the pastry to the baking sheet. Using the back of a small knife, scallop the edges of each piece of pastry. Then, using the tip of the knife, score a line 1cm/½in from the edge of each rectangle to form a border. Chill the pastry shapes for 30 minutes. Meanwhile, preheat the oven to 200°C/400°F/Gas 6.

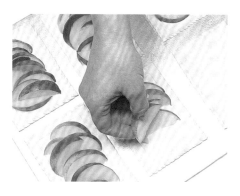

4 Halve the nectarines and remove the stones (pits), then cut the fruit into thin slices. Arrange the nectarine slices in the centre of the pastry rectangles, leaving the border uncovered. Sprinkle the fruit with the caster sugar and a little freshly grated nutmeg.

5 Bake for 12–15 minutes until the edges of each pastry case are puffed up and the fruit is tender.

6 Transfer the tarts to a wire rack to cool slightly before removing and serving warm. In a small bowl, offer a little crème fraîche or whipped cream, if you like.

COOK'S TIP
These free-form puff pastry tarts can be made in other shapes if you wish. Cut the pastry into diamonds instead of rectangles, or into rounds, using a large pastry cutter or an upturned plate as a guide. Whatever shape you use, be sure to allow for a border of pastry so that it can rise properly around the fruit.

MINI MILLE-FEUILLE

THIS PÂTISSERIE CLASSIC IS A DELECTABLE COMBINATION OF TENDER PUFF PASTRY WITH LUSCIOUS PASTRY CREAM. AS IT IS DIFFICULT TO CUT, MAKING INDIVIDUAL SERVINGS IS A BRILLIANT SOLUTION.

3 Bake the pastry rounds for 15–20 minutes until golden, then transfer to wire racks to cool.

4 Whisk the egg yolks and sugar for 2 minutes until light and creamy, then whisk in the flour until just blended. Bring the milk to the boil over a medium heat and pour it over the egg mixture, whisking to blend. Return to the pan, bring to the boil and boil for 2 minutes, whisking constantly.

5 Remove the pan from the heat and whisk in the Kirsch or liqueur. Pour into a bowl and press a piece of clear film (plastic wrap) on to the surface to prevent a skin from forming. Set aside.

SERVES FOUR

INGREDIENTS
  450g/1lb rough puff or puff pastry
  6 egg yolks
  65g/2½oz/⅓ cup caster
    (superfine) sugar
  45ml/3 tbsp plain (all-purpose) flour
  350ml/12fl oz/1½ cups milk
  30ml/2 tbsp Kirsch or cherry liqueur
  450g/1lb/2⅔ cups raspberries
  icing (confectioners') sugar,
    for dusting

1 Lightly butter two large baking sheets and sprinkle them with just a little very cold water. On a lightly floured surface, roll out the pastry to a thickness of 3mm/⅛in.

2 Using a 10cm/4in plain pastry cutter or a plate as a guide, cut out 12 rounds from the pastry. Lift the rounds on to the baking sheets and prick each a few times with a fork. Chill for 30 minutes. Meanwhile preheat the oven to 200°C/400°F/Gas 6.

6 To assemble, carefully split the pastry rounds in half. Spread each round with a little pastry cream. Arrange a layer of raspberries over the cream and top with a second pastry round.

7 Spread with a little more cream and a few more raspberries. Top with a third pastry round and dust with icing sugar.

ALMOND CREAM PUFFS

THESE SWEET LITTLE PIES CONSIST OF CRISP, FLAKY LAYERS OF PASTRY SURROUNDING A DELICIOUS, CREAMY FILLING. THEY ARE BEST SERVED WARM, SO REHEAT ANY THAT BECOME COLD BEFORE EATING.

MAKES TEN

INGREDIENTS
    275g/10oz puff pastry
    2 egg yolks
    15ml/1 tbsp plain (all-purpose) flour
    30ml/2 tbsp ground almonds
    30ml/2 tbsp caster (superfine) sugar
    a few drops of vanilla or almond
        essence (extract)
    150ml/¼ pint/⅔ cup double (heavy)
        cream, whipped
    milk, to glaze
    icing (confectioners') sugar

VARIATION

Another tasty option is to use desiccated (dry unsweetened shredded) coconut instead of ground almonds.

1 Roll out the pastry thinly on a lightly floured surface, and cut out ten 7.5cm/ 3in plain rounds and ten 6.5cm/2½in fluted rounds. Keep the smaller rounds for the tops, and use the larger ones to line a patty or cupcake tin. Chill for about 10 minutes. Preheat the oven to 200°C/400°F/Gas 6.

2 Whisk the egg yolks with the flour, almonds, sugar and vanilla essence. Fold in the cream and spoon into the pastry cases. Brush the rims with milk, add the tops and seal the edges. Glaze with milk. Bake for 20–25 minutes until golden. Cool slightly. Dust with icing sugar before serving.

POACHED PEAR TARTLETS
WITH CHOCOLATE SAUCE

PUFF PASTRY IS SHAPED AND TOPPED WITH SPICY POACHED PEARS. THE CHOCOLATE SAUCE COMPLEMENTS THE PASTRIES BEAUTIFULLY.

SERVES SIX

INGREDIENTS

   3 firm pears, peeled
   450ml/¾ pint/scant 2 cups water
   strip of thinly pared orange rind
   1 vanilla pod (bean)
   1 bay leaf
   50g/2oz/¼ cup granulated sugar
   350g/12oz puff pastry
   40g/1½oz/⅓ cup cocoa
     powder (unsweetened)
   75ml/5 tbsp double (heavy) cream
   15g/½oz/1 tbsp butter, softened
   15ml/1 tbsp soft light brown sugar
   25g/1oz/¼ cup walnuts, chopped
   1 egg, beaten
   15g/½oz/1 tbsp caster (superfine) sugar

1 Cut the pears in half and scoop out just the cores with a melon baller or small spoon.

2 Put the water in a small pan with the orange rind, vanilla pod, bay leaf and sugar. Bring to the boil, stirring well. Add the pears and more water to cover.

3 Cover and cook very gently for about 15 minutes, or until just tender. Remove the pears with a slotted spoon and set aside to cool slightly while you make the pastry. Reserve the syrup.

4 Meanwhile, roll out the pastry on a lightly floured work surface and cut out six pear shapes, slightly larger than the pear halves. Place the pastry shapes on greased baking sheets and chill for 30 minutes.

5 Remove the orange rind, vanilla pod and bay leaf from the reserved syrup, then return the syrup to the heat and boil rapidly for 10 minutes. Blend the cocoa powder with 60ml/4 tbsp cold water in a separate pan.

6 Stir a few spoonfuls of the syrup into the cocoa paste, then whisk the paste into the syrup in the pan. Continue to cook until reduced to about 150ml/ ¼ pint/⅔ cup. Remove the pan from the heat and add the cream to the syrup. Stir well.

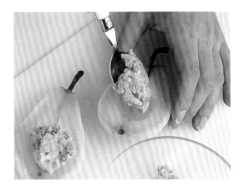

7 Preheat the oven to 200°C/400°F/ Gas 6. In a bowl, mix together the butter, sugar and walnuts. Gently pat the pears dry with kitchen paper, then spoon a little filling into each cavity.

8 Lightly brush the pastry pear shapes with a little beaten egg. Put a pear half, filled side down, in the centre of each pastry shape.

9 Lightly sprinkle the pastries with a little caster sugar. Bake for 12 minutes, or until the pastry has puffed up around the pear and is golden brown. Drizzle over some of the warm chocolate sauce and serve immediately.

COOK'S TIP
Decorate these tartlets with small fresh bay leaves, if you wish.

PLUM AND MARZIPAN PASTRIES

READY-ROLLED PUFF PASTRY HAS BEEN USED HERE FOR SPEED AND CONVENIENCE. IF YOU MAKE YOUR OWN, THE SQUARES SHOULD MEASURE 15CM/6IN.

MAKES SIX

INGREDIENTS
    375g/13oz ready-rolled puff pastry
    3 red plums
    90ml/6 tbsp plum jam
    115g/4oz/½ cup white marzipan,
      coarsely grated
    1 egg, beaten
    50g/2oz/½ cup flaked
      (sliced) almonds
For the glaze
    30ml/2 tbsp plum jam
    15ml/1 tbsp water

1 Preheat the oven to 220°C/425°F/ Gas 7. Unroll the pastry, cut it into six equal squares and then place on one or two dampened baking sheets.

2 Halve and stone (pit) the red plums. Using a small spoon, place 15ml/1 tbsp plum jam into the centre of each puff pastry square, leaving a border all round. Divide the marzipan among them. Place half a plum, hollow-side down, on top of each marzipan mound.

3 Brush the edges of the pastry with a little beaten egg. Bring up the corners of the pastry and lightly press the edges together, then open out the corners at the top. Glaze the pastries with some more beaten egg, then press a sixth of the flaked almonds on each.

4 Bake the pastries for 20–25 minutes, or until lightly golden.

5 Meanwhile, to make the glaze, heat the jam and water in a pan, stirring until smooth. Press the mixture through a sieve into a bowl, then lightly brush it over the tops of the pastries while they are still warm. Leave the pastries to cool on a wire rack before serving at room temperature.

PEACH AND REDCURRANT TARTLETS

TART REDCURRANTS AND SWEET PEACHES MAKE A WINNING COMBINATION IN THESE SIMPLE TARTLETS.
SMALL BUNCHES OF REDCURRANTS MAKE EASY ORNAMENTS, DUSTED WITH A LITTLE ICING SUGAR.

MAKES FOUR

INGREDIENTS
    25g/1oz/2 tbsp butter, melted
    16 sheets of filo pastry, each
        measuring 15cm/6in square, thawed
        if frozen
    150ml/¼ pint/⅔ cup double
        (heavy) cream
    130g/4½oz peach and mango
        fromage frais or yogurt
    vanilla essence (extract)
    15ml/1 tbsp icing (confectioners')
        sugar, sifted, plus extra for dusting
    2 peaches, halved and stoned (pitted)
    50g/2oz/½ cup redcurrants, plus
        redcurrant sprigs, to decorate

COOK'S TIP
To strip redcurrants from their stalks,
pull the stalks through the tines of a fork
so that they drop into a bowl.

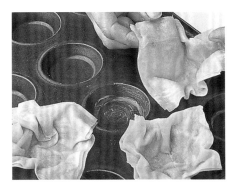

1 Preheat the oven to 190°C/375°F/
Gas 5. Use a little of the butter to lightly
grease four individual tartlet tins (mini
quiche pans). Brush the pastry squares
with a little more butter, stack them in
fours, then place in the tartlet tins to
make four pastry cases. Bake for about
15 minutes until golden. Cool the filo
cases on a wire rack before removing
them from the tins.

2 To make the filling, whip the cream
to soft peaks, then lightly fold in the
fromage frais or yogurt with a few drops
of the vanilla essence and icing sugar.
Divide among the pastry cases.

3 Slice the peaches and arrange the
slices on top of the filling, with a few
redcurrants. Decorate with redcurrant
sprigs and dust with icing sugar.

FILO, ICE CREAM AND MINCEMEAT PARCELS

LOOKING RATHER LIKE CRISP FRIED PANCAKES, THESE GOLDEN PARCELS REVEAL WARM PIECES OF MINCEMEAT AND MELTING VANILLA ICE CREAM WHEN CUT OPEN. THEY CAN BE ASSEMBLED DAYS IN ADVANCE, READY FOR EASY, LAST-MINUTE FRYING.

MAKES TWELVE

INGREDIENTS
  1 firm pear, peeled and cored
  225g/8oz/1 cup mincemeat
  finely grated rind of 1 lemon
  12 sheets of filo pastry, thawed
   if frozen
  1 egg, beaten
  250ml/8fl oz/1 cup vanilla ice cream
  oil, for deep-frying
  caster (superfine) sugar, for dusting

1 Chop the pear and place in a bowl. Stir in the mincemeat and lemon rind.

2 Keeping the rest of the filo covered under a damp dishtowel, lay one sheet on a board and cut it into two 20cm/8in squares. Brush with beaten egg, then cover with the second square of filo.

3 Lay 20ml/4 tsp of the mincemeat mixture on the filo, placing it 2.5cm/1in away from one edge and spreading it slightly to cover a 7.5cm/3in area.

4 Spoon 20ml/4 tsp of the vanilla ice cream over the mincemeat. Brush around the edges of the filo pastry with a little of the remaining beaten egg.

5 Fold over the two opposite sides of the pastry to cover the filling. Roll up, starting from the filled end. Transfer to a baking sheet and freeze. Make and freeze 11 more rolls in the same way.

6 Shortly before you are ready to serve, pour oil into a heavy pan to a depth of 7.5cm/3in. Heat it to 185°C/365°F, or until a cube of bread added to the oil browns in 30 seconds.

7 Fry several parcels at a time for 1–2 minutes until golden, turning them during cooking. Drain on kitchen paper while frying the remainder. Dust with caster sugar and serve immediately.

VARIATION
Use mango ice cream instead of vanilla for a sensational change.

WALNUT AND VANILLA ICE PALMIERS

THESE WALNUT PASTRIES CAN BE SERVED FRESHLY BAKED, BUT FOR CONVENIENCE, MAKE THEM AHEAD AND REHEAT THEM IN A MEDIUM OVEN FOR 5 MINUTES.

MAKES SIX

INGREDIENTS
  75g/3oz/¾ cup walnut pieces
  350g/12oz puff pastry
  1 egg, beaten
  45ml/3 tbsp caster (superfine) sugar
  about 200ml/7fl oz/scant 1 cup
   vanilla ice cream

1 Preheat the oven to 200°C/400°F/ Gas 6. Lightly grease a large baking sheet with butter. Chop the walnuts finely. On a lightly floured surface roll the pastry to a thin rectangle measuring 30 × 20cm/12 × 8in.

2 Trim the edges of the pastry, then brush with the beaten egg. Sprinkle all but 45ml/3 tbsp of the walnuts and 30ml/2 tbsp of the sugar over the pastry.

3 Run the rolling pin over the walnuts to press them gently into the pastry, then roll up the pastry from one short edge to the centre, then roll up the other side until the two rolls meet.

4 Brush the points where the rolls meet with a little beaten egg. Using a sharp knife, cut the pastry into 1cm/½in slices.

5 Lay the slices on their sides and flatten them with a rolling pin. Transfer to the baking sheet. Brush the slices with more beaten egg and sprinkle with the reserved walnuts and sugar.

6 Bake for 15 minutes, or until pale golden. Serve the palmiers warm, in pairs, sandwiched with ice cream.

ALMOND AND DATE FILO PARCELS

IT IS WORTH BUYING A POT OF GOOD HONEY, SUCH AS ORANGE BLOSSOM OR HEATHER, FOR DIPPING THESE DELICIOUS PASTRIES INTO — IT MAKES ALL THE DIFFERENCE.

MAKES ABOUT THIRTY

INGREDIENTS
15ml/1 tbsp sunflower oil
225g/8oz/2 cups blanched almonds
115g/4oz/⅔ cup pitted dates
25g/1oz/2 tbsp butter, softened
5ml/1 tsp ground cinnamon
1.5ml/¼ tsp almond essence (extract)
40g/1½oz/⅓ cup icing
  (confectioners') sugar
30ml/2 tbsp orange flower water
10 sheets of filo pastry, thawed
  if frozen
50g/2oz/¼ cup butter, melted
120ml/4fl oz/½ cup clear honey
dates, to serve (optional)

1 Heat the oil in a small pan, add the almonds and fry until golden, stirring constantly. Drain them on kitchen paper, allow to cool, then grind in a very clean coffee or spice mill. Pound the dates by hand or process in a blender or a food processor.

2 Combine the almonds, pitted dates softened butter, cinnamon, almond essence and icing sugar in a mixing bowl, blender or food processor. Add a little orange flower water to taste. Mix or process the mixture to a smooth paste. If the paste feels stiff, work in a little extra flower water, but only 5ml/1 tsp at a time, until smooth.

3 Preheat the oven to 180°C/350°F/ Gas 4. Brush a sheet of filo pastry with melted butter and cut into three equal strips, keeping the remaining sheets covered with a damp dishtowel.

4 Place a walnut-size piece of the almond and date paste at the end of each strip. Fold one corner of the pastry over the filling to make a triangle and then continue folding to make a neat triangular package. Brush with butter. Repeat to make about 30 pastries.

5 Place the pastries on a buttered baking sheet and bake for 30 minutes until golden. Cook them in batches, if possible, as once cooked they must be dipped immediately in honey.

6 While the filo parcels are cooking, pour the clear honey and a little orange flower water into a pan and heat very gently. As soon as the pastries are cooked, lower them one by one into the honey mixture and turn them so that they are coated. Transfer to a plate and cool, then serve, with dates if you like.

APRICOT FILO PURSES

THESE LITTLE FILO PARCELS CONCEAL A DELECTABLE APRICOT AND MINCEMEAT FILLING. THEY PROVIDE THE PERFECT EXCUSE FOR USING UP ANY MINCEMEAT AND MARZIPAN.

MAKES EIGHT

INGREDIENTS
  350g/12oz filo pastry, thawed
    if frozen
  50g/2oz/¼ cup butter, melted
  8 apricots, halved and
    stoned (pitted)
  60ml/4 tbsp mincemeat
  12 ratafia biscuits (almond
    macaroons), crushed
  30ml/2 tbsp grated marzipan
  icing (confectioners') sugar,
    for dusting

COOK'S TIP
Filo pastry dries out quickly, so keep any squares not currently being used covered under a clean damp dishtowel.

1 Preheat the oven to 200°C/400°F/ Gas 6. Cut the sheets of filo pastry into 32 squares, each about 18cm/7in. Brush four of the squares with a little melted butter and stack them, giving each layer a quarter turn to create a star shape. Repeat with the remaining filo squares to make eight stars.

2 Place an apricot half, hollow side up, in the centre of each pastry star. Mix the mincemeat, crushed ratafias and marzipan together and spoon a little of the mixture into the hollow in each apricot half.

3 Top with another apricot half, then bring the corners of each pastry star together and gently squeeze to make a gathered purse.

4 Place the purses on a baking sheet and brush each with a little melted butter. Bake for about 20 minutes, or until the pastry is golden and crisp. Lightly dust with icing sugar and serve the purses immediately. Whipped cream, flavoured with a little brandy, makes an ideal accompaniment.

BAKLAVA

THE ORIGINS OF THIS RECIPE LIE IN TURKEY AND GREECE, WHERE THE COFFEE IS BLACK, THICK AND VERY STRONG. COFFEE IS USED IN THIS WELL-KNOWN PASTRY CONFECTION, WHICH IS TRADITIONALLY SERVED ON RELIGIOUS FESTIVAL DAYS, BUT MAKES A LUXURIOUSLY SWEET DESSERT OR TREAT AT ANY TIME. YOU MIGHT LIKE TO OFFER SOME STRONG TURKISH COFFEE WHEN SERVING THIS DESSERT.

MAKES SIXTEEN

INGREDIENTS
 50g/2oz/½ cup blanched
  almonds, chopped
 50g/2oz/½ cup pistachio
  nuts, chopped
 75g/3oz/6 tbsp caster
  (superfine) sugar
 75g/3oz/6 tbsp butter, melted
 6 sheets of filo pastry, thawed
  if frozen
For the syrup
 115g/4oz/½ cup caster
  (superfine) sugar
 7.5cm/3in piece cinnamon stick
 1 whole clove
 2 green cardamom pods, crushed
 75ml/5 tbsp very strong
  brewed coffee

1 Preheat the oven to 180°C/350°F/ Gas 4. Add the chopped almonds, nuts and sugar to a small bowl and mix well, stirring to thoroughly coat the nuts in sugar. Brush a shallow 18 × 28cm/ 7 × 11in baking tin with a little of the melted butter.

2 Using the tin as a guide, cut the six sheets of filo pastry with a very sharp knife so that they fit the tin exactly. It is easiest to cut through all the sheets in one go, rather than working through them singly. Lay a sheet of pastry in the tin and brush it all over with some of the melted butter.

3 Lay a second sheet of filo in the tin and brush with butter. Add a third sheet, brushing with a little butter. Sprinkle the filo with half of the nut mixture, making sure it is evenly distributed.

4 Layer three more sheets of filo pastry on top of the nut mixture, brushing each layer with butter as you go. Then spread the remaining nut mixture over the pastry, smoothing it evenly over the entire surface. Top with the remaining sheets of pastry, brushing each sheet with a little more butter as before, and liberally brushing the top layer too. Gently press down with your hand all around the edges to seal.

COOK'S TIP
While assembling the baklava, keep the pile of filo pastry sheets covered with a clean damp dishtowel to prevent them from drying out and becoming brittle, which makes the pastry difficult to handle. Work quickly to minimize the risk of the pastry drying out.

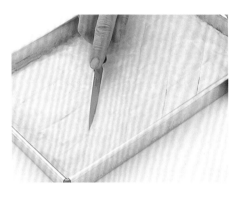

5 Using a very sharp knife, mark the top of the baklava into diamonds. Place in the preheated oven and bake for 20–25 minutes, or until golden brown and crisp all over.

6 Meanwhile, make the syrup. Put the sugar, spices and coffee in a small pan and heat gently until the sugar has dissolved – be careful not to burn the sugar as there is a high proportion of it to the liquid. Cover the pan and set aside for 20 minutes, to give the spices time to flavour the syrup.

7 Remove the baklava from the oven. Reheat the syrup over a gentle heat, then strain it over the pastry, ensuring an even coverage. Leave to cool in the tin. If you can, set it aside for 6 hours or preferably overnight to allow the flavours to mingle. When ready to serve, cut the baklava into diamonds, following the lines scored prior to baking, then remove from the tin.

VARIATIONS
• Try different nuts in the baklava filling if you prefer. Walnuts, pecan nuts and hazelnuts can all used to great effect.
• If you would prefer a syrup that does not include coffee, substitute the coffee for 75ml/5 tbsp water and add two strips of thinly pared lemon rind. This will give the baklava a delightful mildly spiced citrus flavour.
• Decorate each baklava diamond with extra nuts if you like.

ELEGANT FRUIT TARTS

Of all pastries, shortcrust is probably the most popular. Many of the pastries in this chapter are made exclusively with butter, which gives them the best flavour; others contain a small amount of white vegetable fat to make the pastry even more crumbly. Shortcrust has a particular affinity with fruit, a fact that is celebrated in sweet treats like Blueberry Frangipane Flan, Rustic Apple Tart and utterly irresistible Fresh Orange Tart with its creamy citrus custard filling.

ORANGE SWEETHEART TART

*STUNNING TO LOOK AT AND DELECTABLE TO EAT, THIS TART HAS A CRISP SHORTCRUST PASTRY CASE,
SPREAD WITH APRICOT JAM AND FILLED WITH FRANGIPANE, THEN TOPPED WITH TANGY ORANGE SLICES.*

SERVES EIGHT

INGREDIENTS
   200g/7oz/scant 1 cup granulated
     sugar
   250ml/8fl oz/1 cup fresh orange
     juice, strained
   2 large navel oranges
   75g/3oz/¾ cup blanched almonds
   50g/2oz/¼ cup butter
   1 egg
   15ml/1 tbsp plain (all-purpose) flour
   45ml/3 tbsp apricot jam
For the pastry
   175g/6oz/1½ cups plain
     (all-purpose) flour
   2.5ml/½ tsp salt
   75g/3oz/6 tbsp butter, diced
   45ml/3 tbsp chilled water

1 To make the pastry, sift the flour and
salt into a mixing bowl. Rub or cut in
the butter until the mixture resembles
fine breadcrumbs. Sprinkle over the
water and mix to a dough. Knead on a
floured surface for a few seconds until
smooth. Wrap the dough in clear film
(plastic wrap) and chill for 30 minutes.

2 After the pastry has rested, roll it
out on a floured surface to a thickness
of 5mm/¼in. Use to line a 20cm/8in
heart-shaped tart tin. Trim the edges
and chill until required.

3 Put 150g/5oz/¾ cup of the sugar into
a pan and pour in the orange juice.
Bring to the boil and boil steadily for
about 10 minutes, or until the liquid is
thick and syrupy.

4 Cut the oranges into 5mm/¼in slices,
leaving the peel on. Add to the syrup.
Simmer gently for 10 minutes, or until
glazed. Transfer the slices to a wire rack
to dry. When cool, cut in half. Reserve
the orange syrup. Preheat the oven to
200°C/400°F/Gas 6, with a baking sheet
placed in it.

5 Grind the almonds finely in a food
processor, blender or nut grinder. With
an electric mixer, cream the butter and
remaining sugar until light and fluffy.
Beat in the egg and 30ml/2 tbsp of the
orange syrup. Add the ground almonds
and mix well, then add the flour.

6 Melt the jam over a low heat, then
brush it evenly over the inside of the
pastry case. Pour in the almond
mixture. Bake for 20 minutes, or until
set. Leave to cool in the tin.

7 Starting at the top of the heart shape
and working down to the point, arrange
overlapping orange slices on top of the
tart. Boil the remaining syrup until
thick. Brush on top to glaze.

RUSTIC APPLE TART

THIS EASY APPLE TART LOOKS AS THOUGH IT HAS COME STRAIGHT FROM THE KITCHEN OF A FRENCH FARMHOUSE. COOKING THE APPLES BEFORE PUTTING THEM ON THE PASTRY PREVENTS A SOGGY CRUST.

SERVES SIX

INGREDIENTS
    900g/2lb cooking apples, peeled,
      quartered and cored
    15ml/1 tbsp lemon juice
    50g/2oz/¼ cup caster
      (superfine) sugar
    40g/1½oz/3 tbsp butter
    crème fraîche or lightly whipped
      cream, to serve
For the pastry
    225g/8oz/2 cups plain
      (all-purpose) flour
    pinch of salt
    15ml/1 tbsp caster (superfine) sugar
    150g/5oz/⅔ cup butter, diced
    1 egg yolk
    30ml/2 tbsp chilled water

1 To make the pastry, sift the flour, salt and sugar into a bowl. Rub or cut in the butter until the mixture resembles fine breadcrumbs. Combine the egg and water, sprinkle over the dry ingredients and mix to a dough. Knead for a few seconds until smooth. Wrap in clear film (plastic wrap) and chill for 30 minutes.

2 Slice the apple quarters and place in a bowl. Sprinkle with the lemon juice and sugar, and toss to combine.

3 Melt the butter in a large heavy frying pan over a medium heat and add the apples. Cook, stirring frequently, for about 12 minutes until the apples are just turning golden brown. Remove the frying pan from the heat and set aside. Preheat the oven to 190°C/375°F/Gas 5.

4 On a lightly floured work surface, roll out the pastry to a 30cm/12in round and trim the edge if uneven. Carefully transfer the pastry to a baking sheet. Heap the apple slices on the pastry, leaving a 5cm/2in border all round the edge of the pastry.

6 Gather the pastry border around the apple slices, enclosing those closest to the rim and leaving the centre open. Bake the tart for 35–40 minutes until the pastry is crisp and golden brown. Serve warm, with crème fraîche or whipped cream.

CARAMELIZED UPSIDE-DOWN PEAR PIE

IN THIS GLORIOUSLY STICKY DESSERT, THE PASTRY IS BAKED ON TOP OF THE FRUIT, WHICH GIVES IT A CRISP AND FLAKY TEXTURE. WHEN INVERTED, THE PIE LOOKS WONDERFUL.

SERVES EIGHT

INGREDIENTS
   5–6 firm, ripe pears
   175g/6oz/¾ cup caster
      (superfine) sugar
   115g/4oz/½ cup butter
   whipped cream, to serve
For the pastry
   115g/4oz/1 cup plain
      (all-purpose) flour
   1.5ml/¼ tsp salt
   130g/4½oz/9 tbsp cold butter, diced
   40g/1½oz/3 tbsp white vegetable
      fat, diced
   60ml/4 tbsp chilled water

1 To make the pastry, combine the flour and salt in a bowl. Cut or rub in the butter and vegetable fat until the mixture resembles coarse breadcrumbs. Stir in just enough water to bind. Wrap the dough in clear film (plastic wrap) and chill for 30 minutes. Preheat the oven to 200°C/400°F/Gas 6.

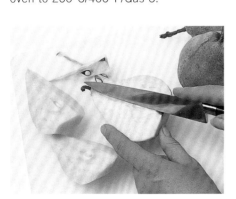

2 Peel, quarter and core the pears. Toss with some of the sugar in a bowl.

3 Melt the butter in a 27cm/10½in heavy ovenproof omelette pan. Add the remaining sugar. When it changes colour, arrange the pears in the pan.

4 Continue cooking, uncovered, for about 20 minutes, or until the fruit has completely caramelized.

5 Leave the fruit to cool in the pan. Meanwhile, on a lightly floured surface, roll out the pastry to a round that is slightly larger than the diameter of the pan. Place the pastry on top of the pears and carefully tuck the pastry in around the edges.

6 Bake for 15 minutes, then lower the oven temperature to 180°C/350°F/ Gas 4. Bake for a further 15 minutes, or until the pastry is golden.

7 Let the pie cool in the pan for a few minutes. To unmould, run a knife around the pan's edge, then, using oven gloves, invert a plate over the pan and quickly turn the two over together.

8 If any pears stick to the pan, remove them gently with a metal spatula and replace them carefully on the pie. Serve warm in slices with a little whipped cream, if you like.

VARIATIONS
• To make Caramelized Upside-down Apple Pie, replace the pears with 8–9 firm, tart apples – Cox's Orange Pippins would be a good choice. You will need more apples than pears as they shrink during cooking.
• Nectarines or peaches also work well, as does rhubarb. Rhubarb is tart, so you may need more sugar.
• For a more exotic pie, use sliced mango.
• Children like banana upside-down pie. Buy small bananas, peel them and slice them in half lengthways, then arrange the slices in the pan.

ALSACE PLUM TART

FRUIT AND CUSTARD TARTS ARE TYPICAL OF THE ALSACE REGION OF FRANCE. SOME HAVE A YEAST DOUGH BASE INSTEAD OF PASTRY. USE OTHER SEASONAL FRUITS OR A MIXTURE IF YOU LIKE.

SERVES SIX TO EIGHT

INGREDIENTS
    450g/1lb ripe plums, halved
      and stoned (pitted)
    30ml/2 tbsp Kirsch or plum brandy
    30ml/2 tbsp seedless raspberry jam
    2 eggs
    50g/2oz/¼ cup caster
      (superfine) sugar
    175ml/6fl oz/¾ cup double
      (heavy) cream
    grated rind of ½ lemon
    1.5ml/¼ tsp vanilla essence (extract)
For the pastry
    200g/7oz/1¾ cups plain
      (all-purpose) flour
    pinch of salt
    25g/1oz/¼ cup icing
      (confectioners') sugar
    100g/3½oz/scant ½ cup butter, diced
    2 egg yolks
    15ml/1 tbsp chilled water

1 To make the pastry, sift the flour, salt and sugar into a bowl. Rub or cut in the butter until the mixture resembles fine breadcrumbs. Mix the egg yolks and water together, sprinkle over the dry ingredients and mix to a soft dough.

2 Lightly knead on a floured work surface for a few seconds until smooth. Wrap in clear film (plastic wrap) and chill for 30 minutes.

4 Roll out the pastry thinly and use to line a 23cm/9in flan tin (quiche pan). Cover and chill for 30 minutes. Prick the base all over with a fork and line with foil. Add a layer of baking beans and bake for 15 minutes until slightly dry and set. Remove the foil and beans.

6 Lower the oven temperature to 180°C/350°F/Gas 4. Beat the eggs and sugar until well combined, then beat in the cream, lemon rind, vanilla essence and any juice from the plums.

3 Preheat the oven to 200°C/400°F/ Gas 6. Mix the plums with the Kirsch or plum brandy in a bowl and set aside for 30 minutes.

5 Lightly brush the base of the pastry case with a thin layer of jam, bake for 5 minutes more, then transfer to a wire rack to cool.

7 Arrange the plums, cut side down, in the pastry case, then pour over the custard mixture. Bake for 30 minutes, or until a knife inserted in the centre comes out clean. Serve the tart warm.

PEAR AND ALMOND CREAM TART

THIS GLORIOUS TART MAKES A TRULY INDULGENT DESSERT. VARY IT ACCORDING TO THE SEASON — IT IS EQUALLY SUCCESSFUL MADE WITH NECTARINES, PEACHES, APRICOTS OR APPLES.

SERVES SIX

INGREDIENTS
  3 firm pears
  a little lemon juice
  15ml/1 tbsp peach brandy
    or water
  60ml/4 tbsp peach preserve, strained
For the pastry
  200g/7oz/1¾ cups plain
    (all-purpose) flour
  pinch of salt
  25g/1oz/¼ cup icing
    (confectioners') sugar
  100g/3½oz/scant ½ cup butter, diced
  2 egg yolks
  15ml/1 tbsp chilled water
For the almond cream filling
  100g/3½oz/generous ¾ cup blanched
    almonds
  50g/2oz/¼ cup caster
    (superfine) sugar
  65g/2½oz/5 tbsp butter
  1 egg, plus 1 egg white
  a few drops of almond
    essence (extract)

1 To make the pastry, sift the flour with the salt and sugar. Rub or cut in the butter until the mixture resembles fine breadcrumbs. Mix the egg yolks and water, sprinkle over the dry ingredients and mix to a dough. Knead for a few seconds until smooth. Wrap in clear film (plastic wrap) and chill for 30 minutes.

2 Roll out the pastry and use to line a 23cm/9in flan tin (quiche pan), then chill. Meanwhile, make the filling. Pulse the almonds and caster sugar in a food processor until finely ground but not pasty. Add the butter and process until creamy, then mix in the egg, egg white and almond essence.

3 Place a baking sheet in the oven and preheat to 190°C/375°F/Gas 5. Thinly peel and halve the pears, remove their cores and rub them lightly with lemon juice. Put them cut side down on a chopping board and slice thinly crossways, keeping the slices together.

4 Pour the almond cream filling into the pastry case. Slide a palette knife under one pear half and press the top with your fingers to fan out the slices. Quickly transfer to the tart, placing the fruit on the filling like spokes of a wheel. Remove a few slices from each half before arranging and use to fill in any gaps in the centre.

5 Place the tart on the hot baking sheet and bake for 50–55 minutes, or until the filling is set and well browned. Cool on a wire rack.

6 Meanwhile, heat the brandy or water and the preserve in a small pan, then brush over the top of the hot tart to glaze. Serve at room temperature.

APRICOT FRANGIPANE TART <u>WITH</u> KIRSCH

TAKE A LIGHT PASTRY CASE, FILL IT WITH MOIST ALMOND SPONGE TOPPED WITH FRESH APRICOTS AND CRUSHED MACAROONS, AND THE RESULT IS SIMPLY SENSATIONAL.

SERVES SIX

INGREDIENTS
   12 apricots, stoned (pitted), some
     halved, some thickly sliced
   75g/3oz ratafia biscuits (almond
     macaroons), crushed
   natural (plain) yogurt or single (light)
     cream, to serve
For the pastry
   225g/8oz/2 cups plain
     (all-purpose) flour
   115g/4oz/½ cup butter, diced
   10ml/2 tsp finely grated lime rind
   60–90ml/4–6 tbsp chilled water
For the filling
   25g/1oz/2 tbsp butter, softened
   30ml/2 tbsp soft light brown sugar
   15ml/1 tbsp plain (all-purpose) flour
   50g/2oz/½ cup ground almonds
   1 egg, beaten
   45ml/3 tbsp Kirsch

1 To make the pastry, sift the flour into a mixing bowl, then rub or cut in the butter until the mixture resembles fine breadcrumbs. Stir in the grated lime rind and add enough chilled water to make a soft dough. Wrap in clear film (plastic wrap) and chill for 30 minutes.

2 Meanwhile, make the filling. Cream the butter with the sugar in a large bowl, then stir in the flour, ground almonds, egg and Kirsch.

3 Preheat the oven to 200°C/400°F/ Gas 6. Roll out the pastry on a floured surface to a 40 × 16cm/16 × 6½in rectangle and use to line a 35 × 12cm/ 14 × 4½in flan tin (quiche pan). Spread the filling in the base of the flan case and arrange the apricots on top. Scatter over the crushed ratafia biscuits.

4 Bake for about 40 minutes, or until the pastry is golden. Serve warm or cold, with yogurt or cream.

BLUEBERRY FRANGIPANE FLAN

THERE'S SOMETHING IRRESISTIBLE ABOUT THIS TANGY LEMON PASTRY CASE WITH ITS SWEET ALMOND FILLING AND RINGS OF RIPE BLUEBERRIES. THE JAM AND LIQUEUR GLAZE ADDS AN INDULGENT FINISH.

SERVES SIX

INGREDIENTS
30ml/2 tbsp ground coffee
45ml/3 tbsp near-boiling milk
50g/2oz/¼ cup butter
50g/2oz/¼ cup caster
  (superfine) sugar
1 egg
115g/4oz/1 cup ground almonds
15ml/1 tbsp plain (all-purpose) flour
225g/8oz/2 cups blueberries
30ml/2 tbsp seedless blackberry jam
15ml/1 tbsp Amaretto liqueur
crème fraîche or sour cream, to serve
For the pastry
  175g/6oz/1½ cups plain
    (all-purpose) flour
  115g/4oz/½ cup butter, diced
  25g/1oz/2 tbsp caster
    (superfine) sugar
  finely grated rind of ½ lemon
  15ml/1 tbsp chilled water

1 Preheat the oven to 190°F/375°C/ Gas 5. To make the pastry, sift the flour into a large bowl and rub or cut in the butter until the mixture resembles fine breadcrumbs. Add the caster sugar and lemon rind, stir well, then add the water and mix to a firm dough. Wrap the pastry in clear film (plastic wrap) and chill for 20 minutes.

2 Roll out the pastry on a lightly floured surface and use to line a 23cm/9in loose-based flan tin (quiche pan). Prick the base with a fork. Line the pastry with baking parchment and baking beans and bake for 10 minutes.

3 Remove the baking parchment and beans and bake for 10 minutes more. Remove the pastry case from the oven.

4 Meanwhile, mix the coffee and milk in a large mixing bowl. Leave to infuse for 4 minutes. Cream the butter and sugar until pale. Beat in the egg, then add the almonds and flour. Strain in the milky coffee through a fine sieve and gently fold it in.

5 Spoon the coffee mixture into the pastry case and spread evenly. Scatter the blueberries over the top and push them down slightly into the mixture. Bake for about 30 minutes until firm, covering with foil after 20 minutes.

6 Remove from the oven and allow to cool slightly. Melt the jam and liqueur in a small pan and brush over the flan. Remove from the tin and serve warm.

SUMMER BERRY TART

A SIMPLE CRISP PASTRY CASE IS ALL THAT IS NEEDED TO SET OFF THIS CLASSIC FILLING OF VANILLA-FLAVOURED CUSTARD TOPPED WITH LUSCIOUS BERRY FRUITS.

SERVES SIX TO EIGHT

INGREDIENTS
   3 egg yolks
   50g/2oz/¼ cup caster
      (superfine) sugar
   30ml/2 tbsp cornflour (cornstarch)
   30ml/2 tbsp plain (all-purpose) flour
   5ml/1 tsp vanilla essence (extract)
   300ml/½ pint/1¼ cups milk
   150ml/¼ pint/⅔ cup double
      (heavy) cream
   800g/1¾lb/4½–5 cups mixed
      summer berries, such as
      raspberries, blueberries,
      loganberries or boysenberries
   60ml/4 tbsp redcurrant jelly
   30ml/2 tbsp raspberry liqueur
   fresh mint leaves, to decorate
      (optional)
For the pastry
   185g/6½oz/1⅔ cups plain
      (all-purpose) flour
   pinch of salt
   115g/4oz/½ cup butter, diced
   1 egg yolk
   30ml/2 tbsp chilled water

1   To make the pastry, sift the flour and salt into a mixing bowl. Rub or cut in the butter until the mixture resembles fine breadcrumbs. Mix the egg yolk with the chilled water and sprinkle over the dry ingredients. Mix to a firm dough.

COOK'S TIP
If you are planning to serve the tart within an hour or so of filling, you can finish the fruit with a simple dusting of icing sugar instead of the glaze.

2   Put the dough on to a lightly floured surface and knead for a few seconds, until smooth. Wrap in clear film (plastic wrap) and chill for 30 minutes.

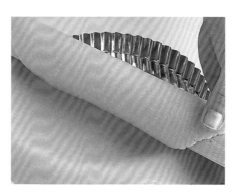

3   Roll out the pastry and use to line a 25cm/10in petal-shaped flan tin (quiche pan) or a 23cm/9in round pan. Wrap in clear film and chill.

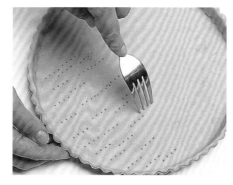

4   Put a baking sheet in the oven and preheat to 200°C/400°F/Gas 6. Prick the base of the pastry, line with foil and baking beans and bake for 15 minutes. Remove the foil and beans and bake for 10 minutes more. Leave to cool.

5   Beat the egg yolks, sugar, cornflour, flour and vanilla together. Bring the milk to the boil in a pan. Slowly pour on to the egg mixture, whisking all the time.

6   Pour the custard into the cleaned pan and cook over a low heat, stirring constantly, until it has thickened. Return to a clean mixing bowl, cover the surface with a piece of clear film and set aside to cool. Whip the cream until thick, then fold into the custard. Spoon the custard into the pastry case and spread out evenly.

7   Arrange the fruit on top of the custard. Gently heat the redcurrant jelly and liqueur together until melted. Allow to cool, then brush over the fruit. Serve the tart within 3 hours of assembling, decorated with mint, if using.

EXOTIC FRUIT TRANCHE

THIS IS A GOOD WAY TO MAKE THE MOST OF A SMALL SELECTION OF EXOTIC FRUIT.

SERVES EIGHT

INGREDIENTS
150ml/¼ pint/⅓ cup double (heavy)
  cream, plus extra to serve
250g/9oz/generous 1 cup mascarpone
  cheese
25g/1oz/¼ cup icing (confectioners')
  sugar, sifted
grated rind of 1 orange
450g/1lb/3 cups mixed prepared
  seasonal fruits
90ml/6 tbsp apricot conserve, sieved
15ml/1 tbsp white or coconut rum
For the pastry
175g/6oz/1½ cups plain
  (all-purpose) flour
50g/2oz/¼ cup butter, diced
25g/1oz/2 tbsp white vegetable fat
50g/2oz/¼ cup caster
  (superfine) sugar
2 egg yolks
about 15ml/1 tbsp chilled water
115g/4oz/scant ½ cup apricot
  conserve, sieved and warmed

1 To make the pastry, sift the flour into a large mixing bowl and rub or cut in the fat until the mixture resembles fine breadcrumbs. Stir in the caster sugar. Add the egg yolks and enough chilled water to make a soft dough.

2 Roll out the pastry thinly between two sheets of clear film (plastic wrap) and use to line a 35 × 12cm/14 × 4½in fluted tranche tin. Allow the excess pastry to hang over the edge of the tin and chill for 30 minutes.

3 Preheat the oven to 200°C/400°F/ Gas 6. Prick the base of the pastry case and line with baking parchment and baking beans. Bake for 10–12 minutes. Lift out the paper and beans and return the pastry to the oven for 5 minutes. Trim off the excess pastry and brush the inside of the case with the warmed apricot conserve to form a seal. Leave to cool on a wire rack.

4 Whip the cream to soft peaks, then stir it into the mascarpone with the icing sugar and orange rind. Spread evenly in the cooled pastry case and top with the prepared fruits. Gently warm the apricot conserve with the rum in a pan, and drizzle or brush over the fruits to make a glaze. Serve with extra cream.

COOK'S TIPS
• Use fruits such as mango, papaya, star fruit, kiwi fruit and blackberries.
• If you don't have a tranche tin, use a 23cm/9in flan tin (quiche pan).

PRUNE TART <u>WITH</u> CUSTARD FILLING

BRANDY-SOAKED PRUNES AND CLASSIC CUSTARD FILLING COMBINE TO SIMPLE BUT DELICIOUS EFFECT.

<u>SERVES SIX TO EIGHT</u>

INGREDIENTS

225g/8oz/1 cup stoned
  (pitted) prunes
50ml/2fl oz/¼ cup brandy
300ml/½ pint/1¼ cups milk
a few drops of vanilla
  essence (extract)
4 egg yolks
45ml/3 tbsp caster
  (superfine) sugar
30ml/2 tbsp cornflour (cornstarch)
25g/1oz/¼ cup flaked
  (sliced) almonds
icing (confectioners') sugar,
  for dusting
thick cream, to serve

For the pastry
175g/6oz/1½ cups plain
  (all-purpose) flour
pinch of salt
50g/2oz/¼ cup caster
  (superfine) sugar
90g/3½oz/scant ½ cup butter, diced
1 egg

1 Place the prunes in a small mixing bowl and pour in the brandy. Set the prunes aside in a warm place to soak. Meanwhile, preheat the oven to 200°C/400°F/Gas 6.

2 To make the pastry, place the flour, salt, sugar and diced butter in a food processor. Set aside 5ml/1 tsp of the egg white and add the remaining egg to the food processor. Process until the mixture forms a soft, pliable dough. Shape into a ball and leave to rest for 10 minutes.

3 Lightly flour a 28 × 18cm/11 × 7in loose-based tin. Roll out the pastry and use to line the tin. Chill for 30 minutes.

4 Line the pastry case with foil and fill with baking beans, then bake for about 15 minutes. Remove the foil and beans, and bake for 10–15 minutes more. Brush the base of the pastry with the reserved egg white while the pastry is still hot. Set aside to cool slightly.

5 Pour the milk into a pan and add the vanilla. Bring to the boil. In a small mixing bowl, whisk the egg yolks and sugar until thick, pale and fluffy, then whisk in the cornflour. Strain in the milk and whisk until there are no lumps.

6 Return to the cleaned pan and bring back to the boil, whisking to remove any lumps. Cook for about 2 minutes until thick and smooth, then set aside to cool. Press baking parchment on to the surface to prevent a skin from forming.

7 Stir any prune liquid into the custard, then spread the custard over the pastry case. Arrange the prunes randomly on top, sprinkle with the almonds and dust with icing sugar. Bake for 10 minutes more. Serve hot or warm with cream.

COOK'S TIP
Don't worry if you have to push the pastry slightly to fit the tin; this pastry is soft and easy to mould.

DATE AND ALMOND TART

FRESH DATES MAKE AN UNUSUAL BUT DELICIOUS FILLING FOR A TART, ESPECIALLY WHEN TEAMED WITH A SPONGE FILLING FLAVOURED WITH GROUND ALMONDS AND ORANGE FLOWER WATER.

SERVES SIX

INGREDIENTS
  90g/3½oz/scant ½ cup butter
  90g/3½oz/scant ½ cup caster
    (superfine) sugar
  1 egg, beaten
  90g/3½oz/scant 1 cup
    ground almonds
  30ml/2 tbsp plain (all-purpose) flour
  30ml/2 tbsp orange flower water
  12–13 fresh dates, halved and
    stoned (pitted)
  60ml/4 tbsp apricot jam
For the pastry
  175g/6oz/1½ cups plain
    (all-purpose) flour
  75g/3oz/6 tbsp butter, diced
  1 egg
  15ml/1 tbsp chilled water

1 Preheat the oven to 200°C/400°F/ Gas 6 and place a baking sheet in it to preheat. To make the pastry, sift the flour into a bowl, then rub or cut in the butter until the mixture resembles fine breadcrumbs. Add the egg and water, then work to a dough. Wrap in clear film (plastic wrap) and chill for 20 minutes.

2 Roll out the pastry on a lightly floured surface and use to line a 20cm/8in flan tin (quiche pan). Prick the base with a fork, then chill until required.

3 Cream the butter and sugar in a small mixing bowl with a wooden spoon until light, then beat in the egg. Stir in the ground almonds, flour and 15ml/ 1 tbsp of the orange flower water and mix thoroughly.

4 Spread the almond filling evenly over the base of the pastry case. Arrange the dates, cut side down, on the mixture. Bake the tart on the hot baking sheet for 10–15 minutes, then lower the oven temperature to 180°C/350°F/Gas 4. Bake for 15 minutes more, or until pale golden and set.

5 Transfer the tart to a wire rack to cool. Meanwhile, in a small pan, gently heat the apricot jam, then press through a sieve into a bowl. Stir in the remaining orange flower water. Lightly brush the apricot glaze over the tart and serve at room temperature.

RASPBERRY AND CRÈME BRÛLÉE TART

FRESH RASPBERRIES AND A CRUNCHY CARAMEL TOPPING CONTRAST WITH THE THICK VANILLA-SCENTED CUSTARD FILLING IN THIS LOVELY SUMMERY TART.

SERVES EIGHT

INGREDIENTS
  1 vanilla pod (bean)
  450ml/¾ pint/scant 2 cups double
    (heavy) cream
  1 whole egg, plus 3 egg yolks
  30ml/2 tbsp caster (superfine) sugar
  150g/5oz/scant 1 cup
    fresh raspberries
  5 tbsp icing (confectioners') sugar
For the pastry
  150g/5oz/1¼ cups plain
    (all-purpose) flour
  pinch of salt
  25g/1oz/¼ cup icing
    (confectioners') sugar
  75g/3oz/6 tbsp butter, diced
  2 egg yolks
  finely grated rind of 1 orange
  15ml/1 tbsp egg white, lightly beaten

1 To make the pastry, sift the flour, salt and icing sugar into a mixing bowl. Rub or cut in the butter until the mixture resembles fine breadcrumbs.

2 Mix the egg yolks and orange rind together, add to the dry ingredients and mix to a soft dough. Knead on a lightly floured work surface for a few seconds, until smooth. Wrap in clear film (plastic wrap) and chill for 30 minutes.

3 Roll out the pastry and use to line a fluted 23cm/9in flan tin (quiche pan). Cover and chill for a further 30 minutes. While the pastry case is chilling, put a baking sheet in the oven and preheat to 200°C/400°F/Gas 6.

4 Prick the base of the pastry all over with a fork and line with foil and baking beans. Place on the hot baking sheet and bake blind for 10 minutes. Remove the foil and beans and bake the pastry for 5 minutes more.

5 Lightly brush the base and sides of the pastry case with egg white, then return to the oven for 3–4 minutes. Lower the oven temperature to 160°C/325°F/Gas 3.

6 Halve the vanilla pod lengthways. Place in a small pan with the cream. Slowly bring to the boil, then remove the vanilla pod. In a mixing bowl or pouring jug (pitcher), whisk the egg and egg yolks with the sugar until pale. Slowly whisk in the hot cream.

7 Sprinkle the raspberries over the base of the pastry case, arranging them so that they are fairly evenly distributed. Pour over the custard, then bake the tart for 17–20 minutes, or until very lightly set. Place on a wire rack to cool. Chill for at least 4 hours, or overnight.

8 To add the crunchy caramel topping, first protect the edges of the pastry case with pieces of foil. Dredge a thin layer of icing sugar over the custard, right to the edge of the pastry case. Place under a hot grill (broiler) for 1 minute, or until the sugar melts and turns a dark golden colour. Take care not to over-grill or the custard will separate. Chill for about 10 minutes, to allow the caramel to harden slightly, then serve in slices.

ONE-CRUST RHUBARB PIE

THIS METHOD CAN BE USED FOR ALL SORTS OF FRUIT AND IS REALLY FOOLPROOF. IT DOESN'T MATTER HOW ROUGH THE PIE LOOKS WHEN IT GOES INTO THE OVEN; IT COMES OUT LOOKING FANTASTIC!

4 Cut the rhubarb into pieces about 2.5cm/1in and place in a large bowl. Add the sugar and ginger and mix well.

5 Pile the rhubarb mixture into the middle of the pastry round. Carefully draw the pastry up roughly around the filling so that it encloses it but does not cover it completely. Some of the fruit should remain visible in the centre.

6 Lightly glaze the pastry rim with any remaining egg yolk and sprinkle the chopped hazelnuts and golden sugar over. Bake for 30–35 minutes, or until the pastry is golden brown. Serve warm.

SERVES SIX

INGREDIENTS
  1 egg yolk, beaten
  25g/1oz/3 tbsp semolina
  450g/1lb rhubarb
  75g/3oz/6 tbsp caster
    (superfine) sugar
  1–2 pieces stem (crystallized) ginger
    in syrup, drained and
    finely chopped
  25g/1oz/¼ cup chopped hazelnuts
  30ml/2 tbsp golden granulated sugar
For the pastry
  225g/8oz/2 cups plain
    (all-purpose) flour
  pinch of salt
  115g/4oz/½ cup butter, diced
  45–60ml/3–4 tbsp chilled water

1 To make the pastry, sift the flour and salt into a small bowl. Rub or cut in the butter until the mixture resembles fine breadcrumbs. Sprinkle over 45ml/3 tbsp of the water and mix together to a soft dough, adding more water if needed. Wrap in clear film (plastic wrap) and chill for 30 minutes.

2 Preheat the oven to 200°C/400°F/ Gas 6. On a lightly floured surface, roll out the pastry to a 35cm/14in round. Lay it over the rolling pin and transfer it to a large baking sheet.

3 Brush a little egg yolk over the pastry round. Sprinkle the semolina evenly over the centre of the pastry, leaving a wide margin all round.

COOK' TIP
Egg yolk glaze brushed on to the pastry gives it a nice golden sheen. However, be careful not to let the glaze drip on to the baking sheet, or it will burn and be difficult to remove.

FRESH ORANGE TART

FINELY GRATED ORANGE RIND GIVES THIS RICH SHORTCRUST PASTRY ITS WONDERFUL COLOUR AND FLAVOUR. A CREAMY CUSTARD FILLING AND FRESH ORANGES TURN IT INTO A SOPHISTICATED DESSERT.

SERVES NINE

INGREDIENTS
   2 eggs, plus 2 egg yolks
   150g/5oz/⅔ cup caster
    (superfine) sugar
   150ml/¼ pint/⅔ cup single
    (light) cream
   finely grated rind and juice
    of 1 orange
   6–8 oranges
   fresh mint sprigs, to decorate
For the pastry
   175g/6oz/1½ cups plain
    (all-purpose) flour
   90g/3½oz/scant ½ cup butter, diced
   15ml/1 tbsp caster (superfine) sugar
   finely grated rind of 1 orange
   1 egg yolk
   about 10ml/2 tsp orange juice

1 To make the pastry, sift the flour and rub or cut in the butter. Stir in the sugar and orange rind. Beat the egg yolk with the orange juice, then add to the dry ingredients and mix to a firm dough.

2 Lightly and quickly knead the dough until smooth. Roll out and use to line a 20cm/8in square fluted tin. Wrap and chill for 30 minutes.

3 Put a baking sheet in the oven and preheat to 200°C/400°F/Gas 6. Prick the pastry case all over with a fork and line with foil and baking beans. Place on the hot baking sheet and bake blind for 12 minutes. Remove the foil and beans and bake the pastry for a further 5 minutes.

4 Whisk the eggs, yolks and sugar in a bowl until foamy. Whisk in the cream, followed by the orange rind and juice. Pour into the pastry case and bake for 30–35 minutes until firm. Remove from the oven and leave to cool on a wire rack still in the tin.

5 Peel the oranges, removing all the white pith and separate the segments by cutting between the membranes. Arrange the segments in rows on top of the tart. Chill until ready to serve, then carefully remove the tart from the tin and decorate with sprigs of fresh mint.

RICH AND INDULGENT PASTRY DESSERTS

Not all sweet pies and pastries are filled with fruit.

For pure indulgence, velvety smooth Coffee Custard Tart is

unbeatable. You'll find it here alongside decadent chocolate desserts

such as Dark Chocolate and Hazelnut Tart, a creamy Baked

Cheesecake with Kissel, and classics, such as American Pumpkin Pie,

Yorkshire Curd Tart and that most classic of

French pastries, Lemon Tart.

AMERICAN PUMPKIN PIE

THIS SPICY SWEET PIE IS TRADITIONALLY SERVED AT THANKSGIVING, OR AT HALLOWE'EN TO USE THE
PULP FROM THE HOLLOWED-OUT PUMPKIN LANTERNS.

SERVES EIGHT

INGREDIENTS
    900g/2lb piece of pumpkin
    2 large eggs
    75g/3oz/scant ½ cup soft light
      brown sugar
    60ml/4 tbsp golden (light
      corn) syrup
    250ml/8fl oz/1 cup double
      (heavy) cream
    15ml/1 tbsp mixed spice
    2.5ml/½ tsp salt
    icing (confectioners') sugar,
      for dusting
For the pastry
    200g/7oz/1¾ cups plain
      (all-purpose) flour
    2.5ml/½ tsp salt
    90g/3½oz/scant ½ cup butter, diced
    1 egg yolk
    15ml/1 tbsp chilled water

3 Preheat the oven to 200°C/400°F/ Gas 6. Roll out the pastry on a lightly floured surface and use to line a 23cm/ 9in loose-based flan tin (quiche pan). Prick the base all over with a fork and line with foil and baking beans. Chill the pastry case for 15 minutes. Bake for 10 minutes, then remove the foil and beans and bake the pastry case for a further 5 minutes.

4 Lower the oven temperature to 190°C/375°F/Gas 5. Tip the pumpkin pulp into a mixing bowl and beat in the eggs, sugar, syrup, cream, mixed spice and salt to make a smooth filling. Pour the mixture into the pastry case. Bake for 40 minutes, or until the filling has set. Dust the surface generously with icing sugar and serve the pie in slices at room temperature.

1 To make the pastry, sift the flour and salt into a mixing bowl. Rub or cut in the butter until the mixture resembles fine breadcrumbs, then mix in the egg yolk and enough chilled water to make a soft dough. Roll the dough into a ball, then wrap it in clear film (plastic wrap) and chill for at least 30 minutes.

2 Meanwhile, peel the pumpkin and remove the seeds. Cut the flesh into cubes. Place the pieces in a heavy pan and add enough water to cover. Bring to the boil and simmer for 15–20 minutes until tender. Mash the flesh well until smooth, then spoon the pumpkin into a sieve and set over a bowl to drain.

BUTTERNUT SQUASH AND MAPLE PIE

THIS AMERICAN-STYLE PIE HAS A RICH SHORTCRUST PASTRY CASE AND A CREAMY FILLING, SWEETENED WITH MAPLE SYRUP AND FLAVOURED WITH FRESH GINGER AND A DASH OF BRANDY.

SERVES TEN

INGREDIENTS
1 small butternut squash
60ml/4 tbsp water
2.5cm/1in piece of fresh root ginger,
  peeled and grated
120ml/4fl oz/½ cup double
  (heavy) cream
90ml/6 tbsp maple syrup
45ml/3 tbsp light muscovado
  (molasses) sugar
3 eggs, lightly beaten
30ml/2 tbsp brandy
1.5ml/¼ tsp grated nutmeg
beaten egg, to glaze
For the pastry
  175g/6oz/1½ cups plain
    (all-purpose) flour
  pinch of salt
  115g/4oz/½ cup butter, diced
  10ml/2 tsp caster (superfine) sugar
  1 egg, lightly beaten

1 To make the pastry, sift the flour and salt into a mixing bowl. Rub or cut in the butter until the mixture resembles fine breadcrumbs. Add the sugar and the egg. Mix to a dough. Wrap in clear film (plastic wrap). Chill for 30 minutes.

2 Halve the butternut squash, peel and scoop out the seeds. Cut the flesh into cubes and put in a pan with the water. Cover and cook gently for 15 minutes. Remove the lid, stir in the ginger and cook for a further 5 minutes until all the liquid has evaporated and the squash is tender. Cool slightly, then purée in a food processor until smooth.

3 Roll out the pastry and use to line a 23cm/9in flan tin (quiche pan). Gather up the trimmings, re-roll them thinly, then cut them into maple leaf shapes. Brush the edge of the pastry case with beaten egg and attach the maple leaf shapes at regular intervals to make a decorative rim. Cover with clear film and chill for 30 minutes.

4 Put a heavy baking sheet in the oven and preheat to 200°C/400°F/Gas 6. Prick the pastry base with a fork and line with foil and fill with baking beans. Bake blind on the hot baking sheet for 12 minutes.

5 Remove the foil and beans and bake for a further 5 minutes. Brush the base of the pastry case with beaten egg and return to the oven for about 3 minutes. Lower the oven temperature to 180°C/350°F/Gas 4.

6 Mix 200g/7oz/scant 1 cup of the butternut purée with the cream, syrup, sugar, eggs, brandy and grated nutmeg. (Discard any remaining purée.) Pour into the pastry case. Bake for about 30 minutes, or until the filling is lightly set. Cool slightly, then serve with cream.

CIDER PIE

FEW CAN RESIST THIS DELECTABLE PIE, WITH ITS RICH CIDER FILLING. SUGGEST THE SEASON WITH PRETTY PASTRY DECORATIONS OF APPLES, DOTTED AROUND THE EDGE OF THE PIE.

SERVES SIX

INGREDIENTS
    600ml/1 pint/2½ cups cider
      (hard cider)
    15g/½oz/1 tbsp butter
    250ml/8fl oz/1 cup maple syrup
    60ml/4 tbsp water
    2 eggs, at room temperature,
      separated and yolks beaten
    5ml/1 tsp grated nutmeg
    icing (confectioners') sugar,
      for dusting
For the pastry
    175g/6oz/1½ cups plain
      (all-purpose) flour
    1.5ml/¼ tsp salt
    10ml/2 tsp granulated sugar
    115g/4oz/½ cup cold butter, diced
    about 60ml/4 tbsp chilled water

1 To make the pastry, sift the flour, salt and sugar into a mixing bowl. Rub or cut in the butter until the mixture resembles fine breadcrumbs.

2 Sprinkle the chilled water over the flour mixture. Combine with a fork until the dough holds together. If the dough is too crumbly, add a little more water. Gather the dough into a ball and flatten into a round. Wrap in clear film (plastic wrap) and chill for 30 minutes.

COOK'S TIP
Cut apple shapes from the pastry trimmings, bake them for 10 minutes alongside the pie, then arrange on top of the baked pie before dusting with icing sugar.

3 Meanwhile, pour the cider into a pan and boil until only 175ml/6fl oz/¾ cup remains, or approximately one-third, then set aside to cool.

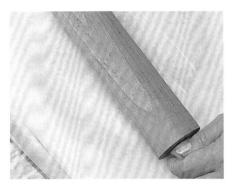

4 Roll out the pastry between two large sheets of baking parchment or clear film to a thickness of 3mm/⅛in. Use to line a 23cm/9in pie dish.

5 Trim the edge, leaving a 1cm/½in overhang. Fold the overhang under to form a rim. Using a fork, press the rim down and scallop the edge. Chill for at least 20 minutes. Preheat the oven to 180°C/ 350°F/Gas 4.

6 Place the butter, maple syrup, water and reduced cider in a pan and simmer gently for 5–6 minutes. Cool slightly, then whisk in the egg yolks.

7 Place the egg whites in a large bowl, and whisk vigorously until they form stiff peaks. Using a wooden spoon, gently fold in the cider mixture.

8 Pour the filling into the pastry case so that it fills the case evenly. Lightly dust with the grated nutmeg. Bake for 30–35 minutes, or until the filling is firmly set and golden. Dust with icing sugar and serve immediately.

DARK CHOCOLATE AND HAZELNUT TART

THIS CRISP, HAZELNUT-FLAVOURED PASTRY TASTES WONDERFUL WITH A RICH CHOCOLATE FILLING.

3 Roll out the pastry on a floured surface and use to line a 23cm/9in loose-based heart-shaped flan tin (quiche pan). Trim the edges. Cover and chill for a further 30 minutes.

4 Re-roll the pastry trimmings into a long strip, about 30cm/12in long. Cut this into six strips, each 5mm/¼in wide, and make two plaits (braids) with three pastry strips in each. Curve into a heart shape and press gently to join together at both ends. Carefully place the heart on a baking sheet lined with baking parchment and chill.

5 Put a heavy baking sheet in the oven and preheat to 200°C/400°F/Gas 6. Prick the base of the pastry case with a fork. Line with foil and baking beans and bake blind for 10 minutes. Remove the foil and beans and bake for a further 5 minutes. Bake the pastry plait on the shelf below for 10 minutes, or until lightly browned.

SERVES TEN

INGREDIENTS
   300ml/½ pint/1¼ cups double
     (heavy) cream
   150ml/¼ pint/⅔ cup creamy milk
   150g/5oz dark (bittersweet)
     chocolate, chopped
   4 eggs
   50g/2oz/¼ cup caster (superfine) sugar
   5ml/1 tsp vanilla essence (extract)
   15ml/1 tbsp plain (all-purpose) flour
   115g/4oz/1 cup toasted hazelnuts
   10ml/2 tsp icing
     (confectioners') sugar
For the pastry
   150g/5oz/1¼ cups plain
     (all-purpose) flour
   pinch of salt
   45ml/3 tbsp caster (superfine) sugar
   50g/2oz/½ cup ground
     hazelnuts, toasted
   90g/3½oz/scant ½ cup butter, diced
   1 egg, lightly beaten

1 To make the pastry, sift the flour, salt and sugar into a mixing bowl, then mix in the toasted hazelnuts. Rub or cut in the butter until the mixture resembles fine breadcrumbs.

2 Make a well in the centre, add the beaten egg and mix to a firm dough. Knead the dough on a lightly floured surface for a few seconds until smooth. Wrap in clear film (plastic wrap) and chill for 30 minutes.

6 Pour the cream and milk into a pan and bring to the boil. Add the chocolate and stir until melted. Whisk the eggs, caster sugar, vanilla and flour together. Pour the hot chocolate cream over the egg mixture, whisking all the time. Stir in the chopped hazelnuts.

7 Pour the chocolate and hazelnut mixture into the pastry case and bake for 25 minutes, or until just set. Allow to cool, then remove from the tin and transfer to a serving plate. Place the pastry rope on top, then lightly dust with icing sugar.

CHOCOLATE, PEAR AND PECAN PIE

A CLASSIC PIE GETS A TEMPTING NEW TASTE WITH DARK CHOCOLATE AND JUICY PEARS.

SERVES EIGHT TO TEN

INGREDIENTS
   3 small pears, peeled
   165g/5½oz/scant ¾ cup caster
     (superfine) sugar
   150ml/¼ pint/⅔ cup water
   pared rind of 1 lemon
   50g/2oz plain (semisweet) chocolate,
     broken into pieces
   50g/2oz/¼ cup butter, diced
   225g/8oz/scant ¾ cup golden
     (light corn) syrup
   3 eggs, beaten
   5ml/1 tsp vanilla essence (extract)
   150g/5oz/1¼ cups pecan
     nuts, chopped
For the pastry
   175g/6oz/½ cup plain
     (all-purpose) flour
   115g/4oz/½ cup butter, diced
   25g/1oz/2 tbsp caster
     (superfine) sugar
   1 egg yolk
   10–15ml/2–3 tsp chilled water

1 To make the pastry, sift the flour into a mixing bowl and rub or cut in the butter. Stir in the sugar. Mix the egg yolk with 10ml/2 tsp of the water, add to the dry ingredients and mix to a dough, adding more water if necessary. Knead for a few seconds until smooth. Wrap the dough in clear film (plastic wrap) and chill for 30 minutes.

2 Preheat the oven to 200°F/400°C/ Gas 6. Roll out the pastry and line a deep 23cm/9in fluted flan tin (quiche pan). Chill the case for 20 minutes, then line it with foil and baking beans. Bake for 10 minutes. Lift out the foil and beans and bake for 5 minutes more. Set aside to cool.

3 Cut the pears in half and remove the cores with a small spoon. Place 50g/ 2oz/¼ cup of the sugar in a pan with the water. Add the lemon rind and bring to the boil. Add the pears. Cover, lower the heat and simmer for 10 minutes. Remove the pears from the pan and set aside to cool. Discard the liquid.

4 Place the chocolate into a heatproof bowl and melt over a pan of simmering water. Beat in the butter, then set aside. In a separate pan, heat the remaining sugar and syrup together until most of the sugar has dissolved. Bring to the boil and simmer for 2 minutes.

5 Whisk the eggs into the chocolate mixture until combined, then whisk in the syrup mixture. Stir in the vanilla essence and pecan nuts.

6 Place the pear halves flat side down on a board. Using a fine sharp knife, make lengthways cuts all along each pear, taking care not to cut all the way through. Using a palette knife (metal spatula), lift the pears into the pastry case and arrange. Pour the pecan mixture over the top, so that the pears are still visible through the mixture.

7 Bake for 25–30 minutes, or until the filling is set, then leave to cool on a wire rack before removing the pie from the tin and serving, in slices.

WALNUT PIE

SWEETENED WITH COFFEE-FLAVOURED MAPLE SYRUP, THIS PIE HAS A RICH AND STICKY TEXTURE. THE WALNUTS CAN BE REPLACED BY PECAN NUTS FOR AN AUTHENTIC AMERICAN PIE.

SERVES EIGHT

INGREDIENTS
    30ml/2 tbsp ground coffee
    175ml/6fl oz/¾ cup maple syrup
    25g/1oz/2 tbsp butter, softened
    175g/6oz/¾ cup soft light
      brown sugar
    3 eggs, beaten
    5ml/1 tsp vanilla essence (extract)
    115g/4oz/1 cup walnut halves
For the pastry
    150g/5oz/1¼ cups plain
      (all-purpose) flour
    pinch of salt
    25g/1oz/¼ cup icing
      (confectioners') sugar
    75g/3oz/6 tbsp butter, diced
    2 egg yolks

2 Knead the pastry on a lightly floured surface for a few seconds until smooth. Wrap in clear film (plastic wrap) and chill for 30 minutes.

3 Roll out the pastry and use to line a 20cm/8in fluted flan tin (quiche pan). Line with baking parchment and baking beans and bake for about 10 minutes. Remove the paper and beans and bake for a further 5 minutes until brown. Set the pastry case aside. Lower the oven temperature to 180°C/350°F/Gas 4.

4 Heat the coffee and maple syrup in a pan until almost boiling. Set aside to cool slightly. Mix the butter and sugar in a bowl, then gradually beat in the eggs. Strain the reserved maple syrup mixture into the bowl, add the vanilla essence and stir well.

1 Preheat the oven to 200°C/400°F/ Gas 6. To make the pastry, sift the flour, salt and icing sugar into a mixing bowl. Rub or cut in the butter until the mixture resembles fine breadcrumbs. Add the egg yolks and mix well to form a soft dough.

5 Arrange the walnuts in the pastry case, then carefully pour in the filling. Bake for 30–35 minutes, or until lightly browned and firm. Allow to cool for a few minutes before serving warm with crème fraîche or vanilla ice cream.

ALMOND AND PINE NUT TART

STRANGE THOUGH IT MAY SEEM, THIS TRADITIONAL TART IS AN ITALIAN VERSION OF THE HOMELY BAKEWELL TART FROM DERBYSHIRE IN ENGLAND.

SERVES EIGHT

INGREDIENTS
  115g/4oz/½ cup butter, softened
  115g/4oz/½ cup caster
    (superfine) sugar
  1 egg, plus 2 egg yolks
  150g/5oz/1¼ cups ground almonds
  115g/4oz/1⅓ cups pine nuts
  60ml/4 tbsp seedless raspberry jam
  icing (confectioners') sugar,
    for dusting
For the pastry
  175g/6oz/1½ cups plain
    (all-purpose) flour
  65g/2½oz/⅓ cup caster
    (superfine) sugar
  1.5ml/¼ tsp baking powder
  pinch of salt
  115g/4oz/½ cup chilled butter, diced
  1 egg yolk

1 To make the pastry, sift the flour, sugar, baking powder and salt on to a clean, dry cold surface or marble pastry board. Make a well in the centre and put in the diced butter and egg yolk. Gradually work the flour mixture into the butter and egg yolk, using just your fingertips, until you have a soft, pliable dough.

2 Press the dough into a 23cm/9in loose-based fluted flan tin (quiche pan). Chill for 30 minutes.

3 Cream the butter and sugar with an electric mixer until light, then use a wooden spoon to beat in the egg and egg yolks a little at a time, alternating them with the almonds. Beat in the nuts.

4 Preheat the oven to 160°C/325°F/ Gas 3. Spread the jam evenly over the pastry base, then spoon in the filling. Bake for 30–35 minutes until golden, or until a skewer inserted in the centre of the tart comes out clean.

5 Transfer to a wire rack and leave to cool, then carefully remove the side of the tin, leaving the tart on the tin base. Dust with icing sugar and serve with whipped cream.

COOK'S TIP
This pastry is too sticky to roll out, so simply mould it into the base and sides of the tin with your fingers.

HONEY AND PINE NUT TART

WONDERFUL TARTS OF ALL DESCRIPTIONS ARE TO BE FOUND THROUGHOUT FRANCE, AND THIS RECIPE RECALLS THE FLAVOURS OF THE SOUTH, WITH ITS SUNNY MEDITERRANEAN INFLUENCES.

3 Roll out the pastry on a lightly floured surface and use to line a 23cm/9in flan tin (quiche pan). Prick the base with a fork, then chill for 10 minutes. Line with baking parchment and fill with baking beans. Bake for 10 minutes. Remove the paper and beans and set the pastry case aside.

4 Cream the butter and caster sugar together until light and fluffy. Beat in the eggs one at a time. In a small pan, gently heat the honey until it melts, then add it to the butter mixture with the lemon rind and juice. Mix well. Stir in the pine nuts and salt, blending well, then pour the filling evenly into the pastry case.

SERVES SIX

INGREDIENTS
   115g/4oz/½ cup butter, diced
   115g/4oz/½ cup caster
     (superfine) sugar
   3 eggs, beaten
   175g/6oz/⅔ cup sunflower honey
   grated rind and juice of 1 lemon
   225g/8oz/2⅔ cups pine nuts
   pinch of salt
   icing (confectioners') sugar,
     for dusting
For the pastry
   225g/8oz/2 cups plain
     (all-purpose) flour
   115g/4oz/½ cup butter, diced
   30ml/2 tbsp icing
     (confectioners') sugar
   1 egg
   15ml/1 tbsp chilled water

1 Preheat the oven to 180°C/350°F/ Gas 4. To make the pastry, sift the flour into a large mixing bowl and rub or cut in the butter until the mixture resembles fine breadcrumbs.

2 Stir in the icing sugar. Add the egg and water and mix to form a soft dough. Knead lightly until smooth.

5 Bake for about 45 minutes, or until the filling is lightly browned and set. Leave the tart to cool slightly in the tin, then remove and dust generously with icing sugar. Serve warm, or at room temperature, with crème fraîche or vanilla ice cream, if you like.

LEMON TART

THIS CLASSIC FRENCH TART IS ONE OF THE MOST DELICIOUS DESSERTS THERE IS. A RICH LEMON CURD
IS ENCASED IN A CRISP PASTRY CASE. CRÈME FRAÎCHE IS AN OPTIONAL – BUT NICE – EXTRA.

SERVES SIX

6 eggs, beaten
350g/12oz/1½ cups caster
  (superfine) sugar
115g/4oz/½ cup butter
grated rind and juice of 4 lemons
icing (confectioners') sugar
  for dusting
For the pastry
225g/8oz/2 cups plain
  (all-purpose) flour
115g/4oz/½ cup butter, diced
30ml/2 tbsp icing
  (confectioners') sugar
1 egg
5ml/1 tsp vanilla
  essence (extract)
15ml/1 tbsp chilled water

1 Preheat the oven to 200°C/400°F/
Gas 6. To make the pastry, sift the flour
into a mixing bowl and rub or cut in the
butter until the mixture resembles fine
breadcrumbs. Stir in the icing sugar.

2 Add the egg, vanilla essence and
most of the chilled water, then work to a
soft dough. Add a few more drops of
water if necessary. Knead quickly and
lightly until smooth.

3 Roll out the pastry on a floured
surface and use to line a 23cm/9in flan
tin (quiche pan). Prick the base all over
with a fork. Line with baking parchment
and fill with baking beans. Bake the
pastry case for 10 minutes. Remove the
paper and beans and set the pastry
case aside while you make the filling.

4 Put the eggs, sugar and butter into
a pan, and stir over a low heat until all
the sugar has dissolved. Add the lemon
rind and juice, and continue cooking,
stirring constantly, until the lemon curd
has thickened slightly.

5 Pour the curd mixture into the pastry
case. Bake for about 20 minutes, or
until the lemon curd filling is just set.
Transfer the tart to a wire rack to cool.
Dust the surface of the tart generously
with icing sugar just before serving.

BAKED CHEESECAKE WITH KISSEL

AS WITH ALL CLASSIC CHEESECAKES, THIS SIMPLE GERMAN VERSION IS BAKED IN A RICH SHORTCRUST PASTRY CASE, FLAVOURED HERE WITH LEMON. KISSEL IS A TRADITIONAL RED BERRY COMPÔTE.

SERVES EIGHT TO TEN

INGREDIENTS
  675g/1½lb/3 cups quark or low-fat
    soft white cheese
  4 eggs, separated
  150g/5oz/⅔ cup caster
    (superfine) sugar
  45ml/3 tbsp cornflour (cornstarch)
  150ml/¼ pint/⅔ cup sour cream
  finely grated rind and juice of
    ½ lemon
  5ml/1 tsp vanilla essence (extract)
  fresh mint sprigs, to decorate
For the pastry
  225g/8oz/2 cups plain
    (all-purpose) flour
  115g/4oz/½ cup butter, diced
  15ml/1 tbsp caster (superfine) sugar
  finely grated rind of ½ lemon
  1 egg, beaten
For the kissel
  450g/1lb/4–4½ cups prepared red
    berry fruit
  50g/2oz/¼ cup caster
    (superfine) sugar
  120ml/4fl oz/½ cup water
  15ml/1 tbsp arrowroot

1 To make the pastry, sift the flour into a large mixing bowl. Rub or cut in the butter until the mixture resembles fine breadcrumbs. Stir in the sugar and lemon rind, then add the beaten egg and mix to a dough. Wrap in clear film (plastic wrap) and chill for 30 minutes.

2 Roll out the pastry and use to line a 25cm/10in loose-based fluted flan tin (quiche pan). Chill for 1 hour.

3 Place the quark or soft white cheese in a fine sieve set over a bowl and leave to drain for 1 hour.

4 Preheat the oven to 200°C/400°F/ Gas 6. Prick the base of the chilled pastry case all over with a fork, fill it with crumpled foil and bake for about 5 minutes. Remove the foil and bake for a further 5 minutes. Remove the pastry case from the oven and lower the oven temperature to 180°C/350°F/Gas 4.

5 Put the drained quark or soft cheese in a bowl with the egg yolks and caster sugar and mix together.

6 Blend the cornflour in a cup with a little of the sour cream, then add to the cheese mixture along with the remaining sour cream, the lemon rind and juice and vanilla essence. Mix thoroughly with a wooden spoon.

7 Whisk the egg whites in a grease-free bowl until stiff, then fold into the cheese mixture, one-third at a time. Pour the filling into the pastry case and bake for 1–1¼ hours, or until golden and firm. Switch off the oven and leave the door slightly ajar. Let the cheesecake cool down in the oven, then remove it and chill for 2 hours.

8 To make the kissel, put the prepared fruit, caster sugar and water into a pan and cook over a low heat until the sugar dissolves and the juices begin to run. Remove the fruit with a slotted spoon and put in a bowl. Set aside. Retain the fruit juices in the pan.

9 Mix the arrowroot with a little cold water in a cup. Stir the mixture into the reserved fruit juices in the pan and bring to the boil, stirring constantly. Return the fruit to the pan, mix well, then allow to cool.

10 Serve the well-chilled cheesecake in slices, spooning a little of the kissel over each portion. Decorate with sprigs of mint and fresh berries.

YORKSHIRE CURD TART

THE DISTINGUISHING CHARACTERISTIC OF YORKSHIRE CURD TARTS IS ALLSPICE, OR "CLOVE PEPPER"
AS IT WAS KNOWN LOCALLY. THIS TART TASTES SUPERB AND IS NOT TOO SWEET.

2 Put the dough on a floured surface, knead lightly and briefly, then form into a ball. Roll out the pastry thinly and use to line a 20cm/8in fluted loose-based flan tin (quiche pan). Cover with clear film (plastic wrap) and chill for about 15 minutes.

3 Preheat the oven to 190°C/375°F/ Gas 5. Mix the sugar with the ground allspice in a bowl, then stir in the eggs, lemon rind and juice, butter, curd cheese and raisins. Mix well.

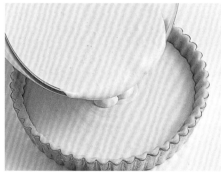

4 Pour the filling into the pastry case, then bake for 40 minutes, or until the pastry is cooked and the filling is lightly set and golden brown. Cut the tart into wedges while it is still slightly warm, and serve with cream, if you like.

SERVES EIGHT

INGREDIENTS
  90g/3½oz/scant ½ cup soft light
    brown sugar
  large pinch of ground allspice
  3 eggs, beaten
  grated rind and juice of 1 lemon
  40g/1½oz/3 tbsp butter, melted
  450g/1lb/2 cups curd
    (farmer's) cheese
  75g/3oz/scant ½ cup raisins
For the pastry
  225g/8oz/2 cups plain
    (all-purpose) flour
  115g/4oz/½ cup butter, diced
  1 egg yolk
  15–30ml/1–2 tbsp chilled water

1 To make the pastry, place the flour in a large mixing bowl and rub or cut in the butter until the mixture resembles fine breadcrumbs. Stir the egg yolk into the flour and add just enough of the water to bind the mixture together to form a dough.

COOK'S TIP
Although it is not traditional, mixed spice (apple pie spice) would make a good substitute for the ground allspice.

COFFEE CUSTARD TART

FOR SHEER DECADENCE, TRY THIS CRISP WALNUT PASTRY CASE, FLAVOURED WITH VANILLA AND FILLED WITH A SMOOTH CREAMY COFFEE CUSTARD. IT IS BAKED UNTIL LIGHTLY SET AND TOPPED WITH CREAM.

SERVES SIX TO EIGHT

INGREDIENTS
    1 vanilla pod (bean)
    30ml/2 tbsp ground coffee
    300ml/½ pint/1¼ cups single
      (light) cream
    150ml/¼ pint/⅔ cup milk
    2 eggs, plus 2 egg yolks
    50g/2oz/¼ cup caster
      (superfine) sugar
    icing (confectioners') sugar,
      for dusting
    whipped cream, to serve
For the pastry
    175g/6oz/1½ cups plain
      (all-purpose) flour
    30ml/2 tbsp icing
      (confectioners') sugar
    115g/4oz/½ cup butter, diced
    75g/3oz/¾ cup walnuts, chopped
    1 egg yolk
    5ml/1 tsp vanilla essence (extract)
    10ml/2 tsp chilled water

1 To make the pastry, sift the flour and sugar into a mixing bowl. Rub or cut in the butter until the mixture resembles fine breadcrumbs. Stir in the walnuts.

2 In a small bowl, mix together the egg yolk, vanilla and water. Add to the dry ingredients and mix to a smooth dough. Wrap in clear film (plastic wrap) and chill for about 20 minutes. Put a heavy baking sheet in the oven and preheat to 200°C/400°F/Gas 6.

3 Roll out the pastry and use to line a 20cm/8in flan tin (quiche pan) or flan ring, using a knife to trim the edges. Chill again for 20 minutes.

4 Prick the base all over with a fork. Fill the pastry case with foil and baking beans and bake on the baking sheet for 10 minutes. Remove the foil and beans, and bake the case for 10 minutes more. Reduce the oven temperature to 150°C/300°F/Gas 2.

5 Meanwhile, split the vanilla pod and scrape out the seeds. Put both in a pan with the coffee, cream and milk. Heat until almost boiling, remove from the heat, cover and infuse for 10 minutes. Whisk the eggs, egg yolks and caster sugar together in a bowl.

6 Return the cream mixture to the heat, bring to the boil, then pour on to the egg mixture, stirring constantly. Strain into the pastry case. Bake for 40–45 minutes, or until lightly set. Cool on a wire rack. Serve dusted with icing sugar and topped with whirls of cream.

CLASSIC DECORATED PIES

There are some sweet pies that are so popular that recipes for them are found all over the world. Classics like Deep-dish Apple Pie and Blueberry Pie come into this category, along with Linzertorte, Shoofly Pie and Treacle Tart. Over the centuries, cooks creating these pies have lovingly decorated them. Some are topped with pastry shapes that hint at what lies beneath, others have lattice or crumble crusts, a few conceal their fillings under swirls of meringue, but all are delectable.

DEEP-DISH APPLE PIE

This all-time classic favourite is made with rich shortcrust pastry. Inside, sugar, spices and flour create a deliciously thick and syrupy sauce with the apple juices.

SERVES SIX

INGREDIENTS
  115g/4oz/½ cup caster
    (superfine) sugar
  45ml/3 tbsp plain (all-purpose) flour
  2.5ml/½ tsp ground cinnamon
  finely grated rind of 1 orange
  900g/2lb tart cooking apples
  1 egg white, lightly beaten
  30ml/2 tbsp golden granulated sugar
  whipped cream, to serve
For the pastry
  350g/12oz/3 cups plain
    (all-purpose) flour
  pinch of salt
  175g/6oz/¾ cup butter, diced
  about 75ml/5 tbsp chilled water

1 To make the pastry, sift the flour and salt into a mixing bowl and rub or cut in the butter until the mixture resembles fine breadcrumbs.

2 Sprinkle over the water and mix to a firm, soft dough. Knead lightly for a few seconds until smooth. Wrap in clear film (plastic wrap) and chill for 30 minutes.

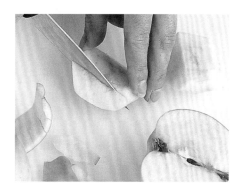

3 Combine the caster sugar, flour, cinnamon and orange rind in a bowl. Peel, core and thinly slice the apples. Add to the sugar mixture in the bowl, then toss gently with your fingertips until they are all evenly coated.

4 Put a baking sheet in the oven and preheat to 200°C/400°F/Gas 6. Roll out just over half the pastry and use to line a 23cm/9in pie dish that is 4cm/1½in deep, allowing the pastry to overhang the edges slightly. Spoon in the filling, doming the apple slices in the centre.

5 Roll out the remaining pastry to form the lid. Lightly brush the edges of the pastry case with a little water, then place the lid over the apple filling.

6 Trim the pastry with a sharp knife. Gently press the edges together to seal, then knock up the edge. Re-roll the pastry trimmings and cut out apple and leaf shapes. Brush the top of the pie with egg white. Arrange the pastry apples and leaves on top.

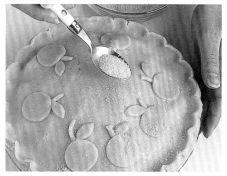

7 Brush again with egg white, then sprinkle with golden granulated sugar. Make two small slits in the top of the pie to allow steam to escape.

8 Bake for 30 minutes, then lower the oven temperature to 180°C/350°F/Gas 4 and bake for a further 15 minutes until the pastry is golden and the apples are soft – check by inserting a small sharp knife or skewer through one of the slits in the top of the pie. Serve hot, with some whipped cream.

BLUEBERRY PIE

AMERICAN BLUEBERRIES OR EUROPEAN BILBERRIES CAN BE USED FOR THIS PIE. YOU MAY NEED TO ADD A LITTLE MORE SUGAR IF YOU ARE LUCKY ENOUGH TO FIND NATIVE BILBERRIES.

SERVES SIX

INGREDIENTS
  800g/1¾lb/7 cups blueberries
  75g/3oz/6 tbsp caster (superfine)
    sugar, plus extra for sprinkling
  45ml/3 tbsp cornflour
    (cornstarch)
  grated rind and juice of ½ orange
  grated rind of ½ lemon
  2.5ml/½ tsp ground cinnamon
  15g/½oz/1 tbsp butter, diced
  1 egg, beaten
  whipped cream, to serve
For the pastry
  275g/10oz/2½ cups plain
    (all-purpose) flour
  pinch of salt
  75g/3oz/6 tbsp butter, diced
  50g/2oz/¼ cup white vegetable fat
  60–75ml/4–5 tbsp chilled water

1 To make the pastry, sift the flour and salt into a large mixing bowl. Rub or cut in the fat until the mixture resembles fine breadcrumbs.

2 Sprinkle over most of the water and mix to a soft dough. Add more water if necessary. Knead lightly. Wrap in clear film (plastic wrap) and chill.

3 Preheat the oven to 200°C/400°F/ Gas 6. Roll out half the pastry and use to line a 23cm/9in pie dish, allowing the excess pastry to overhang the edge.

4 In a bowl, mix the blueberries, caster sugar, cornflour, orange rind and juice, lemon rind and cinnamon. Spoon into the pastry case and dot with the butter.

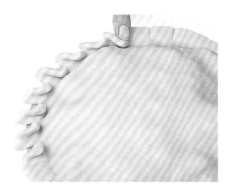

5 Roll out the remaining pastry and use to make a lid for the pie. Trim off the excess, leaving a rim all round. Cut the rim at 2.5cm/1in intervals, then fold each pastry section over on itself to form a triangle. Re-roll the trimmings and cut out pastry decorations from them. Attach them to the pastry lid with a little of the beaten egg.

6 Glaze the pastry with the beaten egg and sprinkle with caster sugar. Bake for 30 minutes, or until golden. Serve warm or cold with whipped cream.

PEACH LEAF PIE

JUICY, LIGHTLY SPICED PEACH SLICES ARE COVERED WITH A CRUST MADE ENTIRELY FROM INDIVIDUAL PASTRY LEAVES TO MAKE THIS SPECTACULAR PIE.

SERVES EIGHT

INGREDIENTS
 1.2kg/2½lb ripe peaches
 juice of 1 lemon
 115g/4oz/½ cup granulated sugar
 45ml/3 tbsp cornflour (cornstarch)
 1.5ml/¼ tsp grated nutmeg
 2.5ml/½ tsp ground cinnamon
 25g/1oz/2 tbsp butter, diced
 1 egg, beaten with 45ml/1 tbsp
   water, to glaze
For the pastry
 225g/8oz/2 cups plain
   (all-purpose) flour
 4ml/¾ tsp salt
 115g/4oz/½ cup cold butter, diced
 40g/1½oz/3 tbsp white vegetable
   fat, diced
 75–90ml/5–6 tbsp chilled water

1 To make the pastry, sift the flour and salt into a large mixing bowl. Add the butter and vegetable fat, and rub in with your fingertips or cut in with a pastry blender until the mixture resembles coarse breadcrumbs.

2 Sprinkle over the dry ingredients just enough of the water to bind the mixture and use a fork to bring it together to form a soft dough. Gather the dough into two balls, one slightly larger than the other. Wrap separately in clear film (plastic wrap) and chill for 30 minutes. Meanwhile, put a baking sheet in the oven and preheat to 220°C/425°F/Gas 7.

3 Drop a few peaches at a time into a large pan of boiling water, leave for 20 seconds, then transfer to a bowl of cold water. When cool, peel. Slice the peaches and mix with the lemon juice, sugar, cornflour and spices. Set aside.

4 On a lightly floured surface, roll out the larger piece of pastry to a thickness of 3mm/⅛in. Use to line a 23cm/9in pie plate. Chill until required.

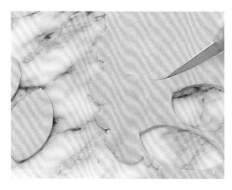

5 Roll out the second piece of pastry and cut out leaf shapes about 7.5cm/3in long. Cut out enough to completely cover the top. Mark veins with a knife.

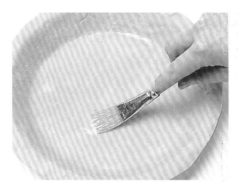

6 Brush the base of the pastry case with egg glaze. Add the peach mixture, piling it into a dome in the centre. Dot with the butter.

7 To assemble the pie top, start from the outside edge. Make a ring of leaves around the edge attaching each leaf to the pastry base with a dab of egg glaze. Place a second ring of leaves above, staggering the positions. Continue with rows of leaves until the pie is covered. Brush with egg glaze.

8 Bake the pie on the hot baking sheet for about 10 minutes. Lower the oven temperature to 180°C/350°F/Gas 4 and continue to bake for 35–40 minutes more, or until golden. Serve hot, with cream, if you like.

COOK'S TIP
Baking the pie on a hot baking sheet helps to make the pastry case crisp on the base. The moisture from the filling might otherwise cause the pastry to become soggy.

LINZERTORTE

USE A GOOD QUALITY JAM OR CONSERVE TO FILL THE CINNAMON AND ALMOND PASTRY CASE IN THIS TRADITIONAL AUSTRIAN SPECIALITY, AND DUST IT WITH ICING SUGAR BEFORE SERVING.

SERVES EIGHT TO TEN

INGREDIENTS

200g/7oz/scant 1 cup butter
200g/7oz/scant 1 cup caster
   (superfine) sugar
3 eggs, plus 2 egg yolks
2.5ml/½ tsp ground cinnamon
grated rind of ½ lemon
115g/4oz/2 cups fine sweet biscuit
   (cookie) crumbs
150g/5oz/1¼ cups ground almonds
225g/8oz/2 cups plain (all-purpose)
   flour, sifted
225g/8oz/¾ cup raspberry jam
icing (confectioners') sugar,
   for dusting

1 Preheat the oven to 190°C/375°F/ Gas 5. Cream the butter and sugar together until light. Slowly add the eggs and 1 of the egg yolks, beating all the time, then add the cinnamon and rind.

2 Stir the crumbs and ground almonds into the mixture. Mix well, then add the sifted flour. Knead the mixture to form a dough, then wrap in clear film (plastic wrap) and chill for about 30 minutes.

3 Roll out two-thirds of the pastry on a lightly floured surface and use to line a deep 25cm/10in loose-based flan tin (quiche pan). Press the pastry into the sides and trim the edge.

4 Spread the raspberry jam generously and evenly over the base of the pastry case. Roll out the remaining pastry into a long rectangle. Cut this into even strips with a sharp knife and arrange in a lattice pattern over the jam filling.

5 Lightly beat the remaining egg yolk in a small bowl, then brush it evenly over the pastry rim and lattice. Bake the flan for 45 minutes, or until golden brown. Leave to cool in the tin before turning out on to a wire rack. Just before serving, sift a little icing sugar over the top of the Linzertorte. Serve with custard, if you like.

ITALIAN CHOCOLATE RICOTTA TART

CREAMY RICOTTA CHEESE PACKED WITH MIXED PEEL AND DARK CHOCOLATE CHIPS IS BAKED IN A CHOCOLATE AND SHERRY PASTRY CASE FOR MAXIMUM FLAVOUR.

SERVES SIX

INGREDIENTS
   2 egg yolks
   115g/4oz/½ cup caster
     (superfine) sugar
   500g/1¼lb/2½ cups ricotta cheese
   finely grated rind of 1 lemon
   90ml/6 tbsp dark (bittersweet)
     chocolate chips
   75ml/5 tbsp chopped mixed peel
   45ml/3 tbsp chopped angelica
For the pastry
   225g/8oz/2 cups plain
     (all-purpose) flour
   30ml/2 tbsp cocoa powder
     (unsweetened)
   60ml/4 tbsp caster (superfine) sugar
   115g/4oz/½ cup butter, diced
   60ml/4 tbsp dry sherry

1 Preheat the oven to 200°C/400°F/ Gas 6. To make the pastry, sift the flour and cocoa into a bowl, then stir in the sugar. Rub or cut in the butter until the mixture resembles fine breadcrumbs, then work in the dry sherry, using your fingertips, until the mixture binds to a firm, smooth dough.

2 Roll out three-quarters of the pastry on a lightly floured surface and use to line a 24cm/9½in loose-based flan tin (quiche pan). Chill for 20 minutes.

COOK'S TIP
This chocolate tart is best served at room temperature, so if made in advance, chill it when cool, then, when needed, bring to room temperature before serving.

3 Beat the egg yolks and sugar in a bowl, then add the ricotta cheese. Beat with a wooden spoon to mix thoroughly. Stir in the lemon rind, chocolate chips, mixed peel and angelica. Scrape the ricotta mixture into the pastry case and level the surface.

4 Roll out the remaining pastry thinly and cut into narrow strips, then arrange these in a lattice over the filling. Bake for 15 minutes, then lower the oven temperature to 180°C/350°F/Gas 4 and bake for 30–35 minutes more until golden brown. Leave to cool in the tin.

SHOOFLY PIE

AN UNSWEETENED PASTRY CASE MADE WITH A SIMPLE COMBINATION OF BUTTER AND CREAM CHEESE COMPLEMENTS THE WONDERFUL DARK SWEET FILLING OF THIS PIE FROM THE AMERICAN DEEP SOUTH.

3 Mix the flour, brown sugar, salt, spices and butter in a bowl. Rub in with your fingertips until the mixture resembles coarse breadcrumbs, then set aside.

4 Roll out the dough thinly on a lightly floured surface to a thickness of about 3mm/⅛in and use to line a 23cm/9in pie plate. Trim and flute the pastry edges. Spoon one-third of the filling mixture into the pastry case.

5 Whisk the eggs with the treacle in a large bowl. Put a baking sheet in the oven to preheat.

6 Pour the boiling water into a small bowl and stir in the bicarbonate of soda; it will foam. Pour immediately into the egg mixture and whisk to blend. Pour into the pastry case and sprinkle the remaining filling mixture over the top in an even layer.

7 Place the pie on the hot baking sheet and bake for about 35 minutes, or until browned. Leave to cool, then serve at room temperature.

SERVES EIGHT

INGREDIENTS
- 115g/4oz/1 cup plain (all-purpose) flour
- 115g/4oz/½ cup firmly packed soft dark brown sugar
- 1.5ml/¼ tsp each salt, ground ginger, cinnamon, mace, and nutmeg
- 75g/3oz/6 tbsp cold butter, diced
- 2 eggs
- 185g/6½oz/½ cup black treacle (molasses)
- 120ml/4fl oz/½ cup boiling water
- 1.5ml/½ tsp bicarbonate of soda (baking soda)

For the pastry
- 115g/4oz/½ cup cream cheese
- 115g/4oz/½ cup butter, diced
- 115g/4oz/1 cup plain (all-purpose) flour

1 To make the pastry, put the cream cheese and butter in a mixing bowl. Sift over the flour.

2 Rub or cut in with a pastry blender to bind the dough together. Wrap in clear film (plastic wrap) and chill for at least 30 minutes. Meanwhile, preheat the oven to 190°C/375°F/Gas 5.

TREACLE TART

TRADITIONAL SHORTCRUST PASTRY IS PERFECT FOR THIS OLD-FASHIONED FAVOURITE, WITH ITS STICKY LEMON AND GOLDEN SYRUP FILLING AND TWISTED LATTICE TOPPING.

SERVES FOUR TO SIX

INGREDIENTS
    260g/9½oz/generous ¾ cup golden
      (light corn) syrup
    75g/3oz/1½ cups fresh
      white breadcrumbs
    grated rind of 1 lemon
    30ml/2 tbsp lemon juice
For the pastry
    150g/5oz/1¼ cups plain
      (all-purpose) flour
    2.5ml/½ tsp salt
    130g/4½oz/9 tbsp chilled
      butter, diced
    45–60/3–4 tbsp chilled water

1 To make the pastry, combine the flour and salt in a bowl. Rub or cut in the butter until the mixture resembles coarse breadcrumbs.

2 With a fork, stir in just enough water to bind the dough. Gather into a smooth ball, knead lightly for a few seconds until smooth then wrap in clear film (plastic wrap) and chill for at least 20 minutes.

3 On a lightly floured surface, roll out the pastry to a thickness of 3mm/⅛in. Transfer to a 20cm/8in fluted flan tin (quiche pan) and trim off the overhang. Chill the pastry case for 20 minutes. Reserve the pastry trimmings.

4 Put a baking sheet in the oven and preheat to 200°C/400°F/Gas 6. To make the filling, warm the syrup in a pan until it melts.

5 Remove the syrup from the heat and stir in the breadcrumbs and lemon rind. Leave to stand for 10 minutes, then add more breadcrumbs if the mixture is too thin and moist. Stir in the lemon juice, then spread the mixture evenly in the pastry case.

6 Roll out the pastry trimmings and cut into 10–12 thin strips.

7 Twist the strips into spirals, then lay half of them on the filling. Arrange the remaining strips at right angles to form a lattice. Press the ends on to the rim.

8 Place the tart on the hot baking sheet and bake for 10 minutes. Lower the oven temperature to 190°C/375°F/Gas 5. Bake for 15 minutes more, until golden. Serve warm with custard.

PLUM CRUMBLE PIE

POLENTA ADDS A WONDERFUL GOLDEN HUE AND CRUNCHINESS TO THE CRUMBLE TOPPING FOR THIS PIE, WHICH MAKES A PERFECT CONTRAST TO THE RIPE, JUICY PLUM FILLING.

3 Preheat the oven to 180°C/350°F/Gas 4. Sprinkle the sugar and polenta into the pastry case. Cut the plums in half and remove the stones, then place the plums, cut side down, on top of the polenta base.

4 Unwrap the piece of chilled dough, crumble it between your fingers into a mixing bowl, then add the oats and mix lightly. Sprinkle the mixture evenly over the plums, then sprinkle the demerara sugar on top.

5 Bake the pie for 50 minutes, or until golden. Leave for 15 minutes before removing the pie from the tin. Leave to cool for a few minutes more on a wire rack before serving in slices with custard or cream.

SERVES SIX TO EIGHT

INGREDIENTS
    10ml/2 tsp caster (superfine) sugar
    15ml/1 tbsp polenta
    450g/1lb dark plums
    25g/1oz/¼ cup rolled oats
    15ml/1 tbsp demerara (raw) sugar
    custard or cream, to serve
For the pastry
    115g/4oz/1 cup plain
      (all-purpose) flour, sifted
    115g/4oz/1 cup wholemeal
      (whole-wheat) flour
    150g/5oz/⅔ cup caster
      (superfine) sugar
    115g/4oz/1 cup polenta
    5ml/1 tsp baking powder
    pinch of salt
    150g/5oz/10 tbsp butter, diced
    1 egg, beaten
    15ml/1 tbsp olive oil
    about 60ml/4 tbsp chilled water

1 To make the pastry, mix the dry ingredients in a large bowl. Rub or cut in the butter until the mixture resembles fine breadcrumbs. Stir in the egg, olive oil and chilled water to form a dough.

2 Grease a 23cm/9in springform cake tin. Press two-thirds of the dough evenly over the base and sides of the tin. Wrap the remaining dough in clear film (plastic wrap) and chill.

VARIATION
Almonds and plums make a good combination. Add 60ml/4 tbsp flaked (sliced) almonds to the oat topping.

CRUNCHY APPLE AND ALMOND FLAN

DO NOT BE TEMPTED TO PUT ANY SUGAR WITH THE APPLES, AS THIS MAKES THEM PRODUCE TOO MUCH LIQUID. ALL THE SWEETNESS IS IN THE PASTRY AND THE CRUNCHY TOPPING.

SERVES EIGHT

INGREDIENTS
115g/4oz/1 cup plain
   (all-purpose) flour
1.5ml/¼ tsp mixed spice
50g/2oz/¼ cup butter, diced
50g/2oz/¼ cup demerara (raw) sugar
50g/2oz/½ cup flaked
   (sliced) almonds
675g/1½lb cooking apples
25g/1oz/3 tbsp raisins
sifted icing (confectioners') sugar,
   for dusting
For the pastry
175g/6oz/1½ cups plain
   (all-purpose) flour
75g/3oz/6 tbsp butter, diced
25g/1oz/¼ cup ground almonds
25g/1oz/2 tbsp caster
   (superfine) sugar
1 egg yolk
15ml/1 tbsp cold water
1.5ml/¼ tsp almond essence (extract)

1 To make the pastry, place the flour in a food processor or mixing bowl and rub in the butter until the mixture resembles fine breadcrumbs. Stir in the ground almonds and sugar. Whisk the egg yolk, water and almond essence together and mix into the dry ingredients to form a soft, pliable dough. Knead until smooth, wrap in clear film (plastic wrap) and leave in a cool place for 20 minutes.

COOK'S TIP
Don't worry if the pie seems too full after adding the apple slices; as the apples cook the filling will drop slightly.

2 Meanwhile, make the topping. Sift the flour and mixed spice into a mixing bowl and rub in the butter with your fingertips. Stir in the demerara sugar and flaked almonds.

3 Roll out the pastry on a lightly floured work surface and use to line a 23cm/ 9in loose-based flan tin (quiche pan), taking care to press the pastry neatly into the edges and to make a lip around the top edge. Use a rolling pin to trim off the excess pastry and give a neat edge. Chill for 15 minutes.

4 Place a baking sheet in the oven and preheat to 190°C/375°F/Gas 5. Peel, core and thinly slice the cooking apples. Arrange the slices in the pastry case in overlapping, concentric circles, doming the centre. Sprinkle over the raisins.

5 Cover the apples with the crunchy topping mixture, pressing it on lightly. Place the flan on the hot baking sheet and bake for 25–30 minutes, or until the top is golden brown and the apples are tender (you can test them with a fine skewer). Leave the flan to cool in the tin for 10 minutes. Serve warm or cold, dusted with sifted icing sugar.

CRUNCHY-TOPPED COFFEE MERINGUE PIE

FOR A SPECIAL TREAT, TRY THIS SWEET PASTRY CASE FILLED WITH COFFEE CUSTARD AND TOPPED WITH MERINGUE — CRISP ON THE OUTSIDE AND SOFT AND CHEWY UNDERNEATH.

SERVES SIX

INGREDIENTS
  30ml/2 tbsp ground coffee
  350ml/12fl oz/1½ cups milk
  25g/1oz/¼ cup cornflour (cornstarch)
  130g/4½oz/generous ½ cup caster
    (superfine) sugar
  4 egg yolks
  15g/½oz/l tbsp butter
For the pastry
  175g/6oz/1½ cups plain
    (all-purpose) flour
  15ml/1 tbsp icing
    (confectioners') sugar
  75g/3oz/6 tbsp butter, diced
  1 egg yolk
  finely grated rind of ½ orange
  15ml/1 tbsp orange juice
For the meringue
  3 egg whites
  1.5ml/¼ tsp cream of tartar
  150g/5oz/⅔ cup caster
    (superfine) sugar
  15ml/1 tbsp demerara (raw) sugar
  25g/1oz/¼ cup skinned hazelnuts

1 Preheat the oven to 200°C/400°F/ Gas 6. To make the pastry, sift the flour and icing sugar into a bowl. Rub or cut in the butter until the mixture resembles fine breadcrumbs. Add the egg yolk, orange rind and juice and mix to form a firm dough. Wrap in clear film (plastic wrap) and chill for 20 minutes.

2 Roll out the pastry and use to line a 23cm/9in loose-based flan tin (quiche pan). Cover again with clear film and chill for 30 minutes more.

3 Prick the pastry all over, line with foil and baking beans and bake for about 15 minutes, removing the foil and beans for the last 5 minutes. Lower the oven temperature to 160°C/325°F/Gas 3.

4 Put the coffee in a small bowl. Heat 250ml/8fl oz/1 cup of the milk until near-boiling and pour over the coffee. Leave to infuse (steep) for 4–5 minutes, then strain. Blend the cornflour and sugar with the remaining milk in a pan and whisk in the coffee-flavoured milk.

5 Bring the mixture to the boil, stirring until thickened. Remove from the heat.

6 In a bowl, beat the egg yolks. Stir a little of the coffee mixture into the egg yolks, then add to the remaining coffee mixture in the pan with the butter. Cook the filling over a low heat for 4 minutes, or until very thick. Pour the coffee filling into the pastry case.

7 To make the meringue, whisk the egg whites and cream of tartar in a small bowl until stiff peaks form. Whisk in the caster sugar, a spoonful at a time.

8 Spoon the meringue over the filling and spread right up to the edge of the pastry, swirling into peaks. Sprinkle with demerara sugar and hazelnuts, leaving some whole and chopping others into pieces. Bake for 30–35 minutes, or until the topping is golden brown and crisp. Serve the pie warm, or cool on a wire rack and serve cold.

COOK'S TIP
The pastry case can be made up to 36 hours in advance, but once filled and baked the pie should be eaten on the day it is made.

LEMON MERINGUE PIE

CRISP SHORTCRUST IS FILLED WITH A MOUTHWATERING LEMON CREAM FILLING AND HEAPED WITH SOFT GOLDEN-TOPPED MERINGUE. THIS CLASSIC DESSERT NEVER FAILS TO PLEASE.

SERVES SIX

INGREDIENTS
   3 large eggs, separated
   150g/5oz/⅔ cup caster
     (superfine) sugar
   grated rind and juice of 1 lemon
   25g/1oz/½ cup fresh
     white breadcrumbs
   250ml/8fl oz/1 cup milk
For the pastry
   115g/4oz/1 cup plain
     (all-purpose) flour
   pinch of salt
   50g/2oz/¼ cup butter, diced
   50g/2oz/¼ cup lard or white
     vegetable fat, diced
   15ml/1 tbsp caster
     (superfine) sugar
   15ml/1 tbsp chilled water

1 To make the pastry, sift the flour and salt into a mixing bowl. Rub or cut in the fats until the mixture resembles fine breadcrumbs. Stir in the caster sugar and enough chilled water to make a soft dough. Roll it out on a lightly floured surface and use to line a 21cm/8½in pie plate. Chill until required.

2 Meanwhile, place the egg yolks and 30ml/2 tbsp of the caster sugar in a bowl. Add the lemon rind and juice, the breadcrumbs and milk, mix lightly and leave to soak for 1 hour.

3 Preheat the oven to 200°C/400°F/ Gas 6. Beat the filling until smooth and pour into the chilled pastry case. Bake for 20 minutes, or until the filling has just set. Remove the pie from the oven and cool on a wire rack for 30 minutes or until a slight skin has formed on the surface. Lower the oven temperature to 180°C/350°F/Gas 4.

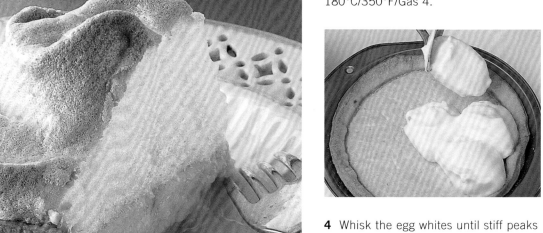

4 Whisk the egg whites until stiff peaks form. Gradually whisk in the remaining caster sugar to form a glossy meringue. Spoon on top of the lemon filling and spread right to the edge of the pastry, using the back of a spoon. Swirl the meringue slightly.

5 Bake the pie for 20–25 minutes, or until the meringue is crisp and golden brown. Allow to cool on a wire rack for 10 minutes before serving.

RHUBARB MERINGUE PIE

THE SHARP TANG OF RHUBARB WITH ITS SWEET MERINGUE TOPPING WILL REALLY TANTALIZE THE TASTE BUDS. THIS PIE IS DELICIOUS HOT OR COLD WITH CREAM OR VANILLA ICE CREAM.

SERVES SIX

INGREDIENTS
675g/1½lb rhubarb, chopped
250g/9oz/generous 1 cup caster
   (superfine) sugar
grated rind and juice of 3 oranges
3 eggs, separated
75ml/5 tbsp cornflour (cornstarch)
whipped cream, to serve
For the pastry
200g/7oz/1¾ cups plain
   (all-purpose) flour
25g/1oz/¼ cup ground walnuts
115g/4oz/½ cup butter, diced
30ml/2 tbsp sugar
1 egg yolk, beaten with
   15ml/1 tbsp water

1 To make the pastry, sift the flour into a bowl and add the walnuts. Rub or cut in the butter until the mixture resembles very fine breadcrumbs. Stir in the sugar and egg yolk mixture to make a firm dough. Knead lightly, wrap in clear film (plastic wrap) and chill for 30 minutes.

2 Preheat the oven to 190°C/375°F/ Gas 5. Roll out the pastry on a lightly floured surface and use to line a 23cm/ 9in fluted flan tin (quiche pan). Prick the base all over with a fork. Line the pastry with foil and baking beans, then bake for 15 minutes.

3 Meanwhile, to make the filling, put the chopped rhubarb in a large pan with 75g/3oz/6 tbsp of the sugar. Add the orange rind. Cover and cook over a low heat until tender.

4 Remove the foil and beans from the pastry case, then brush all over with a little egg yolk. Bake the pastry case for about 15 minutes, or until the pastry is crisp and golden.

5 Mix together the cornflour and the orange juice in a mixing bowl. Remove the rhubarb from the heat, stir in the cornflour mixture, then return the pan to the heat and bring to the boil, stirring constantly. Cook for 1–2 minutes more. Cool slightly, then beat in the remaining egg yolk. Pour into the pastry case.

6 Whisk the egg whites until they form soft peaks, then whisk in the remaining sugar, 15ml/1 tbsp at a time, whisking well after each addition.

7 Swirl the meringue over the rhubarb and orange filling to cover completely. Bake for 25 minutes until the meringue is golden brown. Serve the pie warm, or transfer it to a wire rack and leave to cool for about 30 minutes. Serve in slices with whipped cream.

MISSISSIPPI MUD PIE

THIS IS THE ULTIMATE IN CHOCOLATE DESSERTS — A DEEP PASTRY CASE, FILLED WITH CHOCOLATE CUSTARD AND TOPPED WITH A FLUFFY RUM MOUSSE AND A SMOTHERING OF WHIPPED CREAM.

SERVES SIX TO EIGHT

INGREDIENTS

3 eggs, separated
20ml/4 tsp cornflour (cornstarch)
75g/3oz/6 tbsp caster
   (superfine) sugar
400ml/14fl oz/1¾ cups milk
150g/5oz plain (semisweet)
   chocolate, broken up
5ml/1 tsp vanilla essence (extract)
15ml/1 tbsp powdered gelatine
45ml/3 tbsp water
30ml/2 tsp dark rum
175g/6fl oz/¾ cup double (heavy)
   cream, whipped
a few chocolate curls,
   to decorate
For the pastry
250g/9oz/2¼ cups plain
   (all-purpose) flour
150g/5oz/⅔ cup butter, diced
2 egg yolks
15–30ml/1–2 tbsp chilled water

1 To make the pastry, sift the flour into a bowl and rub or cut in the butter until the mixture resembles breadcrumbs. Stir in the egg yolks with just enough chilled water to make a soft dough.

2 Roll out on a lightly floured surface and use to line a deep 23cm/9in flan tin (quiche pan). Chill for 30 minutes. Preheat the oven to 190°C/375°F/Gas 5. Prick the pastry all over with a fork, line with foil and baking beans, then bake blind for 10 minutes.

3 Remove the foil and beans, return the pie to the oven and bake for about 10 minutes more until the pastry is crisp and golden. Cool in the tin.

4 To make the custard filling, mix the egg yolks, cornflour and 30ml/2 tbsp of the sugar in a bowl. Heat the milk in a pan until almost boiling, then beat into the egg mixture.

5 Return the custard mixture to the cleaned pan and stir over a low heat until the custard has thickened and is smooth. Pour half the custard into a bowl.

6 Melt the chocolate in a heatproof bowl set over a pan of hot water, then add to the custard in the bowl. Add the vanilla essence and mix well. Spread in the pastry case, cover closely with some baking parchment to prevent a skin from forming, cool, then chill until set.

7 Sprinkle the gelatine over the water in a small bowl, leave until spongy, then place over a pan of simmering water until all the gelatine has dissolved. Stir into the remaining custard, along with the rum. Whisk the egg whites until stiff peaks form, whisk in the remaining sugar, then quickly fold into the custard before it sets.

8 Spoon the mixture over the chocolate custard to cover completely. Chill until set, then remove the pie from the tin to serve. Spread whipped cream over the top and decorate with chocolate curls.

BOSTON BANOFFEE PIE

SIMPLY PRESS THIS WONDERFULLY BISCUITY PASTRY INTO THE TIN, RATHER THAN ROLLING IT OUT.
ADD THE FUDGE-TOFFEE FILLING AND SLICED BANANA TOPPING AND IT'LL PROVE IRRESISTIBLE.

SERVES SIX

INGREDIENTS

115g/4oz/½ cup butter, diced
200g/7oz can skimmed, sweetened
   condensed milk
115g/4oz/½ cup soft brown sugar
30ml/2 tbsp golden (light corn) syrup
2 small bananas, sliced
a little lemon juice
whipped cream, to decorate
5ml/1 tsp grated plain
   (semisweet) chocolate

For the pastry

150g/5oz/1¼ cups plain
   (all-purpose) flour
115g/4oz/½ cup butter, diced
50g/2oz/¼ cup caster
   (superfine) sugar

1 Preheat the oven to 160°C/325°F/
Gas 3. In a food processor, process the
flour and diced butter until crumbed.
Stir in the caster sugar and mix to form
a soft, pliable dough.

3 To make the filling, place the butter
in a pan with the condensed milk,
brown sugar and syrup. Heat gently,
stirring, until the butter has melted and
the sugar has completely dissolved.

2 Press into a 20cm/8in loose-based
flan tin (quiche pan). Bake for 30 minutes.

4 Bring to a gentle boil and cook for
7–10 minutes, stirring constantly, until
the mixture thickens and turns a light
caramel colour.

5 Pour the hot caramel filling into the
pastry case and leave until completely
cold. Sprinkle the banana slices with
lemon juice and arrange in overlapping
circles on top of the filling, leaving a
gap in the centre. Pipe a generous swirl
of whipped cream in the centre and
sprinkle with the grated chocolate.

KEY LIME PIE

This pie is one of America's favourites. As the name suggests, it originated in the Florida Keys, but is now hugely popular all over the world.

SERVES TEN

INGREDIENTS
4 eggs, separated
400g/14oz can skimmed, sweetened
    condensed milk
grated rind and juice of 3 limes
a few drops of green food
    colouring (optional)
30ml/2 tbsp caster (superfine) sugar
300ml/½ pint/1¼ cups double
    (heavy) cream
2–3 limes, thinly sliced
thinly pared lime rind and fresh mint
    sprigs, to decorate
For the pastry
225g/8oz/2 cups plain
    (all-purpose) flour
115g/4oz/½ cup chilled butter, diced
30ml/2 tbsp caster (superfine) sugar
2 egg yolks
pinch of salt
30ml/2 tbsp chilled water

3 Preheat the oven to 200°C/400°F/ Gas 6. Trim off the excess pastry from around the edge of the pastry case using a sharp knife, then line the pastry case with baking parchment and fill with baking beans.

4 Bake the pastry case for 10 minutes. Remove the parchment and beans and return the pastry case to the oven for 10 minutes more to lightly brown.

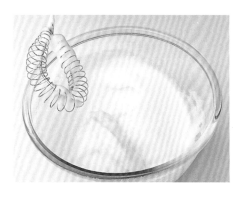

6 Whisk the egg whites in a grease-free bowl until stiff peaks form. Whisk in the sugar, then fold into the lime mixture.

7 Reduce the oven temperature to 160°C/325°F/Gas 3. Pour the lime filling into the pastry case. Bake for about 20 minutes, or until the pie has set and is starting to brown. Cool, then chill.

1 To make the pastry, sift the flour into a large mixing bowl and rub or cut in the butter until the mixture resembles fine breadcrumbs. Add the sugar, egg yolks, salt and enough water to bind together. Knead lightly and briefly to form a soft dough.

2 Roll out the pastry thinly on a lightly floured surface and use to line a deep 21cm/8½in fluted flan tin (quiche pan), allowing the excess pastry to hang over the edge. Prick the base of the pastry case all over with a fork, wrap in clear film (plastic wrap) and chill for at least 30 minutes.

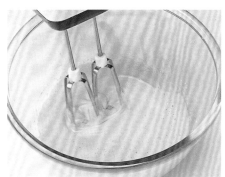

5 Meanwhile, beat the egg yolks in a large bowl until light and creamy, then beat in the condensed milk, along with the lime rind and juice. Add the food colouring, if using, and continue to beat until the mixture is thick.

COOK'S TIP
If short of time, you can make the pastry in a food processor, but take care not to overprocess it. Use the pulse button and process for a few seconds at a time; switch off the motor the moment the dough begins to clump together. Remove and knead lightly, then wrap and chill.

8 Just before serving, whip the cream for the topping and spoon it around the edge of the pie. Cut the lime slices once from the centre to the edge, then twist each slice and arrange. Decorate with lime rind and sprigs of fresh mint.

PUFF, CHOUX AND FILO PASTRY DESSERTS

Puff and similar pastries are repeatedly rolled and folded to trap the air within the buttery layers, expanding on baking to produce wonderfully risen results. Elegant and light, choux is the perfect container for sweet fillings, while bought filo could not be easier to use. Simply brush with melted butter and stack, then cut, fold or scrunch to the desired shape. Whatever the pastry, the result is superb: try Tarte Tatin, Bakewell Tart and Apple Strudel.

PEACH AND BRANDY PIE

SLICES OF JUICY, RIPE PEACHES, GENTLY COOKED IN BUTTER AND SUGAR, ARE ENCASED IN CRISP PUFF PASTRY TO MAKE THIS FRAGRANT FRUIT PIE — SIMPLE BUT DELICIOUS.

5 Preheat the oven to 200°C/400°F/ Gas 6. Remove the clear film from the pastry rounds. Spoon the peaches into the middle of the larger round and use a spoon to spread them out to within about 2cm/2in of the edge.

6 Place the smaller pastry round on top, shaping it in a mound over the peaches. Brush the edge of the larger pastry round with water, then fold this over the top pastry round and press to seal. Twist the edges together to make a pattern all the way round.

7 Make the glaze by mixing the egg and water together in a cup. Lightly brush it over the pastry and sprinkle over the granulated sugar, spreading it evenly over the pastry. Make five or six small crescent-shape slashes on the top of the pastry, radiating from the centre towards the edge.

SERVES EIGHT

INGREDIENTS
   6 large, firm ripe peaches
   40g/1½oz/3 tbsp butter
   45ml/3 tbsp brandy
   75g/3oz/6 tbsp caster
    (superfine) sugar
   450g/1lb puff pastry
   vanilla ice cream, to serve
For the glaze
   1 egg
   5ml/1 tsp water
   15ml/1 tbsp granulated sugar

1 Immerse the peaches in boiling water for about 30 seconds. Lift them out with a slotted spoon, dip in cold water, then peel off the skins. Halve and stone (pit) the peaches, then cut into slices.

2 Melt the butter in a large frying pan. Add the peach slices, then sprinkle with the brandy and sugar. Cook for about 4 minutes, shaking the pan frequently, or until the sugar has dissolved and the peaches are tender. Set the pan aside to cool.

3 Cut the pastry into two pieces, one very slightly larger than the other. Roll out on a lightly floured surface and, using plates or cake tins as a guide, cut the larger piece of pastry into a 30cm/ 12in circle and the smaller one into a 28cm/11in circle.

4 Place the pastry rounds on separate large baking sheets lined with baking parchment, cover with clear film (plastic wrap) and chill for 30 minutes.

8 Bake the pie for about 45 minutes, or until the pastry is risen and golden brown. Serve warm in slices with vanilla ice cream.

STRAWBERRY TART

THIS TART IS BEST ASSEMBLED JUST BEFORE SERVING, BUT YOU CAN BAKE THE PASTRY CASE EARLY IN THE DAY. MAKE THE FILLING AHEAD OF TIME AND PUT IT TOGETHER IN A FEW MINUTES.

SERVES SIX

INGREDIENTS

350g/12oz rough puff or puff pastry
225g/8oz/1 cup cream cheese
grated rind of ½ orange
30ml/2 tbsp orange liqueur or
  orange juice
45–60ml/3–4 tbsp icing
  (confectioners') sugar, plus extra for
  dusting (optional)
450g/1lb/4 cups strawberries, hulled

1 Roll out the pastry on a lightly floured surface to a thickness of about 3mm/⅛in and use to line a 28 × 10cm/11 × 4in tranche tin. Trim the edges of the pastry neatly with a knife, then chill for 30 minutes. Preheat the oven to 200°C/400°F/Gas 6.

2 Prick the base of the pastry all over. Line the pastry case with foil, fill with baking beans and bake for 15 minutes. Remove the foil and beans and bake for 10 minutes more until the pastry is browned. Gently press down on the pastry base to deflate it, then leave to cool on a wire rack.

3 Using a hand-held electric whisk or food processor, beat together well the cream cheese, orange rind, liqueur or orange juice and icing sugar. Spread the cheese filling in the pastry case. Halve the strawberries and arrange them on top of the cheese filling. Dust with icing sugar, if you like.

BAKEWELL TART

ALTHOUGH THE PASTRY BASE MAKES THIS A TART, IN THE ENGLISH VILLAGE OF BAKEWELL, WHERE IT ORIGINATED, IT IS TRADITIONALLY CALLED BAKEWELL PUDDING.

SERVES FOUR

INGREDIENTS
    225g/8oz puff pastry
    30ml/2 tbsp raspberry or apricot jam
    2 eggs, plus 2 egg yolks
    115g/4oz/½ cup caster
      (superfine) sugar
    115g/4oz/½ cup butter, melted
    50g/2oz/⅔ cup ground almonds
    a few drops of almond
      essence (extract)
    icing (confectioners') sugar,
      for dusting

1 Preheat the oven to 200°C/400°F Gas 6. Roll out the pastry on a lightly floured surface and use to line an 18cm/7in pie plate. Trim the edge.

2 Re-roll the pastry trimmings and cut out wide strips of pastry. Use these to decorate the edge of the pastry case by gently twisting them around the rim, joining the strips together as necessary. Prick the pastry case all over, then spread the jam over the base.

3 Whisk the eggs, egg yolks and sugar together in a bowl until the mixture is thick and pale.

4 Gently stir the melted butter, ground almonds and almond essence into the whisked egg mixture.

5 Pour the mixture into the pastry case and bake for 30 minutes, or until the filling is just set and is lightly browned. Dust with icing sugar before serving hot, warm or cold.

COOK'S TIP
Since this pastry case is not baked blind before being filled, place a baking sheet in the oven while it preheats, then place the tart on the hot sheet. This will ensure that the base of the pastry case cooks right through.

APPLE, RAISIN AND MAPLE PIES

CALVADOS ACCENTUATES THE APPLE FLAVOUR OF THESE INDIVIDUAL PUFF PASTRY PIES. SERVE THEM WITH WHIPPED CREAM, FLAVOURED WITH ORANGE LIQUEUR, FOR A DELECTABLE DINNER PARTY DESSERT.

SERVES FOUR

350g/12oz puff pastry
beaten egg or milk, to glaze
whipped cream, flavoured with orange
    liqueur and sprinkled with grated
    orange rind, to serve
For the filling
75g/3oz/scant ½ cup soft light
    brown sugar
30ml/2 tbsp lemon juice
45ml/3 tbsp maple syrup
150ml/¼ pint/⅔ cup water
45ml/3 tbsp Calvados
6 small eating apples, halved, peeled
    and cored
75g/3oz/½ cup raisins

1 To make the filling, mix the sugar, lemon juice, maple syrup and water in a pan. Heat until the sugar has dissolved, then bring to the boil and cook until reduced by half. Stir in the Calvados.

2 Cut four of the apples into eight even segments. Add the apple pieces to the syrup and simmer for 5–8 minutes until just tender. Lift the apple pieces out of the syrup using a slotted spoon and set them aside.

COOK'S TIP
Flavoured cream is delicious with pies and tarts. Lightly whip double cream, stir in a spoonful or two of your favourite liqueur and sweeten to taste. Liqueurs that would go well with these little pies include Grand Marnier, Curaçao, Mandarine Napoléon and Calvados.

3 Chop the remaining apples and add to the syrup with the raisins. Simmer until the mixture is thick, then cool.

4 Preheat the oven to 200°C/400°F/ Gas 6. Roll out the pastry on a floured surface and stamp out eight 15cm/6in rounds with a fluted cutter. Use half the pastry to line four 10cm/4in individual flan tins (mini quiche pans). Spoon in the raisin mixture and level the surface.

5 Arrange the apple segments on top of the raisin mixture. Brush the edge of each pastry case with egg or milk and cover with a pastry lid. Trim, seal and flute the edges.

6 Cut suitable shapes from the pastry trimmings and use to decorate the pies. Brush the tops with beaten egg or milk, then bake for 30–35 minutes. Serve hot, with the flavoured cream.

TARTE TATIN

THIS CLASSIC FRENCH UPSIDE-DOWN TART CAN BE MADE WITH EITHER PÂTE SUCRÉE OR, MORE SIMPLY, WITH PUFF PASTRY, AS IT IS HERE. IT CAN ALSO BE MADE WITH APRICOTS, PEACHES OR PLUMS.

SERVES SIX

INGREDIENTS

   3 eating apples, which will hold their
     shape after cooking
   juice of ½ lemon
   50g/2oz/¼ cup butter, softened
   75g/3oz/6 tbsp caster
     (superfine) sugar
   250g/9oz puff pastry
   single (light) cream, to serve

1 Preheat the oven to 220°C/425°F/ Gas 7. Cut the apples in quarters and remove the cores. Toss the quarters in the lemon juice to prevent the apple from discolouring.

2 Spread the butter over the base of a 20cm/8in heavy ovenproof omelette pan. Sprinkle the caster sugar over the base of the pan and add the apple wedges, skin side down.

3 Cook over a medium heat for about 15 minutes, or until the sugar and butter have melted and the apples are golden.

4 Roll out the pastry and cut it into a 25cm/10in round. Gently place it over the apples, then tuck in the edges with a knife. Bake for 15–20 minutes, or until the pastry is golden.

5 Remove from the oven and loosen the edge with the knife. Invert the serving plate on the omelette pan, then, protecting your hands with oven gloves, hold pan and plate together and quickly turn over. Lift off the pan. Cool slightly before serving with cream.

PEAR TARTE TATIN <u>WITH</u> CARDAMOM

CARDAMOM IS A SPICE THAT IS EQUALLY AT HOME IN SWEET AND SAVOURY DISHES. IT IS DELICIOUS WITH PEARS, AND BRINGS OUT THEIR FLAVOUR BEAUTIFULLY IN THIS SIMPLE TART.

SERVES FOUR TO SIX

INGREDIENTS
  50g/2oz/¼ cup butter, softened
  50g/2oz/¼ cup caster
    (superfine) sugar
  seeds from 10 green
    cardamom pods
  225g/8oz puff pastry
  3 ripe, large round pears

1 Preheat the oven to 220°C/425°F/ Gas 7. Spread the butter over the base of a 18cm/7in heavy ovenproof omelette pan. Sprinkle with the sugar, then sprinkle the cardamom seeds over.

2 On a lightly floured work surface, roll out the pastry to a circle slightly larger than the pan. Prick the pastry all over with a fork, place on a baking sheet and chill.

3 Peel the pears, cut in half lengthways and remove the cores. Arrange the pears, rounded side down, in the pan. Heat until the sugar melts and begins to bubble with the juice from the pears.

4 Once the sugar has caramelized remove the pan from the heat. Place the pastry on top, tucking in the edges with a knife. Bake for 25 minutes.

5 Leave the tart in the pan for about 2 minutes until the juices have stopped bubbling. Invert a serving plate over the pan then, wearing oven gloves to protect your hands, hold the pan and plate together and quickly turn over, gently shaking it to release the tart. It may be necessary to slide a spatula underneath the pears to loosen them. Serve the tart warm, with cream.

GÂTEAU SAINT-HONORÉ

NAMED AFTER THE PATRON SAINT OF BAKERS, THIS SPECTACULAR DESSERT HAS A PUFF PASTRY BASE TOPPED WITH CARAMEL-COATED CHOUX PUFFS AND FILLED WITH CRÈME PÂTISSIÈRE.

SERVES TEN

INGREDIENTS
  175g/6oz puff pastry
For the choux pastry
  300ml/½ pint/1¼ cups water
  115g/4oz/½ cup butter, diced
  130g/4½oz/scant 1¼ cups plain
    (all-purpose) flour, sifted
  2.5ml/½ tsp salt
  4 eggs, lightly beaten
  beaten egg, to glaze
For the crème pâtissière
  3 egg yolks
  50g/2oz/¼ cup caster
    (superfine) sugar
  30ml/2 tbsp plain (all-purpose) flour
  30ml/2 tbsp cornflour (cornstarch)
  300ml/½ pint/1¼ cups milk
  150ml/¼ pint/⅔ cup double
    (heavy) cream
  30ml/2 tbsp orange liqueur, such as
    Grand Marnier
For the caramel
  225g/8oz/1 cup granulated sugar
  120ml/4fl oz/½ cup water

1 Roll out the puff pastry on a lightly floured surface and cut out a 20cm/8in circle. Use a flan ring or an upturned plate as your guide. Place the pastry round on a baking sheet lined with baking parchment, prick all over with a fork and chill while you are making the choux pastry.

2 To make the choux pastry, put the water and butter in a large pan. Heat until the butter has melted, then bring to the boil.

3 Quickly tip in all the flour with the salt, remove the pan from the heat and beat vigorously until the mixture leaves the sides of the pan. Beat in the eggs, a little at a time, to form a paste.

4 Preheat the oven to 200°C/400°F/ Gas 6. Spoon the choux pastry into a piping (pastry) bag fitted with a 1cm/ ½in plain nozzle. Pipe a spiral of choux on to the puff pastry base, starting at the edge and working to the centre.

5 Use the remaining choux pastry to pipe 16 small buns on to a baking sheet lined with baking parchment. Brush the buns and the choux pastry spiral with egg to glaze. Bake the small buns for about 20 minutes and the choux-topped puff pastry on the shelf below for about 35 minutes, or until well risen.

6 Pierce several holes in the top and sides of the spiral, and pierce one small hole in the side of each bun, using a fine skewer. Return the pastry to the oven for 5 minutes more to dry out. Cool on a wire rack.

7 To make the crème pâtissière filling, whisk the egg yolks and caster sugar until light and creamy. Whisk in the flour and cornflour. Bring the milk to the boil in a pan and pour over the egg mixture, whisking all the time. Return the custard to the cleaned pan and cook for 2–3 minutes, until thickened and smooth. Cover with dampened baking parchment and leave to cool.

8 Whip the cream lightly and fold in to the crème pâtissière with the orange liqueur. Spoon half into a piping bag fitted with a small plain nozzle and use to fill the choux buns.

9 To make the caramel, heat the sugar and water in a pan until completely dissolved, stirring occasionally. Bring to the boil and cook until it turns a rich golden colour. Remove the pan from the heat and set over a large bowl half-filled with just boiled water to keep the caramel liquid.

10 Place the puff and choux pastry base on a serving plate. Dip the bases of the choux buns, one at a time, into the caramel and arrange in a ring around the edge of the pastry case.

11 Pipe the remaining crème pâtissière into the centre of the case. Drizzle the tops of the choux buns with the remaining caramel and leave to set. Set aside in a cool place for up to 2 hours before serving.

STRABERRY AND KIRSCH CHOUX RING

KIRSCH AND CREAM MAKE A WONDERFUL COMBINATION WHEN MIXED WITH SUCCULENT STRAWBERRIES IN THIS FEATHERLIGHT PASTRY DESSERT. THE RING IS MADE FROM INDIVIDUAL BALLS OF CHOUX PASTRY, WHICH FUSE TOGETHER AS THEY PUFF UP AND BAKE TO GOLDEN PERFECTION.

SERVES FOUR TO SIX

INGREDIENTS
    350g/12oz/generous 2 cups small
      whole strawberries
    75g/3oz/6 tbsp granulated sugar
    150ml/¼ pint/⅔ cup double
      (heavy) cream
    30ml/2 tbsp Kirsch
    10ml/2 tsp icing (confectioners')
      sugar, sifted, plus extra for dusting
    whipped cream, to serve
For the pastry
    150ml/¼ pint/⅔ cup water
    50g/2oz/¼ cup butter
    65g/2½ oz/9 tbsp plain (all-purpose)
      flour, sifted
    2 eggs, beaten

1 Preheat the oven to 220°C/425°F/ Gas 7. Set aside half the strawberries for later use, choosing the best fruits for decoration, and slice the remainder. Set aside.

2 Draw a fine 15cm/6in circle on a sheet of baking parchment, turn it over and press it on to a lightly greased baking sheet.

3 To make the choux pastry, put the water and butter in a large pan. Heat until the butter has melted, then bring to the boil. Quickly tip in all the flour in one go, remove the pan from the heat and beat vigorously with a wooden spoon until the mixture comes together in a smooth ball and leaves the sides of the pan clean.

4 Beat in the eggs, a small amount at a time, to form a smooth, shiny paste, which is thick enough to hold its shape. You may not need all of the beaten egg. Spoon or pipe the choux pastry in rough balls, making a circle on the baking sheet, using the drawn circle as a guide. The balls should just touch.

5 Bake for 15 minutes, then lower the oven temperature to 190°C/375°F/Gas 5 and cook for a further 20–25 minutes. Make one or two slits in the pastry to let the hot air escape, then leave to cool.

6 Put the granulated sugar into a heavy pan, heat gently until it dissolves, then increase the heat and cook the syrup until it turns a golden caramel colour and a spoonful hardens when dropped into a bowl of cold water.

7 One at a time, spear each reserved whole strawberry on a fork and quickly half-dip them in the caramel, turning to coat. Leave the strawberries to cool on baking parchment.

8 To make the filling, whip the cream in a small mixing bowl until it just starts to thicken. Stir in the Kirsch and icing sugar and continue whisking until stiff. With a wooden spoon, gently fold in the reserved sliced strawberries.

9 Carefully slice the choux ring in half horizontally, generously spoon in the strawberry cream, spreading it evenly, and replace the top. Dust with a little icing sugar. Serve the choux ring with whipped cream and the caramelized strawberries. Serve any leftover cream in a separate bowl.

VARIATION
To make chocolate choux pastry, replace 15ml/1 tbsp of the plain flour with unsweetened cocoa powder.

COOK'S TIP
When making choux pastry, it is very important to add all the flour at once. The easiest way to do this is to sift the flour on to a sheet of baking parchment, then tip it quickly into the pan.

APPLE STRUDEL

THIS CLASSIC RECIPE IS USUALLY MADE WITH STRUDEL DOUGH, WHICH IS WONDERFUL, BUT CAN BE TRICKY AND TIME-CONSUMING, ESPECIALLY FOR A NOVICE. FILO PASTRY MAKES A GOOD SHORTCUT.

SERVES EIGHT TO TEN

INGREDIENTS
   500g/1¼lb filo pastry, thawed
      if frozen
   115g/4oz/½ cup unsalted (sweet)
      butter, melted
   icing (confectioners') sugar,
      for dusting
For the filling
   1kg/2¼lb cooking apples, peeled,
      cored and sliced
   115g/4oz/2 cups fresh white
      breadcrumbs
   150g/5oz/¾ cup granulated sugar
   5ml/1 tsp cinnamon
   75g/3oz/generous ½ cup raisins
   finely grated rind of 1 lemon
   50g/2oz/¼ cup butter

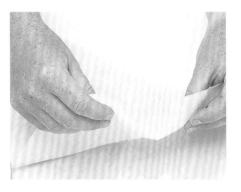

1 Preheat the oven to 180°C/350°F/ Gas 4. To make the filling, place the sliced apples in a large mixing bowl. Add the breadcrumbs, sugar, cinnamon, raisins and grated lemon rind and mix well. Melt the butter in a small pan, then stir it in to the mixture.

2 Lay a sheet of filo pastry on a lightly floured work surface and brush with a little melted butter. Place another sheet on top and brush with melted butter as before. Continue stacking the sheets and brushing with the butter until there are four or five layers in all.

3 Spoon the filling into the centre of the pastry, leaving a 2.5cm/1in border all round. Fold in the two shorter sides, then roll up from one long side, Swiss-roll (jelly-roll) style. Place the strudel on a lightly buttered baking sheet, seam side down. Brush the pastry with the remaining melted butter. Bake for 30–40 minutes, or until golden.

4 Remove the strudel from the oven and place on a wire rack to cool. Dust with icing sugar before cutting into slices for serving.

VARIATION
For extra crunch in the strudel filling, add 75g/3oz/3/4 cup lightly toasted, chopped hazelnuts or almonds.

FRESH CHERRY AND HAZELNUT STRUDEL

SERVE THIS WONDERFUL OLD-WORLD TREAT AS A WARM DESSERT WITH CRÈME FRAÎCHE OR ALLOW TO COOL AND OFFER AS A DELICIOUS ACCOMPANIMENT TO COFFEE OR AFTERNOON TEA.

SERVES SIX TO EIGHT

INGREDIENTS
    75g/3oz/6 tbsp butter
    90ml/6 tbsp light muscovado
        (molasses) sugar
    3 egg yolks
    grated rind of 1 lemon
    1.5ml/¼ tsp grated nutmeg
    250g/9oz/generous 1 cup
        ricotta cheese
    8 large sheets of filo pastry, thawed
        if frozen
    75g/3oz ratafia biscuits (almond
        macaroons), crushed
    450g/1lb/2½ cups cherries, pitted
    30ml/2 tbsp chopped hazelnuts
    icing (confectioners') sugar,
        for dusting

1 Preheat the oven to 190°C/375°F/ Gas 5. Beat 15g/½oz/1 tbsp of the butter with the sugar and egg yolks in a mixing bowl until light and fluffy. Beat in the lemon rind, grated nutmeg and ricotta cheese.

2 Melt the remaining butter in a small pan. Place a sheet of filo on a clean dishtowel and brush it generously with melted butter. Place a second sheet on top and repeat the process. Continue until all the sheets of filo have been used, reserving some of the butter.

3 Sprinkle the crushed ratafias over the top of the filo, leaving a 5cm/2in border all round. Spoon the ricotta mixture over the ratafia biscuits, spread it lightly to cover, then sprinkle over the cherries.

4 Fold in the filo pastry border on all four sides, then using the dishtowel to help you, roll up the strudel, Swiss-roll (jelly-roll) style, beginning from one of the long sides of the pastry and rolling away from you. Grease a large baking sheet with a little of the remaining melted butter.

5 Place the strudel, seam side down, on the baking sheet, brush with the remaining melted butter, and sprinkle the hazelnuts over the surface.

6 Bake for 35–40 minutes, or until the strudel is golden and crisp. Dust with icing sugar and serve with cream.

MANGO AND AMARETTI STRUDEL

FRESH MANGO AND CRUSHED AMARETTI WRAPPED IN WAFER-THIN FILO PASTRY MAKE A SPECIAL TREAT. IT LOOKS REMARKABLY IMPRESSIVE, BUT TAKES VERY LITTLE TIME TO ASSEMBLE AND BAKE. THIS STRUDEL IS EQUALLY DELICIOUS WHEN MADE WITH APRICOTS OR PLUMS.

SERVES FOUR

INGREDIENTS
  1 large mango
  grated rind of 1 lemon
  2 amaretti
  25g/1oz/3 tbsp demerara
    (raw) sugar
  60ml/4 tbsp wholemeal
    (whole-wheat) breadcrumbs
  2 sheets of filo pastry, each
    measuring 48 × 28cm/19 × 11in
  25g/1oz/2 tbsp butter or 20g/¾oz/
    4 tsp soft margarine, melted
  15ml/1 tbsp chopped almonds
  icing (confectioners') sugar,
    for dusting

1 Preheat the oven to 190°C/375°F/ Gas 5. Lightly grease a baking sheet. Cut the flesh from the mango and chop into small cubes (see Cook's Tip). Place in a bowl and sprinkle with the grated lemon rind.

2 Crush the amaretti and mix them with the sugar and breadcrumbs.

3 Lay one sheet of filo pastry on a flat surface and brush with a quarter of the melted butter or margarine. Top with the second sheet, brush with one-third of the remaining fat, then fold both sheets over, if necessary, to make a rectangle measuring 28 × 24cm/11 × 9½in. Brush with half the remaining fat.

4 Sprinkle the filo with the amaretti mixture, leaving a border on each long side. Arrange the mango over the top.

5 Roll up the filo from one long side, Swiss-roll (jelly-roll) fashion.

6 Lift the strudel on to the baking sheet, seam side down. Brush with the remaining melted fat and sprinkle with the chopped almonds.

7 Bake for 20–25 minutes until golden brown, then transfer to a board. Dust with the icing sugar, slice diagonally and serve warm.

VARIATION
Peach and nectarine can also be used instead of mango, as can apricots or red or purple plums.

COOK'S TIPS
• The easiest way to prepare a mango is to hold it upright, then cut a large slice off either side, keeping the knife blade close to the stone. Cross-hatch the flesh on each piece of mango, turn the piece inside-out and cut the cubes of flesh off the skin. Finally, remove the remaining skin from the central slice, and cut the flesh off from around the mango stone. Dice the flesh neatly.
• When buying amaretti, look for the small crunchy, sugar-encrusted biscuits (cookies) that come wrapped in pairs in twists of crisp white paper.

CHOCOLATE, DATE AND ALMOND FILO COIL

EXPERIENCE THE ALLURE OF THE MIDDLE EAST WITH THIS DELECTABLE DESSERT. CRISP FILO PASTRY CONCEALS A CHOCOLATE AND ROSE WATER FILLING STUDDED WITH DATES AND ALMONDS.

SERVES SIX

INGREDIENTS
  275g/10oz filo pastry, thawed
    if frozen
  50g/2oz/¼ cup butter, melted
  icing (confectioners') sugar, cocoa
    powder (unsweetened) and ground
    cinnamon, for dusting
For the filling
  75g/3oz/6 tbsp butter
  115g/4oz dark (bittersweet)
    chocolate, broken up
    into pieces
  115g/4oz/1⅓ cup ground almonds
  115g/4oz/⅔ cup chopped dates
  75g/3oz/¾ cup icing
    (confectioners') sugar
  10ml/2 tsp rose water
  2.5ml/½ tsp ground cinnamon

1 Preheat the oven to 180°C/350°F/ Gas 4. Grease a 22cm/8½in round cake tin. To make the filling, melt the butter with the chocolate in a heatproof bowl set over a pan of barely simmering water, then remove from the heat and stir in the remaining ingredients to make a thick paste. Leave to cool.

2 Lay one sheet of filo on a clean, flat surface. Brush with melted butter, then lay a second sheet on top and brush with more butter.

3 Roll a handful of the chocolate and almond mixture into a long sausage shape and place along one long edge of the layered filo. Roll up the pastry tightly around the filling to make a roll.

4 Fit the filo roll in the cake tin, so that it sits snugly against the outer edge. Make more filo rolls in the same way, adding them to the tin from the outside towards the centre, until the coil fills it.

5 Brush the coil with the remaining melted butter. Bake for 30–35 minutes until the pastry is golden brown and crisp. Transfer the coil to a serving plate. Serve warm, dusted with icing sugar, cocoa and cinnamon.

COOK'S TIP
Filo pastry dries out quickly, so remove one sheet at a time from the pile and cover the rest with a damp dishtowel.

MOROCCAN SERPENT CAKE

THIS IS PERHAPS THE MOST FAMOUS OF ALL MOROCCAN PASTRIES, FILLED WITH LIGHTLY FRAGRANT ALMOND PASTE, AND DUSTED WITH ICING SUGAR AND CINNAMON.

SERVES EIGHT

INGREDIENTS
  8 sheets of filo pastry, thawed
    if frozen
  50g/2oz/¼ cup butter, melted
  1 egg, beaten
  5ml/1 tsp ground cinnamon
  icing (confectioners') sugar,
    for dusting
For the almond paste
  about 50g/2oz/¼ cup butter, melted
  225g/8oz/2⅔ cups ground almonds
  2.5ml/½ tsp almond essence (extract)
  50g/2oz/½ cup icing
    (confectioners') sugar
  1 egg yolk, beaten
  15ml/1 tbsp rose water or orange
    flower water

1 To make the almond paste, mix the melted butter with the ground almonds and almond essence in a bowl. Add the sugar, egg yolk and rose or orange flower water, mix well and knead until soft and pliable. Chill for 10 minutes.

2 Break the paste into 10 even-size balls and, with your hands, roll them into 10cm/4in sausages. Chill again.

3 Preheat the oven to 180°C/350°F/ Gas 4. Place two sheets of filo pastry on the work surface so that they overlap slightly to form an 18 × 56cm/7 × 22in rectangle. Brush the overlapping pastry edges to secure and then lightly brush all over with butter. Cover with another two sheets of filo in the same way and brush again with butter.

4 Place five almond paste sausages along the lower edge of the filo sheet and roll up the pastry tightly, tucking in the ends. Repeat with the remaining filo and almond paste, so that you have two rolls. Brush a large baking sheet with butter. Shape the first roll into a loose coil, then transfer to the baking sheet. Attach the second roll and continue coiling the filo to make a snake. Tuck the end under.

5 In a bowl, beat the egg with half the cinnamon. Brush over the pastry, then bake in the oven for 25 minutes until golden brown. Carefully invert the snake on to another baking sheet and return to the oven for 5–10 minutes more.

7 Transfer the cake to a serving plate. Dust with icing sugar, then sprinkle with the remaining cinnamon. Serve warm.

FILO-TOPPED APPLE PIE

Scrunched up filo pastry, brushed with a little melted butter is the very easiest way to top a pie. A light dusting of icing sugar gives it an attractive finish.

SERVES SIX

INGREDIENTS

900g/2lb cooking apples
75g/3oz/6 tbsp caster
  (superfine) sugar
grated rind of 1 lemon
15ml/1 tbsp lemon juice
75g/3oz/½ cup sultanas
  (golden raisins)
2.5ml/½ tsp ground cinnamon
4 large sheets of filo pastry, thawed
  if frozen
25g/1oz/2 tbsp butter, melted
icing (confectioners') sugar,
  for dusting

VARIATION

Any number of fruit fillings work well in
this pie. A mixture of blackberries and
apples is a good combination.

1 Peel, core and dice the apples. Place
them in a pan with the caster sugar and
lemon rind. Drizzle the lemon juice over.
Bring to the boil, stir well, then cook for
5 minutes or until the apples are soft.
Stir in the sultanas and cinnamon. Pour
the mixture into a 1.2 litre/2 pint/5 cup
pie dish and level the top with a spoon.
Leave to cool.

2 Preheat the oven to 180°C/350°F/
Gas 4. Place a pie funnel in the centre
of the fruit. Brush each sheet of filo
with melted butter. Scrunch up loosely
and place on the fruit to cover it.

3 Bake for 20–30 minutes until the filo
is golden. Dust the pie with icing sugar.
Serve with custard, if you like.

FRESH FIG FILO TART

DESSERTS DON'T COME MUCH EASIER THAN THIS — FRESH FIGS IN CRISP FILO PASTRY, WITH A CREAMY ALMOND BATTER. THE TART TASTES WONDERFUL SERVED WITH CREAM OR YOGURT.

SERVES SIX TO EIGHT

INGREDIENTS

- 5 sheets of filo pastry, each measuring 35 x 25cm/14 x 10in, thawed if frozen
- 25g/1oz/2 tbsp butter, melted
- 6 fresh figs, cut into wedges
- 75g/3oz/¾ cup plain (all-purpose) flour
- 75g/3oz/6 tbsp caster (superfine) sugar
- 4 eggs
- 450ml/¾ pint/scant 2 cups creamy milk
- 2.5ml/½ tsp almond essence (extract)
- 15ml/1 tbsp icing (confectioners') sugar, for dusting

3 Sift the flour into a bowl and stir in the caster sugar. Add the eggs and a little of the milk and whisk until smooth. Gradually whisk in the remaining milk and the almond essence. Pour the batter over the figs.

4 Bake for 1 hour or until the batter has set and is golden. Remove the tart from the oven and allow it to cool in the tin on a wire rack for 10 minutes. Dust with the icing sugar and serve with whipped cream or Greek yogurt.

1 Preheat the oven to 190°C/375°F/ Gas 5. Grease a 25 x 16cm/10 x 6¼in baking tin with butter. Brush each filo sheet in turn with melted butter and use to line the prepared tin.

2 Trim the excess pastry, leaving a little overhanging the edge. Arrange the figs over the base of the tart.

INDEX

A

almonds:
  almond and date filo
    parcels 174
  almond and pine nut
    tart 205
  almond cream puffs 167
  almond macaroons see
    ratafia biscuits
  almond paste see marzipan
  almond pastry 22
  baklava 176
  chocolate, date and almond
    filo coil 248
  crunchy apple and almond
    flan 223
  date and almond tart 192
  gâteau Pithiviers 43
  linzertorte 218
  Moroccan serpent cake 249
  pear and almond cream
    tart 184
Alsace plum tart 184
American pumpkin pie 198
apples 52
  apple, raisin and maple
    pies 237
  apple strudel 244
  baked apple dumplings 150
  crunchy apple and almond
    flan 223
  deep-dish apple pie 214
  filo-topped apple pie 250
  rustic apple tart 181
  tarte Tatin 244
apricots 52–3
  apricot filo purses 175
  apricot frangipane tart with
    Kirsch 186
  chicken and apricot filo
    pie 119
aspic 50
aubergines:
  Greek picnic pie 96
  Mediterranean one-crust pie
    141
  ratatouille and Fontina
    strudel 133
aurora sauce 61
avgolemono sauce 63

B

bacon:
  bacon and egg pie 114
  mini pork and bacon
    pies 86
  quiche Lorraine 91
baked apple dumplings 150

baked cheesecake with
    kissel 208
baked sweet ravioli 152
Bakewell tart 59 236
baking beans 15
    see also blind baking
baking sheets 12
baklava 45 176
bananas 53
  Boston banoffee pie 229
béarnaise sauce 62
béchamel sauce 60
beef:
  beef Wellington 41 127
  Guinness and oyster
    pie 109
  steak and kidney pie with
    mustard gravy 112
beurre blanc 61
biscuit pastry see pâte sucrée
black treacle:
  shoofly pie 220
blind baking 36
blue cheese sauce 60
blueberries:
  blueberry frangipane
    flan 187
  blueberry pie 215
boeuf en croûte see
    beef Wellington
Boston banoffee pie 229
bouchées 42
brandy sauce 66
bream:
  fillets of sea bream in filo
    pastry 128
Brie cheese:
  tomato and black olive
    tart 100
  turkey and cranberry purses
    80
bulgur wheat:
  chicken and apricot filo
    pie 119

butternut squash and maple
    pie 199
butterscotch sauce 67

C

cannoli forms 14
Cantal cheese:
  potato, leek and filo pie 116
caper sauce 61
caramel sauce 67
caramelized onion tart 94
caramelized topping 54
caramelized upside-down pear
    pie 182
Cheddar cheese:
  cheese and onion
    quiche 90
  cheese and spinach
    flan 115
  Mornay sauce 60
  spicy potato strudel 132
  vegetable toppings 49
  vegetarian festive
    tart 102
cheese pastry 16
cherries:
  berry brûlée tartlets 144
  fresh cherry and hazelnut
    strudel 245
Cheshire cheese:
  chestnut, Stilton and ale
    pie 108
  potato, leek and filo
    pie 116
chicken:
  chicken and apricot filo
    pie 119
  chicken and couscous
    parcels 129
  chicken and mushroom
    pie 110
  chicken charter pie 106

chicken, cheese and leek
    parcel 130
  smoked chicken with peach
    mayonnaise in filo
    tartlets 76
  spiced chicken and egg filo
    pie 120
  Tunisian brik 81
chicken livers:
  rich game pie 124
chocolate:
  chocolate, date and almond
    filo coil 248
  chocolate éclairs 158
  chocolate, pear and pecan
    pie 203
  cream filling 57
  dark chocolate and hazelnut
    tart 202
  Greek chocolate mousse
    tartlets 156
  Italian chocolate ricotta
    tart 219
  Mississippi mud pie 228
  mousse 57
  pastry 22
  poached pear tartlets with
    chocolate sauce 168
  sauces 67
  Tia Maria truffle tartlets 147
choux pastry 9
  chocolate éclairs 158
  coffee cream
    profiteroles 157
  gâteau Saint-Honoré 240
  making 26
  mushroom and quail's egg
    gougère 136
  shaping and baking 38
  strawberry and Kirsch choux
    ring 242
cider pie 200

coffee:
  coffee cream
    profiteroles 157
  coffee custard tart 211
  crunchy-topped coffee
    meringue pie 224
  Tia Maria truffle tartlets 147
compôte, red fruit 64
cooling rack 15
cornet moulds 14
Cornish pasties 87
cornmeal pastry 21
  red onion tart with a
    cornmeal crust 95
cottage cheese:
  cheese and spinach
    flan 115
coulis:
  fruit 64
  tomato 61
courgette and dill tart 98
couscous:
  chicken and couscous
    parcels 129
cranberries:
  turkey and cranberry
    pie 113
  turkey and cranberry purses
    80
cream cheese:
  chicken, cheese and leek
    parcel 130
  fillings 58
  pastry 21
  pecan tassies 149
  shoofly pie 220
  strawberry tart 235
creamy caramel sauce 67
crème Anglaise 66
crème Chantilly 57
crème mousseline 55
crème pâtissière 55
crunchy apple and almond
  flan 223
crunchy-topped coffee
  meringue pie 224
curd cheese 58
  lemon curd tarts 148
  red grape and cheese
    tartlets 146
  Yorkshire curd tart 210
custard, savoury 48
custards, sweet:
  Alsace plum tart 184
  coffee custard tart 211
  crunchy-topped coffee
    meringue pie 224
  fillings 54

fresh orange tart 195
Mississippi mud pie 228
prune tart with custard
  filling 191
raspberry and crème brûlée
  tart 193
summer berry tart 188

D
Danish pastries 162
dark chocolate and hazelnut
  tart 202
dark toffee sauce 67
dates:
  almond and date filo parcels
    174
  chocolate, date and almond
    filo coil 248
  date and almond tart 192
decorations 32–4
deep-dish apple pie 214
deep-frying:
  choux pastry 38
  filo pastry 47
  pâte sucrée tubes 41
defrosting pastry 9
docker 15
double-crust pies:
  fillings 48 50–3
  making 29
dried fruit 53
  apple, raisin and maple pies
    237
  Greek fruit and nut
    pastries 151
  moistening 53
  spinach turnovers 83
  see also mincemeat

E
éclairs, chocolate 158
eggs 8
  bacon and egg pie 114
  egg and salmon puff
    parcels 82
  glazes 35
  mini pork and bacon
    pies 87
  salmon in puff pastry 134
  spiced chicken and egg filo
    pie 120
  sweet egg sauces 66
  tuna and egg galette 140
  Tunisian brik 81
egg-set fillings 48
Emmenthal cheese:
  Alsace leek and onion
    tartlets 72

Mornay sauce 60
seafood gougère 136
exotic fruit sauce 65
exotic fruit tranche 190

F
farmer's cheese see
  curd cheese
fats 8
feta cheese:
  cheese scrolls 78
  Greek picnic pie 96
  spinach filo pie 118
feuilletées 44
figs:
  fresh fig filo tart 251
fillets of sea bream in filo
  pastry 128
filo pastry 9
  baking 37
  deep-frying 47
  lining a tin with 30
  shaping 45–7
  using in pies 31
fish:
  egg and salmon puff parcels
    82
  fillets of sea bream in filo
    pastry 128
  fillings 51
  salmon in puff pastry 134
  seafood gougère 138
  smoked salmon quiche with
    potato pastry 92
  tuna and egg galette 140
flaky pastry 9
  making 25
flan pastry 18
flan tins and rings 13
  lining 28
flans, how to bake 36
flour types 8
Fontina cheese:
  ratatouille and Fontina
    strudel 133
  red onion tart with cornmeal
    crust 95
  wild mushroom and Fontina
    tartlets 74
frangipane:
  apricot frangipane tart with
    Kirsch 186
  Bakewell tart 236
  blueberry frangipane
    flan 187
  making a frangipane
    tart 59
  orange sweetheart tart 180

free-form fruit tart 53
freezing pastry 9
French flan pastry 8 18
fresh cherry and hazelnut
  strudel 245
fresh fig filo tart 251
fresh fruit coulis 64
fresh orange tart 195
fromage frais:
  peach and redcurrant
    tartlets 171
fruit:
  in baked custard 54
  coiled fruit parcels 41
  coulis 64
  dumplings 41
  fillings 52–3
  in frangipane 59
  fruit compôte 64
  fruit juice, thickening 52
  fruit sauces 64

galettes 53
glazing 53 59
puréed fillings 56
sauces 64–5

G
galettes:
  fruit and cream 41 53
  tuna and egg galette 140
  vegetable 49
game:
  fillings 50
  hare pot pies 107
  pastry for 27
  rich game pie 124
garlic:
  shallot and garlic tarte Tatin
    with Parmesan pastry 103
gâteau Pithiviers 43
gâteau Saint-Honoré 26 240
gazelles' horns 153
gelatine-set mousse 57
glazing fruit 53 59

glazing pastry 35
glossy hot chocolate
    sauce 67
gluten 8
golden syrup:
    treacle tart 221
gorgonzola cheese:
    blue cheese sauce 60
gougère:
    mushroom and quail's egg
        gougère 136
    seafood gougère 138
grapes:
    red grape and cheese
        tartlets 146
gravy, onion 61
Greek chocolate mousse
    tartlets 156

Greek fruit and nut
    pastries 151
Greek picnic pie 96
Gruyère cheese:
    Alsace leek and onion
        tartlets 72
    cheese and onion quiche 90
    Mornay sauce 60
    mushroom and quail's egg
        gougère 136
    seafood gougère 138
Guinness:
    chestnut, Stilton and ale
        pie 108
    Guinness and oyster
        pie 109

H
hare pot pies 107
hazelnuts:
    dark chocolate and hazelnut
        tart 202
    fresh cherry and hazelnut
        strudel 245

herb shortcrust pastry 16
herbed Greek mini
    tarts 100
hollandaise sauce 62
honey and pine nut tart 206
hot orange and red wine sauce
    65
hot water crust pastry 9
    making 27
    mini pork and bacon
        pies 87
    shaping and baking 39
    using meat in 50

I
ice cream:
    filo, ice cream and
        mincemeat parcels 172

walnut and vanilla ice
    palmiers 172
Italian chocolate ricotta
    tart 219

K
keeping pastry 9
key lime pie 230
kidney beans:
    Mediterranean one-crust pie
        141
kidney, lamb's:
    steak and kidney pie with
        mustard gravy 112

L
lamb pie with pear and mint
    sauce 126
Lancashire cheese:
    potato and leek filo
        pie 116
    spinach filo pie 118
lattice top 33
    cutter 15

leeks:
    Alsace leek and onion
        tartlets 72
    chicken, cheese and leek
        parcel 130
    leek and Roquefort tart with
        walnut pastry 99
    leek, saffron and mussel
        tarts 75
    potato and leek filo pie 116
lemons:
    curd tarts 148
    lemon meringue pie,
        56 226
    lemon tart 207
    mousse 57
limes:
    key lime pie 56 230
    smoked chicken with peach
        mayonnaise in filo
        tartlets 76
linzertorte 218
lobster:
    shellfish in puff pastry 84

M
Maltaise sauce 61
mangoes:
    mango and amaretti
        strudel 246
    mango and tamarillo
        pastries 164
maple syrup:
    apple, raisin and maple pies
        237
    baked apple dumplings 150
    butternut squash and maple
        pie 199
    cider pie 200
    walnut pie 204
marzipan:
    apricot filo purses 175
    mango and tamarillo
        pastries 164
    plum and marzipan
        pastries 170
mascarpone cheese 58
    exotic fruit tranche 190
mayonnaise 63
    smoked chicken with peach
        mayonnaise in filo
        tartlets 76
meat fillings 50
Mediterranean one-crust
    pie 141
meringue cuite 56
    crunchy-topped coffee
        meringue pie 224

lemon meringue pie 226
    rhubarb meringue
        pie 227
milk 66
mille-feuille, mini 166
mince pies 52 154
mincemeat:
    apricot filo purses 175
    filo, ice cream and
        mincemeat parcels 172
    whisky-laced mince pies 154
mini mille-feuille 166
mini pork and bacon
    pies 86
Mississippi mud pie 228
molasses see black treacle
Mornay sauce 60
Moroccan prawn
    packages 79
Moroccan serpent cake 249
moulds 13
mousse fillings 57
    Greek chocolate mousse
        tartlets 156
    Mississippi mud pie 228
mozzarella cheese 49
    prosciutto and mozzarella
        parcels 76
mushrooms:
    chicken and mushroom
        pie 110
    mushroom and quail's egg
        gougère 136
    mushroom, nut and prune
        jalousie 131
    sauce 60
    scallops with wild
        mushrooms 137
    wild mushroom and Fontina
        tartlets 74
mussels:
    leek, saffron and mussel
        tarts 75
    shellfish in puff pastry 84

mustard:
  sauce 61
  steak and kidney pie with
    mustard gravy 112

N
nectarine puff pastry
    tarts 165
nut crust, light 18

O
olive oil pastry 20
olives:
  Mediterranean one-crust pie
    141
  tomato and black olive
    tart 100
one-crust rhubarb pie 194
onions:
  Alsace leek and onion
    tartlets 72
  caramelized onion tart 94
  cheese and onion
    quiche 90
  gravy 61
  red onion tart with a
    cornmeal crust 95
  sauce 60
open pies, fillings for 49–51
oranges:
  fresh orange tart 195
  hot orange and red wine
    sauce 65
  orange sweetheart tart 180
  spiced orange pastry 22
oven temperature 36
oysters:
  Guinness and oyster pie 109

P
palette knife 15
palmiers 44
  walnut and vanilla ice
    palmiers 172
Paris-Brest 26
Parmesan cheese 49
  cheese and spinach
    flan 115
  Greek picnic pie 96
  Mediterranean one-crust pie
    141
  shallot and garlic tarte Tatin
    with Parmesan pastry 103
  vegetarian festive
    tart 102
parsley sauce 60
passionfruit sauce 65
pastry blender 15

pastry boards 12
pastry brush 15
pastry cream 54
pastry cutters 14
pastry pricker 15
pastry wheel 15
pâte à foncer 8
pâte brisée 8
  galettes 41
pâte feuilletée, see puff pastry
pâte sucrée 8 19 41
pâté:
  rich game pie 124
peaches:
  peach and brandy pie 234
  peach and redcurrant
    tartlets 171
  peach leaf pie 216
  smoked chicken with peach
    mayonnaise in filo
    tartlets 76
pears 52
  caramelized upside-down
    pear pie 182
  chocolate, pear and pecan
    pie 203
  lamb pie with pear and mint
    sauce 126
  pear and almond cream
    tart 185
  pear tarte Tatin with
    cardamom 239
  poached pear tartlets with
    chocolate sauce 168
pecan nuts:
  chocolate, pear and pecan
    pie 203
  pecan tassies 149
pie base, pastry 29
pie dishes 13
pie funnel 14 29
  making 39
pie plates 13
pies, how to bake 36
pine nuts:
  almond and pine nut
    tart 205
  honey and pine nut tart 206
pineapple compôte sauce 64
piping equipment 15
pistachio nuts:
  baklava 176
plates, pie 13
plums 53
  Alsace plum tart 184
  plum and marzipan
    pastries 170
  plum crumble pie 222

poached pear tartlets with
    chocolate sauce 168
porcelain flan dishes 14
pork:
  mini pork and bacon
    pies 86
potato:
  pastry 21
  potato, leek and filo
    pie 116
  smoked salmon quiche with
    potato pastry 92
  spicy potato strudel 132
poultry fillings 50
prawns:
  Moroccan prawn
    packages 79
  shellfish in puff pastry 84
profiteroles, coffee cream 157
prosciutto and mozzarella
    parcels 76
prunes:
  mushroom, nut and prune
    jalousie 131
  prune tart with custard
    filling 191
puff pastry 8
  baking 36
  making 23
  shaping 42–4
  using bought puff pastry 25
pumpkin:
  American pumpkin pie 198
puréed fillings 56

Q
quail eggs:
  mushrooms and quail's egg
    gougère 136
quark:
  baked cheesecake with
    kissel 208

quiche 48
  cheese and onion quiche 90
  Greek picnic pie 96
  quiche Lorraine 91
  smoked salmon quiche with
    potato pastry 92

R
raised pie, pastry for 27
  moulds 13
raspberries 52
  mini mille-feuille 166
  raspberry and crème brûlée
    tart 193
ratafia biscuits:
  apricot filo purses 175
  apricot frangipane tart with
    Kirsch 186
  fresh cherry and hazelnut
    strudel 245
ratatouille and Fontina
    strudel 133
red fruit compôte 64
red grape and cheese
    tartlets 146
red onion tart with cornmeal
    crust 95
red wine sauce 60
redcurrants:
  peach and redcurrant
    tartlets 171
rhubarb 52
  one-crust rhubarb pie 194
  rhubarb meringue pie 227
  rhubarb sauce 65
rice:
  egg and salmon puff parcels
    82
  Greek picnic pie 96
  salmon in puff pastry 134
rich flan pastry 18
rich game pie 124

rich shortcrust pastry 8
  making 16
ricotta cheese 58
  baked sweet ravioli 152
  fresh cherry and hazelnut
    strudel 245
  Italian chocolate ricotta
    tart 219
Roquefort cheese:
  Roquefort tart with walnut
    pastry 99
rough puff pastry 9
  making 24
rustic apple tart 181

S
sabayon sauces:
  chilled 66
  classic 63
  warm 66
saffron:
  leek, saffron and mussel
    tarts 75
salmon:
  egg and salmon puff parcels
    82
  salmon in puff pastry 134
  smoked salmon quiche with
    potato pastry 92
sauces 60–7
savoury fillings 48–51

scallops:
  scallops with wild
    mushrooms 137
  seafood in puff pastry 84
sea bream:
  fillets of sea bream in filo
    pastry 128
seafood gougère 138
shallot and garlic tarte
  Tatin 103
shaping pastry 28
shellfish fillings 51
  shellfish in puff pastry 84

shoofly pie 53 220
shortcrust pastry 8
  baking 36
  making 16
  shaping 40–1
short-cut flaky pastry 25
short-cut puff pastry 9
  making 24
shrimp see prawns
simple chocolate sauce 67
single-crust pies:
  fillings 50–3
  making 29
slatted-top pie 43
  mushroom, nut and prune
    jalousie 131
smoked chicken with peach
    mayonnaise in filo tartlets 76
smoked salmon quiche with
    potato pastry 92
soubise sauce 60
spiced chicken and egg filo
    pie 120
spiced orange pastry 22
spicy potato strudel 132
spinach:
  cheese and spinach
    flan 115
  Greek picnic pie 96
  spinach filo pie 118
  spinach turnovers 83
sponge fillings 59
springform cake tins 13
steak and kidney pie with
    mustard gravy 112
Stilton cheese:
  chestnut, Stilton and ale
    pie 108
strawberries 52
  strawberry and Kirsch choux
    ring 242
  strawberry tart 235
strudel pastry 9
  making 27
suet pastry 8 20 30
summer berry tart 188
summer fruit brûlée
    tartlets 144
sweet flan pastry 18

T
tartare sauce 61
tarte Tatin 238
tartlet tins 14
  lining 30
Tia Maria truffle tartlets 147
timers 12
toffee sauce, dark 67

tomatoes:
  tomato and black olive
    tart 100
  tomato coulis 61
tranche tins 13
  lining with filo 30
treacle tart 221
tuna and egg galette 140
turkey:
  turkey and cranberry
    pie 113
  turkey and cranberry
    purses 80

V
vanilla:
  cream cheese filling 58
  sponge filling 59
vegetables 49
vegetarian festive tart 102
velouté sauce 61
vol-au-vents 42–3

W
walnut pastry:
  leek and Roquefort tart with
    walnut pastry 99
  wild mushroom and Fontina
    tartlets 74
walnuts:
  Greek fruit and nut
    pastries 151
  walnut and vanilla ice
    palmiers 172
  walnut pie 204
whisky-laced mince pies 154
white chocolate sauce 67
  coffee cream
    profiteroles 157
white sauce, basic 60
wild mushroom and Fontina
    tartlets 74

wire rack 15
work surfaces 12

Y
yogurt:
  cheese scrolls 78
  chicken and apricot filo
    pie 119
  chicken and couscous
    parcels 129
  exotic fruit sauce 65
  Greek picnic pie 96
  herbed Greek mini
    tarts 100
  peach and redcurrant
    tartlets 171
Yorkshire curd tart 210

Z
zucchini see courgettes

Picture acknowledgements
The Art Archive p6bl; The
Bridgeman Art Library *A
Viennese Patisserie* by Antony
Butler (b. 1927), John Noott
Galleries, Worcestershire, UK
p7; and Mary Evans Picture
Library p6tr.
Note: We have been unable to
trace the copyright holder of
A Viennese Patisserie by Antony
Butler and would be grateful to
receive any information as to
their identity.

Publisher's acknowledgements
The publishers would like to
thank Gill Wing for lending
equipment for photography.
Tel: 020 7226 5392